Running Away

Running Away

Robert Andrew Powell

New Harvest
Houghton Mifflin Harcourt
BOSTON   NEW YORK
2014

This edition published by special arrangement with Amazon Publishing

For information about permission to reproduce
selections from this book, go to www.apub.com.

www.hmhco.com

Library of Congress Cataloging-in-Publication Data is available.
ISBN 978-0-544-26366-6

Book design by Brian Moore

Printed in the United States of America
DOC 10 9 8 7 6 5 4 3 2 1

To David, Jennifer, and Gretchen

THIS BOOK CAPTURES a moment in time. Specifically, February 2007, when I arrived in Boulder, through July 2008, a few months after the Boston Marathon that I moved to Colorado to train for. Not covered are the years spent writing and rewriting and rewriting again until finally, on April 3, 2013, my manuscript found a publisher. Twelve days later, in Boston, two pressure cookers exploded.

The world changes. Meaning adapts to new circumstances. After much thought, I'm leaving this story in its moment. In these pages, Lance Armstrong is merely a suspected drug cheat. Frank Shorter has not publicly detailed his allegations of abuse, and a Subaru hybrid has not yet rolled off the production line. The Boston Marathon exists as it will remain forever into the future: a celebration of human achievement.

Running Away

1

HOW DOES A ghost story start? How about with an old man? The one I'm thinking about is unexceptional on the surface. Handsome, I guess. Quite fit for his age. A little shorter than he used to be, which was never exactly tall. He's never been arrested, was never late with a bill, and he sits through five p.m. mass every Saturday like clockwork. Alive for more than seventy years, he's spent the last thirty in a Midwestern suburb, in a four-story house overlooking a small sylvan lake. He's retired now, finally, from one of those vague business-type jobs — management consultant in his case — that paid him enough money to support a wife, to shepherd four kids through graduate schools, to care for his mother, and to take vacations now and then. Italy one year. Baltimore, for some reason, the next.

This ghost is not dead. Anything but. A female friend, upon being introduced to him, reports that my dad "still has it going on." He and I talk on the phone at least once a week. We talk about the Chicago Cubs and his golf game and whether he's added any beer cans to his collection. We talk about Notre Dame football. We talk about the weather. Gingerly, we dance around what I call my career, and what he once called my permanent vacation. We never talk about the story rattling around my head, the story haunting me.

It goes like this: When my dad was my age, thirty-nine years old, he smoked three packs of cigarettes a day. He drank a couple of beers every evening after work, and never exercised. He was overweight. When he was my age, my dad decided to take up jogging to drop some of those excess pounds. Nothing serious. Just a few laps around the cul-de-sac. It was the 1970s. The American Frank Shorter had won gold and silver medals in two successive Olympic marathons, igniting a running boom. My dad, who set out only to lose some weight, attacked jogging with the same focus with which he approached his work, the same focus that enabled him to rise — completely on his own, seemingly through sheer will — from a working-class assignment in Milwaukee to a station atop the upper middle class. He took up jogging with the same zeal that led him to acquire, by the time he was my age, a wife and four kids and a house on a golf course. And a Chrysler New Yorker that he was terribly proud of. And financial security. And genuine professional success. Within one year of his first step as a jogger, he qualified for and ran the Boston Marathon, finishing the greatest road race in the world in less than three hours.

I was eight years old when he pulled this off. The same year he ran Boston for the first time, the *Boston Globe Sunday Magazine* published a huge feature on him. Six pages long, color photos, and the framework for the story that now lives in my head. The newspaper celebrated the way my dad — smoker, beer drinker, etc. — transformed from couch potato to Boston so quickly. He was painted as superhuman, basically, which is how I've come to view his achievement.

Not long after I turned thirty, around the time my life began to slip away from me, the story in my head started to grow, to metastasize. I can't help but compare his standing then with my current station in life. I do not have four kids. I don't have *any* kids. I don't even have a wife anymore. I definitely don't have a house, much less a house on a golf course. I'm in the prime of my working life, yet I've actually lost money each of the past eight years, a streak that began when I left my wife, which was also the last year I held a steady job. To get by, I've exhausted my life savings. I've spent the past fifteen months living in a converted chicken coop. That's not a joke. In the state of Colorado, where I moved just over a year ago, I have been officially declared indigent.

I'd never been to Colorado before. I'd never even driven through the state. I moved west from Florida because I wanted to place a new story in my head. A story about applying myself and stripping away everything inessential and finally living up to the standard my father had set. In the new story I hoped to author, I am no longer the shiftless son or the floundering son or the son adrift. In the new narrative, I finally become a son without adjectives.

I spent a lot of time picturing how it would all turn out. I imagined molding myself into a person of substance, a guy people can count on, a doer. I saw my life landing back on track. If I got up every day and ran and focused and lived with discipline, I figured, it would follow that I'd also become an adult and find work and fit in with everyone else in America. Maybe I'd find a new wife, too. At no point did I envision a gray February morning in a tacky Southern tourist town. I never saw my head bowed, my eyes fixed on the soft asphalt under my swollen feet. I didn't expect to look down long enough to notice, for the first time, that the black laces on my yellow racing flats have sparkly silver threads woven into them. In this vision that I did not foresee, in a story I did not anticipate writing, I am staring at the ground. My dad stands maybe fifteen feet away, just over the finish line and behind an orange plastic traffic barricade. I am staring at the ground and he is staring at me. The ghost is staring straight at me.

2

MARCH 1. DAY one. Two hundred and fifteen pounds. Body fat 22.5 percent. Twenty frozen minutes.

I get up in the morning a bit after seven. I pull on new black thermal tights and a new Nike compression shirt I bought at the Boulder Running Company, telling the clerk I hadn't seen winter in fifteen years and I didn't know what to wear. I squeeze into a pair of ten-dollar running socks that are supposed to keep my feet from blistering, then tie my ninety-dollar running shoes purchased in Miami about a month ago, which was about a month before I left. Over my compression shirt I layer a cotton sweatshirt from the law school my brother attended and a new Mizuno windbreaker my older sister gave me. A heart-rate monitor hugs my chest just below the nipples. I walk down to Boulder Creek, to a seven-mile concrete path winding through the heart of my new town. Snow dusts the creek bed. Black water gurgles under sheets of cracked ice. I press a button to start my GPS satellite watch, purchased on the last day of December, the last day, according to a resolution, I would spend any more money. And I'm off. The first step. Or, at least, the first step in Colorado.

⚬

This is where my head was at when the story inside it grew so loud I feared an explosion:

On a pillow. Back in Miami. In Little Havana, in a hotel near the river. Specifically, in a small apartment rented month to month ever since I'd left my wife seven years earlier. Outside it's midday, probably close to one o'clock. The sun is hot, as is usually the case in Miami, which is why I have the air conditioner in my bedroom cranked to cold. Even with a comforter pulled over my ears I can hear lobstermen across the street slapping barnacles off traps they'll repair then stack along the riverbank. I can hear the staccato air brakes of semitrailers as they exit I-95, a concrete belt above the water that cuts off Little Havana from the tall buildings of Miami's downtown. Every once in a while a Metro train clacks in the distance, carrying workers to and from their workplaces.

It's dangerously late. I know I've got to walk my dog or she'll make a mess that will embarrass her. I pull my head off the pillow. My forearm is crusted with drool. Slowly, deliberately, I peel away the comforter and drop my feet to the floor. I throw on some shorts and some flip flops, hook a leash onto Valentine's collar, then open the door. Heat waves wash over our bodies. My dog recoils at the light.

I rub sleep out of my eyes as Valentine leads me to her usual spot, about a block away. We walk past the fish market across the street, on the riverbank. I've never seen any fish being sold. Instead, as always, leathery Cubans play dominoes and sip from green bottles of Presidente beer, shouting at each other in Spanish. Closer to us, a fat man reclines on a dented folding chair, rocked back against the iron bars of the fence that rings the hotel. He's here every day, cooling under a pepper tree from maybe six in the morning until dusk. He scratches Valentine's ears when she wanders over to sniff his colostomy bag. Other neighbors squat on their stoops, doing nothing. In Little Havana, the dynamic opposite of Manhattan, there is no hustle. Anything that needs to be done can be put off until mañana, except it seems nobody has anything to do in the first place.

I fit right in. For the past year or two or maybe three, I haven't found much that beats staying in bed. Officially I'm working as a freelance journalist, but it's not going so well. I don't get many assignments anymore, and the last two I was lucky enough to get I just completely screwed up. One was for a business magazine that wanted a story on Miami's boom-and-bust real estate market. After two drafts, the editor sent me an e-mail stating what I already knew, that "this isn't a piece for *Inc.*" The other assignment was for the *New York Times Magazine*. It was a great gig. When I got the work, I crowed to my dad that I was finally making real progress at this journalism thing, that I'd landed a national story that would pay me lots of money and get me exposure and lead, no doubt, to other and better work. And when the editor ultimately killed the story because I "failed to get the goods," I never sent my dad an update. He never again asked about the assignment, though I know he remembers it. By now he's acclimated to my patterns.

I wrote a book a few years ago. That's my big success. I quit my job before I wrote it, and when it came out I thought it was a big deal. I sat back and waited for my life to take off, which it never did. I should be out looking for more stories, I know, trying to hustle up jobs. I should be calling friends for connections to editors in New York. But when I don't do any of that, no one really notices. And the pressure to do all that can grow so strong it paralyzes me. Back in my cool apartment, my couch looks so comfortable over there. I go to it and lie on my back and read the newspaper, Valentine napping at my ankles.

I'm hungry, and my eyes are drooping, but I work through

three sections of the *Times,* saving the sports section for break-fast, which I guess I should call a late brunch. I get up to pull a pair of chocolate fudge Pop-Tarts from the refrigerator. I turn on the radio, NPR news then sports talk with Jim Rome, whom I can pick up only on a scratchy station out of Palm Beach County. I pour a bowl of Cheerios, eating at the table while reading. When I'm done, I put the bowl in the sink then finish the sports sec-tion back on my couch, back on my back, Valentine again at my ankles. I nap for about an hour.

I check my e-mail when I wake. Junk. Nothing from an editor, or from a friend. I move into my office, which is also my bed-room, and lie on my bed until around four thirty p.m. I get up and switch the radio back to NPR. Ooh, I forgot to feed the dog. I feed the dog. Ants swarm over her bowl. The ants carry tiny white dots in their mandibles, which I worry might be eggs. I scrub the bowl in the sink, dry it with a towel and fill it with food. I also spray down the floor with Raid. Valentine eats. *Bon appétit.*

The mail should be here by now. I venture out to check. I take a bag of trash with me to toss into the hotel's Dumpster. It is hot outside, very hot. I practically skip across the blacktop parking lot, thinking about work, which I should get started on. I rush back inside clutching a couple of newly delivered magazines. Slipping into my bedroom, I take a seat at a small desk pushed into a corner. I read a paragraph that I've taped to a wall about Bali and people there who've been beat up by life and now lack any trace of ambition.

∞

I started running on January 1, on the day after what would have been my eleventh wedding anniversary. The running was a New

Year's resolution. In the upcoming year I would limit my time on the Internet, I would stop spending the little money I have, and I would train for a marathon. It was the start of my thirty-ninth year. My dad started running when he was thirty-nine. I hate to run — hate it — but ever since the story germinated in my head, I thought it might be cool to maybe, possibly, try to run a single marathon at age forty. One of those five-hour jogs. Perhaps the New York City Marathon, a race my dad never entered. Then I'd cross the experience off my bucket list.

That first day of January, I jogged on the boardwalk on Miami Beach, eking out two miles without stopping and feeling immensely proud of myself. I came home and wrote in my journal that "running is practice for not quitting, and this year I'm not going to be a quitter." I concluded that this marathon resolution of mine would not be a problem.

"I'm going to pull this off," I wrote.

I missed my first run on January 5. The next day, I ran one mile less than scheduled; when I got to the gym and stepped on the treadmill, I just didn't feel it. By the twenty-fourth I was taking days off so the blisters on my feet could heal. The subsequent Sunday, I just plain skipped my long run. It was too cold, it was too late and too dark. I'd lost the day surfing the Internet endlessly, another resolution broken with malice.

"Very bad!" I wrote in the runner's log that all the marathon guidebooks told me to keep. Right after that, I took two more days off. Very bad.

SUNDAY, FEBRUARY 4:
I stepped out to the cool weather an hour and a half before the kickoff of the Super Bowl. I walked a block. Then I didn't run. I simply didn't run. I felt there wasn't enough time to run before the game started, but that's no excuse. I simply didn't run.

SATURDAY, FEBRUARY 10:
*I said I was going to run the boardwalk, but I didn't. I then
said I was going to run 30 minutes on the gym treadmill, but I
didn't. Whatever. It's a beautiful day. I'm wasting my life.*

Tuesday, February 20: I wake up after noon, again. I am sleepy.
I walk the dog. I surf the Internet. I stroll to the grocery store
up the street to buy more Pop-Tarts and some Diet Mountain
Dew and dental floss and this chicken parmesan frozen-dinner-
in-a-skillet thing I've just discovered. I do not jog. I do not call
friends. I do not talk to anyone. By around eight p.m. I feel motivated to tackle my work, to finally get started. But first there's
a new *Harper's* magazine. And even *Smithsonian* is interesting
when I'm procrastinating. Then it's ten or eleven. I take a break
and eat a Pop-Tart. I think about making a salad because I'm
supposed to be in training and I don't want to gain weight. Then
I, oh, just check my e-mail, which plunges me back into the Internet, and *boom!* The night is gone. I look at a quote taped on
my wall from Emerson, a quote I always read around three a.m.,
when I give up.

> Finish each day and be done with it. You have done what
> you could. Some blunders and absurdities no doubt crept in;
> forget them as soon as you can. Tomorrow is a new day; begin it
> well and serenely and with too high a spirit to be cumbered with
> your old nonsense.

Tomorrow is another day. Tomorrow is a new day. Maybe tomorrow I'll make something of myself. Before I shut down my
laptop, I commence one last Web search, looking—in a self-
destructive way that I'm fully conscious of—specifically for information I know might keep me awake hours longer. I look up

Mrs. Wisconsin, as I often do. She's married still, now with two kids and her second house. I look up a woman who came into my life after Mrs. Wisconsin. This second woman left me for a doctor, then left Miami to make it in television news; I find some of her clips on YouTube and watch them all. I keep going, way back, to look up my ex-wife. At first I find nothing, as usual. But I'm motivated. This night I dig deep enough to Google our old phone number. No links. So I try the address of the house we once owned together, and which I gave her in the divorce. That's when I find this:

MIAMI MORNINGSIDE ESTATE SALE 525 NE 56 ST. Sat. & Sun. 9am-12pm. Beautiful Furn., Designer lamps, Wonderful Kit. Appl. Electronics & So much more! Have moved to Europe so Everything must go!!!

This is significant. This is news. This is what I was looking for, though this isn't what I was in any way expecting to find. My wife — *ex-wife* — has moved to Europe. Blood rushes to my temples. Electric sparks flash across my nervous system, firing up everything. This is problematic. This hurts. Not that she's left Miami; I haven't seen or talked to her in three years. Not because the sale took place a week earlier and I've missed my chance to buy back the mixer we received for a wedding present. I start to freak out — I feel a serious, satisfying pain, perhaps like a stabbing — because she's moved on with her life. Everyone has now moved on with their lives. And I'm still in the apartment I rented temporarily, on a month-to-month basis, when I left her. When I left my wife, my ex-wife, who now lives in Europe.

I can see, suddenly, what will happen if I stay in Miami, in this apartment, in this routine. I can see my uncle Bob, who had moved to Miami to reinvent himself after a divorce. I can see his bathtub. I can see his gun. I look up from my computer. My eyes fall on other quotes taped to the wall, quotes I'd hoped would motivate me to industry.

"Adversity has the same effect on a man that severe training has on the pugilist: it reduces him to his fighting weight."

"Never quit. It's the easiest copout in the world."

"I'm afraid that hard work over a long period of time really does produce results."

I'd printed out the quotes from my computer, cut them into little slips, and pasted them onto the wall near my desk. My eyes dance around the quotes until they settle on one I'd forgotten about. I don't know who said the line, and I can't recall why I glued it to my wall. Perhaps I had anticipated exactly this moment.

"To change one's life: start immediately. Do it flamboyantly. No exceptions."

❦

I start immediately. I rip down thirty-five postcards of Airstream trailers I'd arranged into a rectangle and glued over my couch, the postcards a gift from a woman who used to visit my apartment before she decided to marry her boyfriend. I tear down a bulletin board I've been adding to for seven years, unearthing the initial dog tag bought when I rescued Valentine from a pound, when I tried to rename her Tess but it didn't stick. I find a dozen movie ticket stubs and a ticket to the World Series, Yankees versus Marlins, incredible seats from a friend I lost in the divorce. There's a thirty-fourth birthday card from my ex-wife, which I believe to be the last communication with me she ever attempted.

"You know you're getting older when you hear your favorite song. On an elevator. Have a great day!" There's a stub of an

Aeromexico ticket to Cabo San Lucas, a souvenir from when I first seriously contemplated running away.

I reach into my dresser, pulling out all my clothes. I extract only the shirts and jeans and underwear I absolutely need, then stuff the rest into a plastic bag to take to Goodwill. When the sun comes up, I give away the dresser. A single mother with three kids and temporary custody of a U-Haul carts off my bookshelves and my microwave and my dining room table and the slightly used Italian microfiber couch I'd bought back when I decided Miami was my home and I was never going to leave and I needed to act like I live here. She takes my vacuum, too. Valentine walks around the apartment dazed. Where is all the stuff? What the hell is going on?

From the kitchen I retrieve one steak knife, one fork, one spoon, a lone bowl, a single glass, and one plate. In the bathroom, into the toilet, I flush vials of Zoloft and Lexapro, pills I've been taking for years and which don't seem to be doing me any good. I give my printer to my landlord. Into my car I toss my new running shoes and my new GPS watch and the one bag of clothes. I put my comforter in the front passenger seat, and, the next day, place Valentine atop it. She sits forward like a sphinx as we slip out of Little Havana on a cool morning with absolutely no clouds in a sky that is so pale blue it's almost white. Based on a single *New York Times* article that declared Boulder, Colorado, the epicenter of running in America, if not in the entire world, I head west.

As we pull onto I-95, I take inventory. Fifteen years earlier I'd driven down to Florida to take my first real job. My used car had more than 100,000 miles on it. Just over $30,000 sat in my bank account. I was single. Now, driving out, I have $36,000 in the bank, but only because I cashed in my 401(k). I also have a four-figure bill due for repairing my current car, a used Mazda sedan with more than 100,000 miles on it. I'm single. And divorced. Counterweighing that last negative detail, I now have a dog, and for the first time in years a sense of purpose.

I'm no longer merely going to run a marathon. I'm going to qualify for Boston, in one year of training, just as my dad did. I'm going to match his greatest achievement. That's what I've decided. I'm going to start acting just like him. By doing so, I am certain, I will find my salvation.

There's no traffic heading out of town at this early hour. It takes only about ten minutes to reach the Golden Glades overpass, which soars nine stories above the flat landscape. I can see Dolphin Stadium to the west. I peer into the steel grates on my right, hard by the highway, which I know protect the Parkway hospital psych ward. In my rearview mirror stand the skyscrapers of Miami, which shrink from view as I zoom down the overpass into Broward County. I am out of Miami. I am headed ultimately to a city and to a state to which I've never been. I'm going there to do something—run—that I don't in any way enjoy. I expected to be depressed as I left town, to be cognizant that quitting Miami is quitting yet one more thing in my life. But Miami's behind me and Colorado's up ahead and my dog is beside me and the sun is out and I've got a project and a purpose and damned if I don't feel better already.

3

THE BOULDER ROAD RUNNERS meet socially on the first Monday of every month at the Walnut Brewery, the flagship in a chain of brewpubs fanning from Colorado to fifteen other states. A few days after my first Boulder run, I walk through the brewery's front doors a bit after five o'clock. A hoppy tang smacks my nostrils. Red brick walls support gigantic painted labels of the house beers: Red Moose Ale, Sub Zero Winter Ale, Firehouse Red. University students in leather booths gnaw on buffalo burgers, sip Buffalo Gold lager and watch the Colorado Buffaloes play college basketball on flat-screen televisions. Beer ferments in large steel vats protected behind glass. Kegs rise in stacks above the bar. I find the runners in a back room. They are easy to spot. They're the skinny people.

"I'm an okay runner," says Dan Skarda, the one guy here I know. Dan is as thin as a man can be, almost gaunt. The tight skin wrapped around his cheekbones and forehead is topped by an enviable shock of brown hair. He's wired. He moves and talks with so much energy, even at age forty-seven, that I can tell he's a good athlete. Dan and I attended the same high school in Illinois. His sister and my older sister ran track together, and Dan helped coach their team. He moved to Boulder about a decade ago, primarily for the running. My sister suggested I hunt him down, which I did. It was Dan who encouraged me to show up at the social.

Calling himself "an okay runner" strikes me as false modesty, ridiculously false. He's twice won the Lake County Marathon, held in the northern suburbs where we lived. When he ran the Boston Marathon, in 1984, he finished sixteenth. Overall. He has qualified for and run the US Olympic Marathon Trials. Hoisting my free pint of Sub Zero Winter Ale to my lips as Dan talks, I prepare to dismiss him as a cocky jackass. But once he gives some context, I understand what he means. In Boulder, he's jogged along the Flatirons with Frank Shorter, the two-time Olympic medalist and Boulder resident. He's shared beers with Steve Jones, a Welshman who once held the marathon world record. He's trained with Uta Pippig, a German women's marathon record holder. When he works on his speed at Potts Field, the university's track open to the public on Tuesday mornings, Dan sprints past, and is passed by, members of the Olympic teams of Japan, Kenya, Ethiopia, Romania, Australia, and the United States. He's an okay runner, in Boulder. That guy who won an Olympic gold medal? He's a *good* runner. That other guy who set a world record? He's a good runner, too.

Dan gave me my initial training strategy. I've been running once a day for twenty minutes in a row, nothing more. I give myself a day off on Saturday. On Sunday, for the first of my weekly "long runs," I clipped Valentine to a leash and together we jogged for thirty minutes along Boulder Creek. Distance isn't important right now, Dan says. Nor is speed. I'm just acclimating to the altitude, more than a mile above Miami's sea level. Dan also encouraged me to join the Boulder Road Runners. He doesn't train with the club very often, he tells me, but he is a member in good standing and he wears their singlets when he races. Most of the members here at the bar appear to be in their fifties or higher. For this reason the club is knocked around town as "Older Boulder." Dan points out that a lot of athletes my age in northern Colorado still run at a world-class level, or close to it. As a beginner, I'm better matched with experienced runners who are past their prime.

Dan introduces me to a trio of men standing near our table. One of them is a sports agent, a guy who brings top international runners to Boulder to train. Another is Mike Sandrock, the running columnist for the *Camera*, Boulder's daily newspaper. The third guy is Steve Jones. I do not know who Steve Jones is. When I shake his hand, I do not know he once ran a marathon in Chicago faster than any human had ever run a marathon. I'm still a little nervous, though, and I want to make a good impression. I launch into my spiel about my dad being overweight and a smoker and qualifying for Boston in one year and how I moved here to try to qualify for Boston myself.

"So you're planning to run Boston next month?" Jones interrupts, his face blank. He is looking into my eyes, checking my expression. He is mocking me, basically, seeing if I am as naive as I sound.

"No, you prick, I want to qualify for Boston *next* April, thirteen months from now."

I don't actually call him a prick. I just keep smiling, warm and open and hoping to have my goal ratified in some way; this is the public debut of my mission, my quest. Jones turns to talk to someone else. Dan quickly pulls aside another man he thinks I should know. Carl Mohr, the running club's vice president, is fifty-eight years old. He, too, is a skinny guy, short and youthful with wire glasses and wispy blonde hair. He's run the Boston Marathon six times. I tell him the same thing I just told Steve

Jones. Again I'm trying to convey my enthusiasm, my can-do spirit.

"I presume you're going to ask for a media exemption, right?" Carl asks.

"Oh, no, no. The whole point is to qualify. I don't want to run Boston if I don't qualify."

I smile. See how earnest I am? Carl does not smile back. He scans up and down my body, which in this room of runners appears as hulking as a bricklayer's. He looks at Dan Skarda, raises his eyebrows, draws a sip of his beer. And then, same as Steve Jones, he turns away.

⚯

The good feeling upon leaving Miami didn't last very long. Past Atlanta, the weather chilled. Fog descended on my car, then sleet. Snow stuck to the flat, empty cornfields of Indiana and stayed the rest of the way to my parents' house north of Chicago. My adrenaline faded with the sun. What will I do about money? How can I possibly qualify for Boston if I weigh more than two hundred pounds? And if I don't like to run? And if I've never been good at running? I was tired and anxious as hell and in my parents' house for less than ten minutes when my mom unloaded on me. She called me a crybaby. She brought up my ex-wife. She said I'd had a very nice life all laid out until I screwed it up. She used the word "martyr" eight times. She even smacked me on the shoulder, a first. Didn't hurt — she's sixty-eight years old. Still, it's pretty bracing for a grown man to have his mother punch him and call him a crybaby. Even worse, when she called me a crybaby I broke into tears.

My dad was out of town the night I arrived, which was probably for the best. When he flew in the next day, he talked about how I don't have many options anymore, in general. I left the day after that, driving away from Illinois on a morning as rotten as my mood. A two-front storm they were saying. Tornados in Arkansas and sleet from the Mississippi River on west. Ice coated my Mazda in a clear shell. Red plastic ribbons fluttered on the antennas of stranded cars checked by the police. The arms of a forklift burst out the back of one trailer. A dozen other semi-trailers littered the median, overturned and twisted into giant metal centipedes. I passed each wreck cautiously, hunched over my steering wheel. The needle on my speedometer stayed below 30 all through Iowa.

Beyond Lincoln, Nebraska, where I stopped for a night, the weather warmed. Ice melted off my car's windows, and then off the hood and trunk. Blocks of snow fell from trucks, spinning across the highway like curling stones. By the time I hit the Colorado state line, sun. I slipped off my coat. The highway split, with most of the trucks veering off to Cheyenne. An open road welcomed me into a state I'd never seen.

I paid close attention to the landscape. Rolling plains of copper soil. Trains of coal longer than I imagined possible. Deer leaping near the highway on the approach to Denver, a city of glass towers clustered in the middle of nowhere, for no apparent reason. I skirted the capital and powered through the suburbs of Westminster and Louisville. About twenty miles north of Denver, just beyond the Big Box valhalla of Superior, I crested a hill and my lungs drew an unusually long breath. There, in the valley below, lay Boulder. Jagged mountains loomed to the west, flat slabs of granite jutting out of the prairie like Superman's Fortress of Solitude. In the distance, in Rocky Mountain National Park, Longs Peak towered majestic and white and more than fourteen thousand feet tall. Foothills hugged the city, their gentle brown slopes dotted with pine trees that reminded me, for some reason, of hair plugs. The colors of Boulder in late February are oatmeal grasses and dark evergreens and the black-blue water of the reservoir. I noticed sienna stones stacked into a football stadium, and the orange Italian tiles that roof the university's campus. To my right, to the east, the plains stretched out endlessly, flat and frozen all the way to Lake Michigan, ground I'd just covered.

During the drive out, I'd contemplated the kind of apartment I wanted to live in. Ideally, I decided, kind of half-jokingly, I wanted a prison cell. Nothing but a place to rest between runs. Just a bed and a desk and a bathroom and little else. No distractions. A place to *Focus!* To *Be a Man!* When I toured the Chicken Coop, I gained respect for the power of visualization. A prison cell is what I'd conceived in my mind, and boy, I totally nailed it.

The stock of available housing in Boulder was thinner than I'd counted on; March first isn't the best day for turnover in a college town. Online, during my layover in Lincoln, I'd skimmed ads for "spiritual homes" and "sacred spaces to live." One ad was posted by "a single mother from a long line of women who are strong as ten horses and the most beautiful in all of Persia." "Namaste!" cheered a woman renting out a former massage room that "has good lighting and good vibes." Potential roommates "appreciate the continuum of racial, gender, sexual identity and expression." A "healer, coach, author, and motivational speaker" seeking a roommate for his townhouse in South Boulder described himself as "100% concerned about making the world a better place." His ad was 1,784 words long. His condo is zero waste and wind powered. "I help people plug back in to their spiritual side, overcome obstacles, heal through nature, and achieve their dreams." In a roommate he "prefers someone who brings positive vibes and energy with them ... someone who has a special touch in bringing out the beauty and the best in the world around them ... Speaking Japanese may be a bonus."

The place I ended up renting was advertised as "one bedroom with living room and small bathroom with shower" and "tons of southern sunlight coming in through a large window looking onto yard." I set up a tour soon after I pulled off US 36. As I made my way to the address in the upscale University Hill neighborhood, I passed million-dollar bungalows tucked behind tall trees and shrubbery, which made me optimistic. I envisioned a cozy mother-in-law house, or a widow's cottage above a garage stuffed with Range Rovers. Then I turned onto Rose Hill Drive and saw the dilapidated shack sheathed in baby-blue shingles.

When I first heard it was called the Chicken Coop, I assumed it was because of its ramshackle appearance. The structure looks like one long, weathered railroad car sliced into three apartments, with storage sheds acting as engine and caboose. Turns out the building is called the Chicken Coop because it used to be a chicken coop. Until 1948, chickens lived there, their eggs feeding diners at the Chautauqua meeting hall, at restaurants on Pearl Street, and at the sanitarium over on Mapleton Hill. I moved into the Chicken Coop on March first, the day I started my training in earnest.

There were three units in all. The unit for rent was one small room divided exactly in half by a retainer wall. The back half, which I shall call the bedroom, featured the same sloping flat roof that protected the chickens from the elements. The walls and ceiling in the bedroom were painted white, and there was a light-brown carpet that looked fairly new and was the room's best feature. One bare compact florescent bulb provided all the light.

The front half of the apartment was distinguished by a slim, gabled ceiling and an overhead fan. The window, which was indeed large and sunny, looked onto a narrow yard and a new $2.5 million mansion rising on an adjacent lot. Warm air radiated from a gas heater prettied with peeling flecks of brown paint. The carpet out front was thin and dirty, closely resembled a floor mat, and probably qualified as a Superfund site. The bathroom, tucked in a corner, could fit on an airplane: a toilet, the Coop's lone sink, and an ad-hoc shower demarcated by a plastic map of the earth. There was no kitchen. There was only a small shelf upon which sat a hot plate and a microwave. The refrigerator was a three-foot cube, the kind usually found in a dorm room. While I pored over the lease, Valentine sniffed her way around the perimeter, wondering in her dog brain how the place fit into her prior visions of the American West, of gamboling among aspen and frolicking in the snow.

"This is easily the worst apartment I've rented in my life," I told my new landlord. He chuckled, he believed me, and he knocked $50 a month off the rate he'd quoted, which is still more than I paid to live at the hotel in Miami, a place I've begun remembering fondly. My landlord is a computer executive from California who bought the Coop only a month earlier, and only for the lot. My new roost will be torn down — scraped, to use the Boulder term — in fifteen months, on the very day my lease expires. My rent will offset some of the $700,000 my landlord paid for the place.

"We're going to have to do something with these asbestos tiles first," he said, poking at one of the blue shingles covering the outside facade. "But, um . . . don't worry. They're not harmful or anything."

❧

I spend a couple weeks getting situated. I need a driver's license and registration, car insurance, and health insurance. I bolt new, green plates on my Mazda. When I stop by the public library to pick up a card, a sign posted near the main entrance informs me

I'm no longer my dog's owner, or even her roommate (which is the term I like to use). In Boulder, by law, I'm now Valentine's "guardian."

"Hey, you from Miami?" a guy at Boulder Wine and Spirits asks me. Is it that obvious? I inspect my outfit. I'm wearing a hoodie and jeans, I haven't shaved my beard since Florida, and I'm standing in the beer aisle of a liquor store. I thought I was fitting in. Turns out he overheard me opening a checking account at the bank next door.

"I moved from Fort Lauderdale a year ago," he says. "I spent ten years there. I was even down on South Beach, working at Mansion and other places." Mansion is a Miami nightclub. "I had to get out! I felt my life was spiraling out of control."

He's wearing a T-shirt and a mesh baseball hat embossed with the logo of a football team. A fat black tattoo snakes around his right bicep.

"You'll get used to it," he says. "Everything here is so . . . so . . ." He holds out his hands in a gesture I interpret to mean "slow motion." "For the first six months I was screaming at other drivers and tailgating and all, but now I'm loving it here, man. Give it six months. No, better still, give it a year. But probably six months."

Driving around Boulder, trying not to tailgate, I find three Nepalese restaurants but not a single donut shop. Tibetan prayer flags in primary colors flutter on porches and in front of stores on Pearl Street, the downtown pedestrian mall. Buses, which run on either electricity or natural gas, cover routes named Hop, Skip, and Jump. A bumper sticker encourages me to BE HIGH, BE HAPPY!

Pedestrians in Boulder carry a sense of entitlement. I notice this immediately. In Miami, I was once spit on by the passenger of a pickup truck when I tried to cross a street at a designated crosswalk, with the light. In Boulder, walkers step into traffic nonchalantly, knowing they have the right of way and acting all cocky about it. Waiting at one crosswalk illuminated with flashing yellow lights, I flip my radio to KBCO, Boulder's self-congratulatory adult progressive radio station. As I run the rest of my errands, I listen to Jack Johnson and Beck and some more Jack Johnson and then again to that one same Beck song.

I'm unsettled. I feel out of place, perhaps on another planet. I'm struck by what I don't see in Boulder. I don't see poor people, except at McDonald's, where the entire workforce speaks Spanish. Zoning laws regarding fences and lot lines and mixed-use developments seem to be enforced properly, appropriately. No refrigerators rust in the middle of the street, which is common in Little Havana. Miami is lawless, a state of nature. Boulder seems more like an exclusive gated community, catered by Mexicans.

Being the last-ever occupant of the Coop—human or fowl —frees me as an interior decorator. I'm tempted to spray paint "Helter Skelter" on a wall, but my only beautification involves hanging the calendar my mom gives me every Christmas and a poster I pick up of the American running legend Steve Prefontaine, last seen alive by Frank Shorter before he crashed his convertible and died at age twenty-four.

"To give less than your best is to sacrifice the gift."

I steam-clean the front-room carpet and dust the shelves of a bookcase I found on Craigslist. I buy an old couch from a guy who lives out by Boulder's commuter airport.

"Do you love it?" the guy asks while I appraise the couch's blue denim cushions, which are tagged with orange and purple crayons.

"No," I reply, "but I'll take it."

I pick up a used La-Z-Boy from the founder of the Boulder Fringe Festival, tossing it in the Coop's storage shed along with a floor lamp and a space heater purchased at McGuckin Hardware; this will be my "study." From the shed I pull out an old mattress a previous occupant left behind. I drench it with Lysol, cover it with irregular sheets from Marshall's, and slide it into my back room. At Target I buy a table the length and width of a door, assemble it in the front room and label it my desk. I also invest in new file folders for all the freelance journalism I tell myself I will pick up. At Safeway I stock up on oatmeal, protein bars, Gatorade, and low-calorie frozen dinners I can warm in the microwave. I do not buy ice cream. Or Pop-Tarts. I set up a body-fat-monitoring scale in the bathroom. In the bedroom, I stack my T-shirts and jeans on the floor in the narrow space between the bed and the dividing wall. I fill my small closet with running gear.

With everything squared away, I take Valentine for a long walk around the Hill. We climb south and a little east until we reach the house where a child beauty queen was once murdered, infamously. We both decide JonBenet Ramsey died in a nice neighborhood. Very nice. It's quiet, the dominant soundtrack a gurgling brook that drains into the Creek. Texas license plates — from all the lifestyle relocaters who have moved here recently — hang inside the garages of oversized new houses. In the living rooms of these houses, people my age watch television with their children. The guy who just bought the Coop is younger than me, actually, and already the father of four kids. He also owns a million-dollar house north of Pearl Street and a portfolio of commercial properties. That's depressing. I recall what my mom said back in Illinois, that I had a nice life all laid out for me until I screwed it up. If I'd worked hard and hustled and taken advantage of the head start my parents gave me, I could have lived in this neighborhood, too, I suppose. I try not to think about it. I don't want to be negative.

But wait a minute, I *do* live here. My new driver's license confirms residency on Rose Hill Drive. Back at the Coop, the tenants of the other two units, all shaggy college kids, cover a Weezer song on their guitars while suckling an eight-tentacled octobong. They wave at me when I pass, in part because I bought them a case of Boulder-brewed Avery brown ale as a welcoming gesture. I like that the students are here, that they are playing their guitars loudly (and badly) and even that they are so, so stoned. I'm glad we're all here polluting this upscale street in this upscale neighborhood in this eyesore that used to house poultry. I step inside my section of the Coop, crank up the gas on the heater, and pull Valentine onto the blue denim couch with me.

"We're home, baby!" I coo into her floppy black ears. "We're home!"

4

A TELEVISION FLOATS ABOVE the sales floor at the Fleet Feet running store off Broadway. I'm one of twelve people standing around the TV, watching it. Behind us glimmer display models of New Balance and Adidas trainers, running bras and socks and hats, slick-looking polarized sunglasses and digestible energy goo wrapped in shiny foil pouches. Fleet Feet isn't the biggest running store in town — that would be the Boulder Running Company — so its owners labor to enmesh the store into the community. Fleet Feet sponsors social training runs almost every day of the week. Some of the runs are for newcomers. Other runs are set aside for experienced athletes. One run every Thursday is for women only. We've just finished the Monday evening run, a casual six-mile jog open to all comers. We ran three miles up the Goose Creek canal, then wound our way back to the store. As we cool down, we're drinking water and watching a replay of the Boston Marathon, which took place this morning.

There's a lot to like about Boulder, I've decided. The newspaper article that lured me here, the one that declared Boulder America's running mecca, claimed the city enjoys mild winters and more than three hundred days of sun a year. That seems to be true. In the morning I might step onto a street coated in ice, with a paisley frost blooming across the hood of my car. But by lunchtime I can often walk down Pearl Street in a T-shirt. A blanket of snow covering the city on the last day of March melted away by the first day of April. Unfortunately, so far, most warm weather has been followed by a blast of winter. For one week I watched a lone tulip rise outside my window at the Coop, its petals red at the tip and yellow at the base. Then a frozen rain encrusted the yard, bending the tulip in shame at having displayed the sin of pride. On Easter Sunday, I ran in a blizzard.

The bills from my move are arriving, freaking me out. Beyond the unavoidable costs of relocation—the gas, the motel rooms, the replacement furniture—in one month I spent close to a thousand dollars on running gear. I felt a twinge in one of my knees so I dropped $120 on the appropriately named Brooks Beast, a brick of a shoe built for heavier runners with knee issues. Then my knee felt better and I started losing weight—I shed fifteen pounds in March alone—so I bought a new pair of lighter and more flexible shoes sold under the Asics brand. I needed new shorts and winter-weight shirts and then lighter mesh shirts for the warming days. And water bottles and energy drinks and a nylon running hat. I haven't been buying everything I want, but I don't blanch at buying what I feel I need. This is serious, I tell myself as I hand my Visa and my new Road Runners membership card to the cashier at the Boulder Running Company. I'm all in.

I try to find some work to help pay down the bills. I give my résumé to the dean of the CU School of Journalism but never hear anything back. I apply for a temporary job at Bolder Boulder, the gigantic 10K race started by Frank Shorter and held in the city every Memorial Day. The job looks easy. I only need work a regular shift at the Twenty-Eighth Street Mall, signing up interested runners and selling them sweatshirts and hats with the Bolder Boulder logo. I figure it's a perfect job for right now, a way to meet runners while not requiring a commitment beyond Memorial Day.

"Do you have any retail experience?" asks the temporary store's manager, an effervescent woman named Kristin.

"At a Dairy Queen, when I was sixteen."

"How well do you handle conflict?"

"Well, I'm divorced, so perhaps I can't."

I'm joking, but I don't get the job. I don't get a part-time, seasonal job that pays minimum wage.

So I spend more money instead. I sign up for yoga for athletes, held on Wednesday nights at Fleet Feet. On my first visit, one of the athletes in the class hands the instructor a CD of music, saying about the musician, "He's really big in Tibet. He opened, essentially, for the Dalai Lama at the Pepsi Center." I buy a running guide by Frank Shorter that advises me to swear off cement, so I've moved my Sunday long runs off the Boulder Creek Path and onto mostly dirt trails. I'm running four days a week now, increasing my running distances in slow and steady increments as Shorter also advises in his book. Lastly, I sign up for the Dash 'n' Dine, a series of five-kilometer races at the reservoir, held every Tuesday evening for five weeks. I don't race in the Dash 'n ' Dine. I participate only to expose myself to a racing environment, to the surge of adrenaline at the start, to the swish, click, and tumble of pebbles under a herd of running shoes, a sound that makes me think of waves washing on a beach.

On the TV screen at Fleet Feet, after my Monday workout, the leading American female runner is falling off the pace. She will lose out to a woman from Poland. It's cold and wet in Boston, and terribly windy. All of us in Fleet Feet are interested in the race. To runners, the Boston Marathon is a big deal. To me maybe more than anyone.

☙

I remember walking with my dad after the race. He's already changed into a baby-blue cotton sweat suit with a red zipper. I don't know why I remember those colors, but I do. My mom and his friends have already presented him with a homemade laurel wreath, similar to the one the mayor of Boston crowns atop the winner. That year, 1977, the winner was Jerome Drayton, a thin Canadian with pale skin and wavy black hair, the same basic features as my dad. Because of the similarities in their appearance, and especially because of the wreath on his head, my dad garners attention. A lot of it. A team of Japanese marathoners spills off a motor coach to bow before him and hand him Japanese coins. In my most vivid memory, my dad and I are walking to a parking garage after the race. It is just my dad and me; my siblings and my mom are not around, nor is the reporter who was writing about my dad for the *Boston Globe.* We cross a street near Fenway Park. Traffic is stopped for a light. Even when the light changes, no cars move because people are honking their horns and leaning out their windows to shake my dad's hand and congratulate him on a great race, man, great race.

"Thanks," my dad replies. Smiling, polite, technically honest. "Thanks a lot."

We all meet at the car. I recall driving to a dinner shared with some of my parents' friends. I'm sure it's Italian food, my dad's favorite. I've seen a picture of my dad at the restaurant, sitting next to my younger sister. My dad is hoisting a beer glass large enough to hold a half gallon of Pabst Blue Ribbon. In the photo my dad looks happy; he's about to enjoy his first sip of beer in several months. My sister, just five years old at the time, stares at the goblet with disbelief.

"He's going to drink all that?"

I remember asking my dad if he wanted me to run out to the car to get his wreath. I remember him telling me not to bother.

My mom assembled a collage after the race. She cut up a copy of the big *Globe* profile, mounting excerpts alongside the article's main photo of my dad in his Marquette University tank top. My mom also included a Japanese coin and a map of the course and a folded-up pink washcloth a spectator had handed my dad late in the race, which my dad claims saved his life. The framed collage hung over the piano in the living room of the house we moved to in Illinois, close to the table where I often played the Official Boston Marathon Board Game with my brother and sisters.

"Race 26 miles, 385 yards with thousands of other runners in the privacy of your own home." Draw cards such as "Stop to talk to Wellesley co-eds, lose a turn," and "You get Heartbreak Hill life insurance, go again." The winner of the game is crowned with a cardboard cutout wreath. All finishers receive a bowl of beef stew.

Of the race itself I don't remember very much. I don't remember the start or the finish. I know we moved around the course several times, to places my mom mapped out in advance. I remember seeing him once, sweaty and straining as he approached the Pillar House, a restaurant in Newton where my mom paid five dollars to park. I remember the *Boston Globe* guy growing all excited when he saw my dad on the course. I don't recall talking too much to the guy, the reporter. He was a graduate student at the University of New Hampshire, with shaggy brown hair and a beard. I was eight. I thought he looked like a hippie. As soon as my dad passed the restaurant we took off again, onto a highway so we could reach the finish before he did.

What else do I remember? I remember my dad lost a toenail in the race. I remember watching—studying—my dad in the car as my mom drove from the Prudential Center to the restaurant. His whole body had stiffened up, making it hard for him to fold into the front passenger seat. I remember the expression on his face. Exhausted. Happy in a way. To use a word I didn't know back then, and perhaps didn't learn until I got to Boulder, I'd say he looked transcendent.

The day after the race, a teacher at our grade school computed my dad's numbers. My dad had averaged less than 7 minutes per mile for 26.2 straight miles. "That's unbelievably fast," the teacher concluded. Even before the huge *Boston Globe* article came out, I knew my dad had accomplished something significant.

There is talk that other marathons have grown more prestigious than Boston. London and Berlin, perhaps, two races offering bigger prize money and faster courses ideal for setting world records. Or maybe, in America, New York City and Chicago have become the more important races. But Boston remains the marathon you have to qualify to enter—at my age I'd need to first run a marathon no slower than a 3:15:59 in order to make it into the Boston field. It's also, by far, the marathon that looms largest in my mind.

❧

"Running and finishing the Boston Marathon," says a man in Boulder named Rich Castro, "was one of the most profound accomplishments of my life."

I'm now sitting with Rich at the bar of the Walnut Brewery, the same place that the beer social Dan Skarda took me to was held. It's three days after the marathon. Rich, who is the president of the Boulder Road Runners, occupies the Norm slot at the north end of the bar. He chats up waitresses who swoop in for trays of microbrew, asking one of them about the health of her massage business. He informs the brewmaster, who is stepping out to take a dog for a walk, that he — Rich — is drinking a pale ale, apparently a switch from his usual beer choice. The pale ale bubbles in Rich's personalized mug: giant and brown and ceramic and decorated with a sticker of Ralphie, the University of Colorado's mascot. A small steel tag chained to the mug's handle identifies Rich as the mayor of the Mug Club. He seems to drink here a lot. His mug is stored on a shelf above the bar, along with the mugs of other club members. You have to complete a tour of the world — drink something like 240 pints of microbrew — to have your name inscribed on a plaque behind the bar. Rich tells me he's finishing up his fifth tour.

Rich is a pillar of the Boulder running community. He was the first coach of the university's women's cross country team. He also coached the sprinters on the track team, back in the 1970s when he was a graduate assistant. For the past ten years he has recruited the professionals racing in the Bolder Boulder 10K. He is a member of the Boulder Running Hall of Fame and the Colorado Running Hall of Fame. His stature in the city is confirmed every other minute when someone comes over to shake his hand and ask him for running advice, or to thank him for handling some duty, or just to say hello.

"That was a former punter for the Broncos," Rich says as one of his visitors walks back to his table.

I've come to ask Rich if he'll be my coach. Dan Skarda has warned me there are a lot of people around Boulder who claim to be coaches but who are really just former athletes hanging onto the sport any way they can. He gave me the names of a few guys he feels are more reputable, and Rich Castro is one of them.

I'd wanted to train without a coach. My dad went from zero to Boston all by himself. Training without a coach would show that, like my dad, I'm capable of taking care of my business. But already, after just a month and a half in Colorado, I've started slipping back into my old, bad habits. I'll stay up too late surfing the Internet; I've discovered free WiFi floating across University Hill with temptations I simply can't resist. In the morning, my bed pulsates with warmth and it's always cold out and I'll tell myself it's okay to sleep in, as I need my rest, which is true. My muscles ache. My legs are stiff. On my dad's birthday, April 4, I woke up at 9:15, very late for Boulder. I walked Valentine. I checked my e-mail, then read the paper for a while. I was chilly on my couch in the front room, and increasingly sleepy, so I *climbed back into bed,* a Boulder first. I stayed there until 11:15, completely killing my solid, simple plan to run an hour before lunch. I get my run in, always, but often it is the only thing I accomplish all day. Unlike my dad, I need forced structure. I need someone to guide me.

"Be consistent," Rich says, taking another sip from his ceramic mug. "Live like a clock. That's the best advice I can give you. I live in the same house I've lived in for the past thirty years. I'm married to the same woman for the past twenty-six years. I worked for the same school, CU, for my whole career. I've been going to the same weekly poker game for twenty-five years — I'm about to leave for that right now. There's something to be said for a routine life."

Don't I know it. My dad's entire life is one big, rigid routine. Five o'clock mass every Saturday. Dinner every night at precisely six p.m. After dinner, crack open exactly two light beers while watching sports until it's time for the nine o'clock news on WGN. Watch the news through the weather, then march upstairs to bed, first setting the kitchen table with a bowl of dry oatmeal, a glass of lukewarm orange juice and some vitamins so breakfast is waiting when he wakes up early for his run. On one of my parents' visits to Miami, we invited a friend of mine to join us for dinner at Tobacco Road, the oldest bar in the city. My friend showed up twenty minutes late, which is absolutely, totally normal in Miami — Cuban time — to find we had already ordered, eaten, and were ready to leave.

Rich is a small man. At a few months shy of age sixty he's no longer sculpted like an athlete. He carries a bit of a belly, really. A graying black goatee masks a receding chin. He grew up in La Verne, California, one of nine children of Mexican immigrants. Rich worked in the fields alongside his family, picking fruit or bell peppers depending on the season. When Rich was a boy, a champion decathlete spoke at his grade school. After the speech, Rich went out to a field behind the school, took off his shoes and socks, pulled up his pants, and ran some sprints.

"What are you doing?" asked a teacher. Rich said he was trying to make the Olympics.

At the Walnut Brewery, Rich and I don't talk about how many days a week I should run. How far? How fast? It never comes up. This is supposed to be merely an initial interview, the first of several interviews with several potential coaches. But I am already inclined to go with Rich for his promotion of strict routine. I've never liked my dad's rigidity, yet I can't deny how much my dad accomplishes with his time. Then Rich tells me about his experience running Boston and I know, without a doubt, I won't need to interview any other candidates.

Rich first ran Boston in 1979, in the same race as my dad, who was running Boston for his third and final time. Rich finished in just under two hours and fifty minutes, fantastically fast and ten minutes quicker than my father. Even so, Rich struggled to finish. He'd flown through the first two-thirds of the course. He practically sprinted up Heartbreak Hill, which most people consider the toughest section of the race. But he'd gone out too quickly. By the last leg of the course he found himself so depleted of energy he felt compelled to drop out. He stepped off Beacon Street, onto the sidewalk. A young woman dressed in a vest and a tie like Annie Hall pushed him back onto the course.

"You're not quitting now!" she shouted at him. "Get back out there!"

He got back out there. The last five kilometers passed in a crawl, a "survivor shuffle" to use a running term. Runners he'd passed all race now passed him. He seemed to be moving in slow motion. But he finished, he got his bowl of beef stew and — this is what gets me, this is not something I see coming — he resolved to divorce his first wife.

"I realized if I can do this one thing, if I can finish the Boston Marathon, then I can do anything," he tells me. "So I called her up and said I wanted to go through with the divorce. We went to the courthouse and the judge asked us one question: Is this marriage beyond saving? I looked at her. She said, 'Yes.' I said, 'Yes,' too and that was it. We divided up the property. She bought me out of the house. I took that money and bought a condo, and have owned property in Boulder ever since.

"The marathon was empowering. It taught me I can get through anything and everything, even a divorce, which was the hardest thing I'd ever been through. I'd failed at something I was supposed to succeed at."

With that, Rich takes a last sip of his pale ale. He opens a black nylon wallet embossed with a Nike swoosh, pulling out a twenty to pay his tab. The bartender swipes Rich's Mug Club card. Rich shakes my hand then takes off for the same Thursday night poker game he's been playing for a quarter of a century.

"Live like a clock!" he calls out as he winds his way toward the door. "If you're systematic you can get there, absolutely!"

I sit at the bar a while longer, finishing up a pint of dark lager Rich bought me. I've read the trite kōans about long-distance running, about how if you can finish a marathon you can do anything you set your mind to. I never heard anyone say a marathon gave him the courage to end his marriage. I've never met anyone, ever, who was proud of his or her divorce. Not proud of the divorce, per se, but proud of going through with it. That it was the right thing to do, as difficult as it was.

I sign on with Rich as my coach not because of any particular training style. I don't pick him because his last name allows me the continuity of trading the Castro of Miami for another Castro in Boulder, though that is kinda neat. I go with Rich because he's a good, experienced runner who can bring to my training both structure and solid advice. Mostly, I sign on with Rich Castro because I've been waiting eleven years to find someone who feels the same way about his divorce as I do about mine.

5

D on't lend your uncle Bob any money."
My dad couldn't have been clearer. My uncle Bob,
my mom's younger brother, had lived in Miami for several years before I moved down. All I knew about Bob was his reputation. He'd visited our house outside Chicago once, and I recall him sitting around the living room bar, where my dad displays his beer cans. At the wedding of his daughter, who is one of my two cousins, he declared himself the black sheep of the family. I knew that my younger sister had once visited him in Florida, for a week, and when she came back my mom was angry at the small bikini he let her buy, or had bought for her. My dad's counsel to protect my money from Bob amused me. Like I had any money to lend.

I'd just accepted an entry-level position at a weekly newspaper in Fort Lauderdale. I was twenty-six. It was my first real job, or the first job since the Dairy Queen that didn't involve heavy manual labor. I drove down to Florida in the heat of summer in a twenty-year-old Pontiac station wagon I called the Sweatbox because its only air conditioning came from holes in the floorboards. Bob tracked me down soon after I'd arrived. Actually, he first contacted my boss, leaving her a voice mail message.

"Janine, I don't know who *you* are, but *I'm* Robert Roch and I'm trying to reach a young man with my same first name, who just happens to be my nephew."

That evening, after work, Bob swung by my studio apartment in his Lincoln Continental. He stood a little shorter than me. He wore his thin brown hair buzzed as tight as his beard, which was starting to gray. I could tell he worked out with weights. He looked about the same as he did in an old picture I'd seen, one of him hugging his second wife, now long gone, a blonde with wavy hair and a pink dress and a deep tan that showcased her white teeth. Bob slapped me on the back and led me to his car. We drove to a happy hour at one of the supposedly upscale bars that line the Intracoastal. The specifics of the tavern escape me. What I remember most are the colors. Gold rings, silver chains. Deep green palm fronds. Women with bright blonde hair. Men in floral silk shirts, like the one Bob had on, and brown leather loafers worn without socks, just like Bob.

"What's your job title again?" Bob asked me. "Associate Editor? Man, you're golden. With a title like that you'll be pulling pussy blindfolded."

Oh, please. I was still involved with my college girlfriend, who would become my wife. Even if I wasn't, the vibe at the restaurant frightened me. Everyone seemed a little trashy. All of them were on the prowl. Bob talked to some friends for a while, then came back to opine about the hot chicks in Florida and about how lucky I was to be there and to be young. I recall he took me to dinner afterward with a woman who decorated yacht interiors. She wore a pink dress, like his second wife in that photo. She had long blonde hair, also like his second wife. After dinner, as we waited for the valet to deliver his Lincoln, he audibly regretted the absence of his previous car, a British import. I inferred he could no longer afford the payments on it, or it had been repossessed.

"You should have seen when I had the Jaguar," he said. "The valet would pull up in that car and the pussy would hop right in."

The following Saturday he insisted I join him at his condo, on Williams Island. The island is not the prettiest place, tall white concrete towers surrounding a collection of blue pools, a clubhouse, and a marina. But it's an exclusive address. Professional tennis players keep condos on Williams Island, as do Italian actresses and Venezuelan oligarchs parking their Bolivars in a more stable economy. Bob was clearly proud to live there. He led me and my editor Janine—I thought he should learn *who* she is— around the grounds, from the pool to the Intracoastal Waterway, where his neighbor gave us a ride on a motorboat, and then back to the clubhouse. Bob acted like a sugar baron showing off his tropical plantation.

"Can you believe a bus driver's son is living like this?"

His dad—my mom's dad, my grandpa—had worked for the Chicago Transit Authority. We were supposed to be impressed, I think, at how far Bob had come in life. I was less impressed than I was worried; throughout the tour, evidence accumulated that Bob was living beyond his means. The Jaguar had been repossessed. The cable TV didn't work in his condo. At the pool, he balked when an attendant brought us towels because he didn't want to surrender the three-dollar rental fee. Still, he remained distinctly Bob. When Janine stepped into the pool for a swim, he turned to me and said she wasn't half bad looking and was I going to pull that or what?

Later, in the clubhouse, we sat on stools at the mahogany main bar. A pianist plunked out "Guantanamera." Bob said he wanted to eat something and asked the bartender for the specials. The woman didn't know what they were, excused herself, and soon returned with a short list scribbled on a napkin. I don't recall exactly what specials she announced. Maybe it was chicken Caesar salad and steak tartar and a cold tomato soup splashed with lime. Whatever she began to say, Bob stopped her midrecital.

"Excuse me," he snapped. "Look at me. Look me in the eye, please."

The woman looked him in the eye.

"You're not very good at your job are you?"

We ended up skipping lunch even though Janine and I both offered to pay.

That was the one and only time I visited Williams Island, and the last time I saw Bob. He'd call, but I'd always find something else I just had to do that night, or that day, or that week. It wasn't so much the pussy commentary. And it wasn't specifically his rudeness to the waitstaff, though I couldn't stand that one bit. He simply scared me. I didn't know much about money at that time but I knew he couldn't afford that condo. He obviously couldn't afford the Jaguar that once pulled in the trim; I suspected he couldn't even afford the Lincoln he'd downgraded to. His life looked like one big masquerade. He spent it trolling cheesy nightclubs for women who were themselves trolling for sugar daddies. Bob owned no sugar. It was clear the baronial role he played was pure theater. I worried it would all blow up in his face.

∞

When I first moved down, I was struck by Miami's ugliness. Away from the beach, Miami is dirty and gritty and nothing that ever ends up advertised on television. I'd expected Little Havana to gleam like an Epcot village, but it's all pawn shops and gas stations and little run-down bakeries selling stale bread sprinkled with granules of raw cane sugar. Trash gathers everywhere. Chickens crawl over those abandoned appliances rusting in the streets. The city is chaotic and hostile, which, after a few years, I admit I came to appreciate. It's not Disney World, no. But Disney World is an illusion, artificial. Miami is real.

It's the people who are fake. Sometimes it feels like everyone in Miami is pulling a scam. At the Epicure Market on trendy South Beach, I watched a man simply walk out of the store — saying nothing and leaving his groceries on the belt and his credit card in the checker's hands — when the checker tried to verify the credit card was in fact his. *My* credit card number was stolen at a restaurant in North Bay Village, by a waiter who used it to run up thousands of dollars in illegal purchases, all gasoline for some reason. A Colombo crime family hit man reigned as the city's top nightclub promoter. A magazine publisher advertised his generous sponsorship of the Miami City Ballet, the Museum of Contemporary Art, and the Miami Beach Police Athletic League. I'd seen him in a nightclub once, hosting fashion models at his table. On the day he was thrown in jail on charges of securities fraud, some other fabulist pulled into town, threw around too much money, and smoothly slipped into the vacant space behind the velvet rope.

It was to this city that Bob, a bus driver's son from Chicago, had come to reinvent himself. And it was this city, with these people, to which I brought my new wife.

Most of the details of my marriage have slipped away by now. It's been eleven years. I no longer can really recall most of our time together. What remains are synaptic flashes that come when I'm lying in bed, or running a five-mile loop around the rez, or sitting in the Laundromat watching my jeans tumble dry. I'll be brushing my teeth when suddenly I'll recall the way she threw her arms around my waist when I told her I was leaving. I'll be halfway around the block, waiting for my dog to do her business, when I'll recall how my wife couldn't stop laughing the first time she'd visited my parents' house for our first real date, a concert of zydeco music in a Chicago suburb. I'll be in the snow in Boulder, shivering, watching my dog circle four times as she looks for just the right spot, and I'll be thinking about my ex-wife standing in the front door of my parents' house, my mom inviting her in, and how she was so nervous she could only laugh and laugh and laugh.

There are a few concrete memories that will never disappear, and I cling to one of them when I'm feeling like the biggest shit in the world for cheating on her, for lying to her, and then for leaving her. She can recall this one memory too, I'm sure. It was significant. We were in Miami, at our dining room table, in the house we bought, the house we spent all our free time refurbishing. I held a steady job at a different newspaper. She worked for the school system, making about the same money as me. I had yet to meet Mrs. Wisconsin.

A door-to-door salesman knocked. He was a guy offering us a life insurance policy of some kind. We invited him in, gave him water to drink, and said we'd listen. The salesman — I think he had white hair, I know he was wearing a necktie — couldn't have been very experienced. He should have realized we were easy money. We didn't want to sign anything impulsively, we said, but we'd almost certainly buy a policy if he'd simply call us back in a day or two. He didn't want to wait. He insisted we give him saliva on the spot, and he pulled out two black plastic vials for us to spit into. We declined, with smiles, and again told him to give us a call in a day or two. The salesman never followed up, which was his loss. We'd been sold.

First off, life insurance seemed like something for adults, married adults, people who we were trying to be. Buying a house was also something married adults did, and we'd checked that off the list a year earlier. We'd already bought furniture, including a dresser and matching nightstands in the bedroom and the Swedish Modern table in the dining room at which we'd invited him to sit. We were already fixing up the house on the weekends and almost every night after work. Beyond all that, what sold us on the policy, what closed the deal for us, was one detail. It was a very unusual clause in a life insurance policy, he'd said. Very unusual, he repeated.

My wife didn't make eye contact with me. I didn't make eye contact with her. Neither of us said anything. But we'd been together for more than a decade by then, in total, long enough to know each other instinctively. I knew what she was thinking. I'm sure she knew what I was thinking, in the same way she'd eventually know I was sleeping with one of her lifelong friends. Regarding that very unusual clause, she and I were thinking the exact same thing.

᪕

We'd met at college. Ours was a small, snowy institution in the Midwest, a school where everyone knew everyone else whether they wanted to or not. She enrolled a year after me, and we met soon after she arrived on campus. Although I didn't really pay attention to her at first, I had plenty of opportunity for further observation. By my senior year I realized she possessed the most wonderful laugh I'd ever heard. Looking at her more carefully, I noticed the clarity of her blue eyes. And she liked me. That was probably the biggest factor. It was nice to be liked, by someone. I liked it.

We basically moved in together on campus. In the morning we'd slide across icy sidewalks to grab breakfast at the commons. After studying in the library at night, we'd fall asleep on her bed, my arm draped over her waist. She stuck with me as I found my path. I dropped out of graduate school in Chicago and took jobs digging ditches in the summer and shoveling snow when the weather turned cold. Another job found me chauffeuring handicapped veterans in a rusty white van. After my shift ended, she and I often shared a spaghetti dinner at my apartment in Milwaukee, followed by a muffin at a neighborhood coffee shop.

When I enrolled at a second grad school, back in Chicago, she rode the train down to meet me on weekends. We continued to talk on the phone every night after I accepted an internship in Utah, and then that job in Fort Lauderdale and soon thereafter a better newspaper job in Miami. She finished up her master's degree in school psychology. Our friends began marrying. When her younger sister found a husband, our fate appeared pretty much sealed. It seemed like our turn.

My mom once told me — I don't recall when or why — that my dad was very eager to marry, very aggressive in his courtship. I later asked him about that. He was twenty-five when he wed. He had college and the army out of the way, and a job lined up in the human resources department of a place called Moore Business Forms. It was simply time to get married, right? After he met my mom on a Labor Day trip to Saugatuck, Michigan, he didn't even question marriage as the next logical step. Right? My dad told me he'd never thought about it before, about why he wanted to marry so badly. He never seems to think about any of this.

I didn't think about it either, really. My older sister had married her college boyfriend at twenty-five. My younger sister would eventually marry at twenty-five, to a guy she went to high school with. (My brother, bless him, didn't marry until almost forty. But he's out in Seattle, in his own world.) This sounds ridiculous to say, but I didn't realize I had any options. I was going with the flow. I loved my girlfriend just fine and we were together and I already had a job with medical and dental and I'd started socking away the maximum contributions to my 401(k). When I proposed to her — on the day Kurt Cobain's body was discovered — I was just doing what I thought all responsible, normal young adults do.

It was only after we'd married, and after she moved down to Miami, that I came to feel maybe marriage to each other wasn't in our best interests.

Our first two years were spent in Miami Beach, in an Art Deco apartment close to the water. On Saturdays we'd walk across the boardwalk with our towels, ready to broil away an afternoon. Some nights we'd stroll down Washington Avenue to marvel at the buildings and the people and the implausibility of our presence in South Florida. She took a part-time job at Books & Books on Lincoln Road, soon upgrading to a career position with the school district. We were on track, save one, glaring problem. She hated Miami. The fire ants hiding in the grass. The vacuity. The charlatans living beyond their means. Repeatedly she asked to move back to Milwaukee. She missed her mother, she said. She wanted to go home.

I wasn't yet loving Miami, either, but I was trying to make it work. I wanted to succeed as a journalist. I wanted to socialize at least a little. Passive aggressively she'd sit in the apartment and stew, refusing to engage with anyone or anything in the city. Passive aggressively I'd respond by not sleeping with her. A full year before Mrs. Wisconsin came on the scene, my wife and I spent ten days in North Carolina, in the mountains kneading the western half of the state. We rented a cabin outside of Blowing Rock. In the daylight we hiked the Blue Ridge. At night we went out for dinner, or cooked something back at the cabin. We were alone on that vacation. We didn't have sex once.

Staying married began to feel dishonest. Yet it was the main relationship in my life, the center of my entire existence. I couldn't imagine a world without her. And I knew I couldn't leave. My dad, no way he'd allow that. My mom, either, so religious and wed to my dad for more than forty years. Staying married seemed the one unbreakable rule, in fact, a commandment. My older sister has been married for twenty years. My brother and my younger sister are both married, too, everybody with kids. I am aware of only one person in our extended family who divorced, and that's Uncle Bob, the self-described Black Sheep, the failure in Florida. I felt trapped.

So I kept trying. That's what people are supposed to do, right? Stay on track! I sank all the money I'd been saving into a small house in Miami, a fixer-upper whose restoration became our joint project. I hoped it would become a common bond. I also hoped, as we worked on it, that the fissures in our union would somehow heal themselves. We scraped layers of paint from the doors and walls, patched cracks in the ceiling and bathed the iron window frames in rust inhibitor. An overgrown Brazilian pepper in the backyard gave way to a banana tree and some young palms. Fresh paint appeared on the walls, fresh stain on the floors.

On Friday nights after work we'd change into our grunge clothes, then spend the evening sanding and scraping until our fingers sometimes bled. Later we'd collapse in front of the television, sawdust caked in the corners of our eyes, flecks of paint clinging to our skin like latex glitter. On the night we finally hung the last refinished door on the last refurbished frame, I looked around. The house throbbed with energy invested in its repair. All-Clad pots shined in the kitchen. A desk and chair stood at attention in a room off the garage, a space assigned to be my office. Yet I didn't care. I didn't care at all. I didn't want that house. I did not want to be married, at least not to my wife. By that time, yes, Mrs. Wisconsin was on the scene.

❧

My cousin called about a week after they found Bob's body in his bathtub. She'd flown down from Indiana to clean out his place on Williams Island. She offered me anything I wanted from the condo. Free. It was my understanding the IRS wouldn't let her keep money from whatever she might sell. So after Bob shot himself in the face I ended up with his TV, which I didn't really want.

"He always talked about how you didn't have a TV," my cousin told me, pleased I was taking it.

Before I walked off with the set, she asked if I could find an article about Bob's death, which one of his Williams Island neighbors had seen in the newspaper. I could find it, I replied, and I did. It wasn't an article really, just Bob's name in a list of recent gunshot victims, part of the newspaper's year-long project on gun violence. He was fifty years old, the paper noted. That was it. No notation that his body was cremated, or that my cousin scattered his ashes in the Atlantic Ocean. No indication his gunshot was self-inflicted.

Soon after we'd bought the house, still in a time before Mrs. Wisconsin, my wife started joking, sort of, that she'd stopped wearing a seat belt in the car.

"I'm not afraid to die," she'd crack. She was joking. It was

48

supposed to be funny, though she really did stop wearing her seat belt. I had my own joke. Sometimes I'd sit in my cubicle at work and type out an e-mail on my computer. In the address line I'd put the name of everyone in the office, the reporters and editors and the publisher and the entire art department and all the sales reps in classified and display advertising. For a subject I'd put "Breaking News," which amused me. The body of text was short and to the point.

"I've just killed myself."

Sometimes (usually, often) when I'd write out the e-mail, I'd let my index finger hover over the send button. The door to an emergency exit stood only five yards away. From there, over a metal railing painted a pastel shade of purple, waited an eleven-story drop to the parking lot. No way I'd survive that. One click, one dash, one leap, and for me it would be all over. For my colleagues, who like stories, the e-mail would give them a pretty good story to tell.

The two of us, my wife and I, had thought the same thing. The policy pays out even in the case of suicide. *Good.* Sometimes, when I'm feeling generous, I spin my divorce as a life-affirming gesture, as an effort to save myself. And to get away from my wife so she could save her own life.

It probably means something that we've both left Miami. I stayed in the city for the affair that delivered me nowhere, then for the rebound relationship that ran off with a doctor. By the end, as my fortieth birthday approached, I'd dropped lower than I'd ever been, lower even than during my marriage. There was a bathtub in the apartment I rented after we separated. Every time I brushed my teeth I could see the tub in the medicine cabinet mirror. Just looking at it ran a chill up my neck, settling on a spot near my right temple.

"You're just about out of options," my dad told me when I stopped in Chicago on my drive from Florida to Boulder. Indeed. Absolutely. But remaining in Miami was one of the options I did have. I don't know for sure what would have happened if I'd stayed, but I have my fears.

6

THE SUN THAT regularly shines on Boulder rises from the plains, throwing gold onto Kansas and Nebraska before crawling across the Colorado state line. Sterling, Greeley, Longmont. In Boulder, first light touches the Flatirons, oversized arrowheads pushed up from a prehistoric seabed some 65 million years ago. The towering granite triangles accept sunshine the way a silver screen hosts a Hollywood movie. Eagles and turkey vultures spin overhead. The sun slinks down from the foothills into the valley, washing into Boulder Creek, brightening Pearl Street rooftops and settling finally in auburn fields of open space, glistening a new day.

The woman running next to me is humming. She tells me people never want to run when they're down, so every morning she wills herself into happiness. She is happy and humming as she and I and the rest of the Boulder Road Runners ease into our twenty-minute warm-up. I am not humming. I am groggy. *Down.* I'm an antisocial, self-loathing, suffering runner man. Yes, I notice the way the morning sun ignites the Flatirons, the way small frosty clouds escape our mouths with every exhale. I recognize the romance of being out here early in the morning, in a line of runners quietly clomping along trails of gravel and dirt. I like the Romantic aspect. I just don't like being awake. Or running.

❧

I received a lot of advice in Boulder when I first shared my Boston goal. Several runners advised me to start racking up long miles, right away.

"You gotta build a base," Mike Sandrock, the *Daily Camera*'s running columnist, insisted one morning as he and I huffed our way up the Sanitas mountain trail. "Spend your first six months getting up to sixty miles a week. Go as slow as you need to go, crawl if you feel like it, but get up to sixty miles a week. That'll build your base. You can improve your speed from there."

Rich takes a completely different approach. He believes in putting in as *few* miles per week as possible. More like thirty-five miles total, at least at first. He's not alone in this philosophy. It's a trend touted in running magazines and by prominent bloggers as a way to avoid injuries. A guy I used to play hockey with in Miami, a fitness freak who qualified for Boston in his forties, keeps his legs fresh by training primarily on his bicycle; he never runs more than three days per week. Rich has me running on Tuesdays and Thursdays with his regular training group. I run long on Saturdays now, though my miles those days remain in single figures. Sundays I "recover" from my long run with 6.6 miles with Rich and the club on trails out by the airport. Fridays are my day off. On Mondays and Wednesdays I cross-train on an elliptical machine at the Flatiron Athletic Club, Rich's gym, which he encouraged me to join. I don't know if Rich's training methods are the best, but I know I have to choose one path and stick to it.

"I've surrendered my free will to Rich Castro," I now say when offered training tips.

Because I'm aligned with Rich, my mornings in Boulder are much different than my mornings in Miami. They now begin the night before, when I go to bed as early as I can.

"You've got to start plotting your evenings!" Rich commands. "You've got to start winding down!" Rich is always in bed by eight thirty p.m., even in the summer when it's still light out. Though I continue to stay up past midnight sometimes, I am trying hard to start my wind-down in time to turn the lights off by ten. Rich wakes up at five thirty every morning to stretch and eat some oatmeal, wheat toast, and soy milk.

"I know what I'm going to eat for breakfast every day!"

Five thirty in the morning is out of the question for my alarm, but I still wake early enough to digest the same meal every morning, in my case a chocolate PowerBar and a can of Diet Mountain Dew. That sounds horrible, I know, but Frank Shorter drank flat Coca-Cola during his Olympic victory in Berlin so soda is not without precedent. I walk my dog. I'm sleepy and groggy, but I try to prepare my brain for the upcoming workout.

"You've got to be excited!" Rich advises. "You've got to know exactly what you're going to do and be eager to start doing it."

I try. This morning, before I left the Coop, I pulled out a book of running poetry Rich gave me. He wrote the book himself, *Thoughts on the Run,* by Rich Castro. The cover page features a pressed oak leaf. More pressed leaves are stuck inside. This is the first poem:

> *In me dwells something so simple that it defies explanation*
> *I am shackled by love, but I am not a prisoner.*

For he who makes no friends, will always find his foes
    I choose not to be idle,
so clothed in my own breath on this chilly morning,
    I nourish myself
with the severity of the perfect light found only in the physical world.
    Each run teaches me humility,
for my race is born of fire and wind . . . I chase the sweetness
    found in my trials,
and hoard the life nuggets of personal redemption that I find.
    What I find may be mystical to others,
but we all seek that stillness that can only come with inner peace,
    when we are declared worthy of our endeavors . . .
so that the valiant are released to roar, and feel their power.

❧

The woman next to me continues humming. I'd like to tune her out with music, but I can't. Real runners do not use iPods, I've been told, and everyone in Boulder—almost by definition —is a real runner. So I run without an artificial soundtrack for these first twenty minutes, which are only a warm-up. We trot on a sidewalk fronting a retirement home. Then we climb a pedestrian ramp over the Foothills Parkway, descending into a residential neighborhood much more modest than University Hill. There are about thirty of us altogether.

"Runner up!"

There is another jogger heading toward the pack, coming from the opposite direction. "Runner up!" is what the first person to notice an oncoming athlete is supposed to yell. People also yell "Bike up!" and, perhaps, if a car is coming at us from behind, "Car back!" I have yet to yell one of these warnings. I don't say anything at all if I don't have to.

We pass an elementary school, cutting through its parking lot over to a wide grass field. Netless soccer goals look like uninspired modern sculptures. We pass a dog park, then jog toward one of the city's three recreational centers. We watch our steps for goose droppings on the paved path that bends between a small pond and the rec center's indoor swimming pool. I work the stiffness out of my legs. I try to keep up with everyone. I try not to complain.

"Oh man!" someone says. "Look at that!"

We twist to look, at the Flatirons, which are bathed in a soft, bright light that makes them seem to glow. It's really pretty. In Miami, I liked sunsets more than sunrises. I liked the way the Atlantic Ocean turned a hundred different blues and pinks as the sun fell in the other direction, into the Everglades. Here in Boulder, the sunrise is clearly the better option. I recognize this. I'm grateful for this view of the Flatirons, for this experience.

We turn onto the South Boulder Creek Trail. It's a well-maintained dirt path. The newspaper article that got me out of Miami mentioned that Boulder boasts more than 400 miles of running trails. From Magnolia Road 8,600 feet above sea level to the Creek path's seven miles straight through town to countless loops of the rez and the foothills and the farmland stretching east. The options seem limitless, though on Tuesdays and Thursdays we always run the South Boulder Creek Trail. We run the trail because we are with Rich and Rich says there's something to a life of routine and we are living like clocks.

"Runner up!"

Another man sprints toward us, fast. We skip to the side of the trail, single file, gold shortgrass swatting our tights. The rising sun pulls shadows from each stone crunching under our feet. We curve around a grove of trees, then under South Boulder Road through a tunnel always wet with irrigation runoff. We emerge from the tunnel on a wider dirt trail. Just two hundred yards to the cow gate, where we can rest for a minute. Now one hundred yards. We cross the South Boulder Creek itself, small and swollen with snowmelt rushing down the Rockies. Rich holds the gate open for me. I unzip my windbreaker. I peel off my gloves and today even my hat, hanging everything on the sign that welcomes us to the trailhead. No dogs, the sign reminds us. Watch for cows.

Rich assigns me to the remedial group. It took me several weeks to work my way up to this group, the second string. There are five of us. We start out with one minute "at pace," or the speed we hope to run in a race. The sun shines brighter on the foothills. I spy the red clay of a building designed by I. M. Pei to complement the foothills' natural beauty. Not successfully, I muse as we slow down for a minute. A line of cars as small and orderly as ants marches up the turnpike from Denver, carrying employees of the university or Crispin Porter or IBM. We speed up for another minute, then slow down for another minute. A parallel parade of cars retreats south to Denver, carrying lawyers and oil executives who work in those tall glass buildings downtown. Five seconds, three seconds. One. Six minutes at pace. Go!

Six solid minutes of intense effort. Our shoes kick up gravel. We're running really hard, though I don't know exactly how fast we're going; my job is just to keep up with the pack. I huff so loudly I feel self-conscious. I try to zone out. I try not to think about how much I dislike what we're doing. Arms down, shoulders down, lean forward a bit, swing my knees out ahead of my feet, all things Rich has taught me. Keep my jaw loose. Get a rhythm going. Cows stand to the side of the path. Sometimes in the path.

"Just don't startle them," I've been advised. My legs feel dead. I must push myself. It takes all my energy to do this pushing. Fucking fuck I want to stop. The trail bends gently toward the foothills, into tall grass, then a sharp right to a footbridge often pockmarked with cow patties. Annnnndddd . . . Six Minutes!

Slow but don't stop. A one-minute recovery. We catch our collective breath. The other day, over on a small hill across the creek, we saw two black bears foraging for breakfast. We don't see any bears today. Nobody has the strength anymore for small talk. Five seconds. Four, three. Okay, off again for the second six-minute push.

I struggle to keep up. I *don't* keep up. I'm headed for the half-way point of the trail, another fence to touch and turn around. The four other runners in the remedial group have already touched the fence and are running toward me.

"Keep going, Robert!" someone says.

"Looking good!" shouts someone else. Encouraging words I have a hard time believing. I'm supposed to be optimistic, I know. I'm supposed to be so happy to be here that I feel like humming. I've been advised by one running guidebook to psyche myself up for success by repeating the chant: "I am an animal! I can run forever!" Another recommended chant is more general: "I am awesome!" Sorry, but that's goofy. That's not where I'm at. I spend the entire six minutes dwelling on how much I want to quit. Maybe I don't really want to qualify for Boston. Maybe marathon training is a stupid fucking thing to do.

"Pick up the caboose here!" shouts Rich, who is auditing the remedial group today.

"Cow up!" shouts someone else.

One more brief recovery, which gives me time to catch the pack. One more long, six-minute interval. The last interval is the hardest physically but I often run it the best. I know we're almost done, and when we're done I get to stop. I really want to stop; that PowerBar-and-diet-soda mixture I consumed for breakfast percolates in the back of my throat. We run under the turnpike. Two minutes left. I focus on a tree up ahead, a tall spruce with bare and twisted branches out of a scary children's book. One minute left. I can see the cow gate. The first-string runners are waiting for us. Twenty feet to the cow gate, ten. The cow gate. We stop. I wheeze. I gulp air into my lungs. I let the pleasure of sudden inactivity wash over me. It's kind of postcoital, I acknowledge. It feels so good to stop, it's almost worth it to run. Almost. I've finished last in the remedial group. I feel bad. I know I could have run better.

Fuck it. Whatever. The hardest part of my day is over and it's not even eight a.m. I fetch my jacket and hat and gloves from the trail entrance sign, tying the jacket to my waist on Rich's orders.

"Don't carry your jacket in your hands! You'll screw up your form!"

The twenty-minute jog back to the gym is just that, a jog. Slow, totally casual. It's our cooldown. We steer from the path back into residential streets with Indian names: Iroquois, Illini, Cherokee. Other runners talk about the races they're training for. At Seminole we turn north.

"Car up!"

We move to the side of the street to let the car through. Back over the pedestrian bridge, back past the retirement home, back to the gym. At the sliding front doors of the Flatiron Athletic Club I punch a button on my watch. Seven miles total. One hour of running total, not counting our stops. That's the normal routine. I will go home, where the entire day will stretch out in front of me. Valentine will lounge on the couch, barely lifting her head when I come in. I'll read the letters to the editor in the paper. I'll eat a bowl of Cheerios in chocolate milk, a good recovery meal.

I'll turn on KBCO then lie down on the couch next to my dog. The sun through the big window will feel warm and narcotizing. I will fall asleep, always. I have things to do. I *need* to work. I *need* to make some money. But often, the couch and the nap, that's the rest of my morning. Before that, right now, I will step inside the gym to ice my knees for a while. Rich and I will talk for a few minutes before he heads to the locker room to soak in a hot tub.

"I'm going to start calling you at five thirty in the morning just to make sure you're up," he tells me. "We're going to make an athlete out of you after all."

7

A T MY PARENTS' house in Illinois, my dad keeps everything that is unquestionably *his* in the office. There's a desk and a fax machine, some bookshelves, and a small closet. The desk is old and wood and looks as though it came from a government agency. Atop the desk, pens bloom from an empty can of Planters cocktail peanuts, an old after-dinner snack my dad abandoned on doctor's orders. There are florescent markers, two staplers, three calculators, a chain of paper clips, and a stack of letters from Loyola University Chicago, where he went to graduate school while still in the army.

The bookshelves, waist-high and painted white, line two of the walls. I rarely see my dad reading anything more than a newspaper; whenever I'm around we're watching TV. Yet the bookshelves hold dozens of the pulp fiction paperbacks he must have devoured in his youth. *The Naked Maja, Anatomy of a Murder,* and a few books that don't look so lowbrow: *Crome Yellow* by Aldous Huxley and Remarque's *All Quiet on the Western Front.*

Atop the shelves he has stacked a few old tomes from his work, page-turners such as *Classics in Management* and *A Handbook of Wage and Salary Administration.* There's a videotape, *From Bedside to Bargaining Table,* which must be from his once-frequent negotiations at hospitals, with nurse's unions. THE BEST RN'S BELONG AT BARNES! states a small round button, more hospital–union evidence. There's a yellowed baseball that his mother gave me when I was eight, hit to her by Hank Aaron when she worked at Milwaukee's County Stadium. After she gave it to me, I immediately ran outside and threw grounders in the street, scuffing the ball horrendously. I was eight!

There are no windows in the office. The walls are yellow. One wall near his desk is lined with brown R-Kive boxes, labeled in black Sharpie: "PAWLOWSKI — MISC." and "PAWLOWSKI — RECORDS," both of which are probably the remains of his parents' modest estate. Other boxes:

"FAMILY PICTURES."

"DAVID JENNIFER ROBERT + GRETCHEN, HIGH SCHOOL AND COLLEGES."

"TAXES 2003," with the year written above a "1993" that he scratched out with three neat lines of black ink. There are other boxes for his taxes from each of the past ten years. One last box, "HOUSES 1961 — 63, 64, 66, 68, 70, 72," reveals how many times we moved as a young family.

The other walls are cluttered with awards and certificates, which collectively make up the room's dominant visual. There's a framed document, dated four months before my birth, awarding him "Regular Membership in the American Society for Personnel Administration." In 1973, he qualified for membership in the Admirals Club, the American Airlines bonus program. Another certificate indicates he's a frequent flier of United Airlines, too.

"Well done good and faithful servant, for being a Eucharistic minister."

Golden Gate University in San Francisco commended his "outstanding service as a faculty member." The certificate is dated 1977, a year when we lived in New Hampshire. What's the deal with that? The Falstaff Brewery recognizes him as an Honorary Brewmaster. I'm mystified by a sign stating, "GOD INVENTED WHISKY TO KEEP THE IRISH FROM RULING THE WORLD," as we are in no way Irish, nor am I aware of any Irish enemies my dad or any of us have accrued; he doesn't even drink whisky. Less perplexing is a black-and-white photo of a friend's sailboat upon which we'd visit the Isles of Shoals off the coast of Maine, again back when we lived in New Hampshire. He is a member in good standing of the Beer Can Collectors of America.

Mostly, though, the walls are covered with running awards. There are first place medals and blue ribbons and a blizzard of race numbers embossed on rectangles of white paper. Some of the more important numbers are framed. Lesser numbers have been tucked under frame corners. His number from his first Boston Marathon, in 1977, is framed. Another frame for another year:

THIS IS TO CERTIFY THAT

THOMAS A. POWELL

FINISHED 2046 IN 2:59:57

IN THE 82ND ANNUAL BOSTON MARATHON

FROM HOPKINTON TO BOSTON, 26 MILES, 385 YARDS.

APRIL 18, 1978.

WILL CLONEY, PRESIDENT BOSTON ATHLETIC ASSOCIATION.

There's the plaque he won for finishing first in his age group at the Silver Lake Dodge Washington's Birthday Marathon, his first ever 26.2-mile race. There's a medal from the Ocean State Marathon in Newport, Rhode Island, the third marathon he ran that initial year. There are bibs from the Falmouth Road Race, which is a little over seven miles along the Cape Cod shoreline, and the *Milwaukee Journal* Al's Run, a 10K through his hometown. Four more bibs flap under Leroy Neiman's attempt to paint the Boston Marathon, a poster entitled *The Race*.

One more poster hangs inside the always-open door to the closet, below dried leaves of the wreath friends crowned atop my dad when he finished his first Boston. The poster is of a young man with long and wavy black hair. He's dressed in a red T-shirt and red nylon shorts and is running at sunrise through a golden meadow. The picture was probably taken in Boulder, where the runner in the photo has lived for decades. There is a quote from the man, the only American to win a gold medal in the Olympic marathon and the ignitor of the running boom that ensnared my father:

"Running won't change your life, just the way you live it."

※

Frank Shorter arrived in Boulder in 1970. The Yale graduate had first tried medical school in New Mexico but decided what he really wanted to do was run. His wife, whom he met on the ski slopes at Taos, had lettered on the swim team at CU. Her alma mater in Boulder, a mile above sea level, featured one of the only high-altitude indoor tracks in America, so that's where Shorter went to train for the 1972 Olympics in Munich. Boulder at that time elected Republicans, held an annual rodeo, and, thanks to transplanted hippies who had begun introducing liberal ideas, had legalized the consumption of alcohol only five years earlier. Shorter recalls there being only three other runners in town when he arrived.

When he captured the gold medal in Munich, Shorter was still classified as an amateur athlete; cashing in wasn't the option it is today. To prepare for a career that would earn him some money, he finished law school down in Florida and passed the bar in that state. But all he wanted to do, still, was run. By 1974, with only a year and a half until the next Olympic Games, he and his wife debated their options, couldn't think of a better place to live, and returned to Boulder. Frank Shorter has been here ever since.

"Nothing dominates the culture here," he would say. "Not the university, not Naropa, not the touchy-feelies, not the screaming conservatives, and not the athletes."

∞

From the beginning, Boulder has been a place in which people want to stay. Cheyenne and Arapaho tribes wintered along the Front Range foothills, a natural buffer against the icy winds that ravage the high plains. When prospectors struck silver in nearby Leadville, in 1867, Boulder coalesced into a supply town, sending up salt pork and pickaxes to miners in the mountains. Although the silver trade would soon implode, Boulder's leaders, not wanting to leave, brainstormed ways to keep their town viable. In a fierce fight with Denver and Colorado Springs, Boulder offered up enough free, picturesque real estate to win custody of the state university. A further gift of prime land at the base of the Flatirons convinced Methodist teachers in Texas to set up a Chautauqua, a sort of summer camp for arts and education. A militant faction of Michigan's Kellogg family—Seventh-Day Adventists opposed to sugar on cornflakes and spices such as mustard and paprika on everything else—placed a sanitarium atop Mapleton Hill.

"The great central idea kept before the patient, and exemplified in all his care, is that of health culture," stated the sanitarium's directors. America's first fitness freaks came to Boulder to ride bikes around the foothills and eat zwieback, or twice-baked bread. "Health is the object to be sought, wooed, and won, and every act and relation of life must contribute to the attainment of this end."

Active attempts to make Boulder as great a place as possible continued through the decades. Open space laws prevent developers from carving subdivisions into the rolling countryside. Colorado politicians landed NCAR (the National Center for Atmospheric Research), NIST (the National Institute for Standards and Technology), and a branch of NOAA (the National Oceanic and Atmospheric Administration), diversifying the economy so well that Boulder grew virtually recession proof. The intelligent population fostered by these research institutions and the university — Boulder is consistently ranked one of the smartest cities in America — attracted IBM, Sun Microsystems, and other high-end computer companies, right up to Google, which bought in to Boulder in 2006. Growth is now deliberately limited to only about 1 percent a year. The city's development has been so well managed that current leaders can be selective. When a big advertising company I know from Miami, Crispin Porter + Bogusky, wanted to open a satellite office in Boulder, the agency's directors were summoned to an interview with the mayor.

"This seemed like a good thing," recalls one of the partners, Alex Bogusky. "The mayor of Miami had never asked for a meeting." Crispin Porter were allowed to open up a shop that now employs around nine hundred people.

Although Boulder sits along an earthquake fault line, no seismic shift has ever topped the cultural changes brought on by the 1960s, when the conservative and teetotal town became a way station for hippies traveling to San Francisco. The young idealists, no different at their core from anyone else who's ever visited Boulder, fell for the jagged mountains, abundant sun, mild winters, and cool summers. Experiencing a sort of countercultural Brigham Young moment, many of them decided Boulder was the Place, and that they should stay.

"We wanted to make a living while still holding on to our values," says Mo Siegel, the founder of Celestial Seasonings, the giant tea company that's still here. Smaller health food companies opened, too. A Buddhist and some Beat poets founded Naropa University, giving the counterculture a pseudoacademic home base and forever altering the town's political viewpoint.

Today there are neither candy bars nor sodas for sale in the vending machines at New Vista High School on Baseline Road. Instead there is Vitamin Water, Rice Dream vanilla pies, and Amy's burritos made with organic vegetables and flour. The staff's picks at the Boulder Bookstore one time I stopped in were *Divorce Your Car, Voluntary Simplicity,* and *Getting Out,* the last expounded upon in a card taped to the shelf: "Empire, consumerism, warmongering and environmental blight getting you down? Then try the real world and explore the numerous countries that signed the Kyoto Treaty, said No to the war in Iraq, value joy more than money, and have no desire to run the world. Here is your guidebook for short and long-term emigration."

The education level in town can be disconcerting. One Friday morning, driving back from the grocery store, I was busy copying down the bumper stickers I passed — I BRAKE FOR WHALES and TURN LEFT AT THE NEXT ELECTION — when I saw a young boy and a girl operating a lemonade stand. I don't know what they were doing at home on a Friday but I stopped, of course; I support all lemonade stands as a matter of policy. Turns out they weren't selling lemon-flavored sugar water but twisted pieces of colored paper.

"ORIGAMI 75 CENTS" stated their sign.

I've noticed a hierarchy in car ownership, a caste system as clear as any in India. Entry level is the Subaru Outback: a station wagon with a rack on the roof for bikes, skis, and snowboards. You can drive a Ford or perhaps a Toyota pickup truck around town if you want, but others will presume you're a tourist motoring on to the national park. You're not in the game in Boulder until you're driving at least an Outback. If you're doing a bit better in life, you rise to a Volvo station wagon, boxy and safer and appointed with leather seats and antilock brakes and a killer stereo. For the really well-to-do, for the Brahman, there is the Audi. A station wagon, of course. Shiny as hell, silver or black or perhaps a slick red. Still with the roof rack. An X-Cargo hold strapped to the rack is always a nice touch. It shows you're not just a poseur, even if you are just posing.

There is an alternate option: the Prius, for pure smugness. In Toyota's hybrid sedan you can cruise Boulder like a shark, silently emitting fumes of pure environmental virtue, your self-satisfaction, to me, perhaps more toxic than any carbon dioxide emissions. The two lines will merge someday in an Outback hybrid, the car Boulder is waiting for. The car that will own Boulder.*

New homes in Boulder are tested for energy efficiency before they can be occupied. Boulder is the first American city to enact a carbon tax. It was also the first city in America to institute curbside recycling. The teen space at the main library is a "gay and lesbian safe zone." City buses run on natural gas. Yellow Cabs run on electricity. Even wedding transportation in Boulder is green. Driving up Baseline near Chautauqua one warm Saturday morning, I passed a bride and groom pedaling a tandem bicycle, no doubt heading off to recycle the aluminum cans clanking in their wake. Newspapers may be a dying industry, but I subscribe to the *Camera* and can't wait to open it every morning. The stories are awesome, daily reminders that Boulder is a different kind of place. A man who robbed a bank in South Boulder fled the scene of the crime . . . on a mountain bike. A woman received

---

* And now it exists! The Subaru Crosstrek hybrid, introduced in 2013.

a $1,000 ticket for dying her poodle pink and claiming it was a breast cancer awareness dog.

"A streaker named 'Thomas,' who didn't give his last name, made his way down the Pearl Street Mall at lunchtime Friday and attracted quite a crowd, especially when he began doing aerobics on the lawn of the Boulder County courthouse . . . When asked by officers why he was naked, the man replied: 'It's my true essence.'"

Nearly every week a mountain lion or a black bear enters the city limits, snacking on garbage, tree leaves, and possibly a small dog or two. The predator is usually tranquilized by animal control and trucked high up in the mountains, to places from which the animal sometimes still manages to return. Authors of letters to the *Camera*'s editor argue that the bears and lions (also cougars and coyotes) that enter the city should be killed, to protect the public. Others counter—passionately—that the animals were here first. Because we have intruded on their territory we have an obligation to let them live as they please.

"Never call the authorities!" writes one pro-predator woman. People like her, from what I gather, believe a mountain lion eating your two-year-old child is a great opportunity to teach your four-year-old about the circle of life.

The letters-to-the-editor section of the paper is dependably entertaining whatever the controversy. After wildlife issues, the most common debate involves community standards. For such a famously liberal enclave, Boulder retains a conservative ethos. Letters championing "family values" and "standards of decency" appear in the *Camera* daily. Homeowners on University Hill campaign to rid the neighborhood of students from the, um, university.

"The 18-, 19-, and 20-year olds get more clueless, rude, noisy and filthy," editorializes a woman named Jenny Robertson, a neighbor I've never met but would really, really like to; she sounds like a blast. "These kids should be accountable to all of the laws made to keep Boulder a great place to live. I would like to keep all my neighbors that have young families, work regular jobs during the day or find that 10 p.m. is a good time to go to bed."

Boulder, in general, is a test market for a higher plane of consciousness. It's a high-end city of good intentions with a great location and mild, sunny weather — a deluxe version of what is possible in America. It's also a bubble, a utopia for smart, outdoorsy, activist, environmentally conscious types disconnected from the wider world. Informed about the wider world, absolutely — half the kids in Boulder appear to have been adopted from Asia — but disconnected. The city is known for its runners, but if Boulder were a sport it'd be skiing: affluent, elitist, and snow white.

❦

Frank Shorter's high-altitude success in Boulder inspired athletes from all over the world to relocate here to replicate his training methods. Teams of Kenyans loop around the reservoir with a speed I find shocking. Olympians from other countries pass me the few times I still run the Boulder Creek Path. Every time the Road Runners visit the Potts Field track, elite Japanese women are there with us, progressing through drills with their coach. One weekday morning when I jogged to Potts Field with the Road Runners, an older woman running alongside us chitchatted in a Quebecois accent that reminded me of the singer Celine Dion. It turned out to be Jacqueline Gareau, the answer to a running trivia question. Gareau is the woman who won the Boston Marathon in 1980, the year the notorious imposter Rosie Ruiz crossed the finish line first.

"Boulder is a place where other people can ruin your day," says Tom LeMire, a veteran of the Boulder Road Runners. "You'll be on the bus riding home and you didn't get your workout in and you see these other people who are jogging and you get angry at them."

The city supports athletes of all types. There are skiers and rock climbers and parkour kids who throw themselves off walls and rooftops. Increasing numbers of triathletes ride their high-tech bicycles along US 36 and swim in the reservoir. That said, Boulder retains its strongest association with running. More than 130 kids try out each year for the cross-country team at Boulder High School. Both the men's and women's cross-country teams at the University of Colorado are national powers. The Bolder Boulder 10K that Shorter cofounded attracts more than 50,000 runners every Memorial Day.

Shorter's identification with Boulder is something worth maintaining, he has said, and is one reason he's stayed here even after two divorces. A bronze statue of Shorter stands outside the football stadium, near the finish of that big ten-kilometer race. The facade of a bank located on Broadway, just north of Spruce Street, features a giant mural of Shorter running along the foot-hills. I have yet to see Shorter in person. I'm told he is frequently out of town speaking at road races and running stores around the country. When he is in town he hasn't shown up at the monthly beer socials. It's not like he has anything left to prove, I suppose. His place as the father of the American running boom is secure.

The boom technically started in 1972, ignited by Shorter's Olympic gold medal marathon win. That was the first truly tele-vised Olympics, and ABC made the marathon a centerpiece of its coverage. Even with that sensational start, it took four more years for the sport to really catch on. A series of books by the running guru Jim Fixx helped. So did the New York City Marathon's changing its course to run through all five boroughs. Another elite American runner emerged, Bill Rodgers, and he began claiming wins in Boston. When Shorter won the silver medal at the next Olympic Games, in Montreal, things took off. Shorter became a certified national sensation. His second-place finish humanized him in a way another gold might not have, Shorter admits. In 1976, in very large part because of Shorter, the American running boom definitively exploded. It was the year an overweight family man who worked in personnel relations at a paper supply company in Dover, New Hampshire, took notice. The year 1976 was when my dad started running.

∞

I've started training with Rich's regular Wednesday-morning group, adding an extra day to my weekly schedule. Wednesdays feature a rotating cast of up to a dozen runners, with a core of six or so, including Rich Castro and Carl Mohr, who show up every week. The running columnist Mike Sandrock runs with us sometimes. A guy who organizes triathlon races around Colorado is usually there, too, as is a Canadian entrepreneur with the discombobulating name of Ted Kennedy. We meet at the big house of Carlos Garcia, a Cuban who splits his time between Boulder and a condo on South Beach. Carlos is a committed bachelor and a much better runner than I am. I can't keep up with him during the bulk of the eight-mile workout, but at the start, as we warm up slowly, he and I will sometimes talk about Miami. When he gets a new girlfriend in Boulder he likes to fly her down to South Beach as soon as he can.

"When they come back it's like when I pick up my dog from the pound," he says. He's referring to the way the stunning women of Miami tend to humble the Coloradans. "They have their tails between their legs."

The run is a long, fairly challenging loop. After cutting through the shaded Victorian mansions of Mapleton Hill, we break out to open space at Wonderland Lake. A dirt trail runs parallel to the foothills. We follow it up a tough little incline, out past a dog park into the northernmost section of North Boulder. We slap our hands on a metal gate, then turn around. On the way home, after descending that tricky slope, we curve around Wonderland Lake, passing what I'm told is Frank Shorter's house.

One sunny Wednesday, Rich and Carl and a few others are tapering, or training less strenuously than usual, in preparation for a relay race in Oregon they run every year. I'm not tapering for anything, so when they turn off the course early, just before the nasty little hill, I keep going straight. I always struggle on the hill. It's not all that tall but the path is steep and covered in loose dirt that tends to slip under my shoes. I huff and wheeze and force my legs to turn over until I finally reach the top. At the summit, as I slow to catch my breath, I pass two walkers. One is a tall blonde woman in spandex, attractively applied. She holds a water bottle. Beside her limps an older man, hunched over a bit. His gray hair shows a few streaks of its original black. His thin, practically petite frame disappears under a blousy blue T-shirt. Is it him? We are near his house. I've heard about the kind of women he likes, and this blonde fits the description. I've also heard that the years of running have ravaged his body, which might explain the stoop and the creaky shuffle.

I'm not free to investigate. I stick to my workout, running out past the dog park to the end of the trail. Bright sunshine bounces off my white running cap. I am proud of myself simply for chugging on alone when nobody will notice if I stop. On the way back, I navigate down that difficult hill. At the bottom, I turn as usual to the east, up a path that rolls past Frank Shorter's house. There is that couple again, walking. They notice me approaching and step to the side of the path.

"Way to go!" Frank Shorter chirps as I pass him. It's definitely him. His quick cheer comes out in a falsetto singsong, almost a peep. The Olympic gold medalist, Boulder's most famous citizen, the father of the American running boom, and the man posterized on my father's office wall calls out encouragement. To me. As I run past him. As I run. The man that started the thing that got me here, to this goofy city that is the best of all possible places for a runner to be, encourages me to keep going.

8

I'VE RUN BEFORE. Unlike my dad, who started from scratch at age thirty-nine, I've run a few times. I haven't run enough ever to like it, nor to excel at it in any way. I've never classified myself as a runner; any workouts before Boulder were just for basic, basement-level fitness. But I have run.

In college I'd sometimes earn my beer with a few miles among the corn fields of rural Wisconsin. In Milwaukee after college I twice ran the Al's Run 10K, both times finishing way behind my dad. I also participated in the West End Beer Crawl, a three-mile race (*stroll* is a better word) with cups of cold beer offered along the course instead of water. "Winning" the beer crawl does not involve finishing first. My parents flew down to the Florida Keys one April so my dad and my wife and I could enter the 7 Mile Bridge Run, which until Boulder was the longest run of my life. My dad won his age group. I finished just ahead of the sag wagon, the bus that picks up anyone still on the bridge when they reopen it to Key West–bound tourists. There was a period when I ran the boardwalk in Miami Beach almost regularly, weaving for three miles or so among tourists and Hasidic Jews and sometimes Miss Cable News, the ex-girlfriend of mine who worked out every day, often twice a day. It was that ex who inspired an intense but extremely brief flirtation with serious running that resulted in a man slicing open my knee with a sword.

We'd met at the newspaper where we'd both worked, and for a while we lived together at my apartment, a time I mostly recall as "turbulent." By the night of my thirty-seventh birthday, she and I had been over for half a year. She'd upgraded to her doctor. Everyone reported that she was never happier, that she looked better than ever, and that she and the doctor made "a perfect couple." On my birthday, when she strutted into the American Legion hall where I was drinking a beer with a friend, she did indeed look better than ever, exceptional even by Miami's absurd standards. She granted me ten minutes outside the hall. A halogen security light glowed overhead. I cried a bit. I probed for holes in her relationship with the doctor. She confirmed she had never been happier. I ignored my core certainty that we never were right for each other. I ignored the little detail that she'd reminded me of on the day we broke up: the first time I ever said I loved her, my fingers were wrapped around her neck. I ignored (as I often did at the time) my being in love with a married woman in another state. Gasping warm salty air floating over Government Cut, I vowed to throw away any promise of happiness for the whole rest of my life if she'd just agree to spend that life with me. Which she didn't. She went back to her doctor. I went right home and launched a program of personal improvement.

Fitness was only a part of it. I decided to get my priorities in order overall. I would work like a professional, I declared. I would get in shape. I would turn the ship of my life around. Just declaring these goals felt like an epiphany, like an immediate transformation.

My birthday was on a Saturday. The next morning I got everything organized. I went through all my files, deciding which projects to pursue and which to kill. By Sunday night I'd cleaned my entire apartment, shopped for healthy food for the week, and checked out from the library a Mark Twain classic I'd always meant to read. Most important, I'd drafted an ambitious to-do list for the following day. I scheduled interviews. I arranged research projects and I set aside "quiet time" to brainstorm new plans. My agenda was structured chronologically, from the first thing I needed to do in the morning until I wrapped up my workday at seven o'clock at night. I resolved to check off every single item on the list no matter what. That's what a professional would do. Perhaps that's what a doctor would do. On the first line of the to-do list I wrote my first scheduled activity: run.

I was still renting month-to-month in that hotel by the river, in Little Havana. It's a "transitional neighborhood." Homeless men sleep in the shade under Interstate 95. Human excrement darkens the sidewalks. Trucks back up onto the sidewalks to deliver fish to Garcia's and Joe's seafood restaurants. I'd woken up to teams of police officers in blue DEA Windbreakers socializing after an early-morning raid of a rusty Haitian freighter. Wild dogs roam in packs. A few blocks from my apartment, a neighbor guarded his yard with a flock of ostriches.

I hit the street about an hour after sunup. It was still relatively cool. I'd only scheduled a dinky circuit of not quite three miles; I'd be running every day from there on in, and I didn't want to overtrain on my first outing. Early in the run, as I built up momentum, I loped past some basketball courts and then past the Pleasure Emporium III porn shop, crowded with cars as always. I turned north onto Southeast Second Avenue, a street that crosses the Miami River. The drawbridge yawned open. A sooty tugboat puttered up the river, having just guided a freighter out to Biscayne Bay. I jogged in place until the bridge descended, until the traffic-stopping security gates lifted and I could cross.

Just over the crest of the bridge, I encountered a modest urban obstacle course. Cars whizzed past on my right. In the distance a kid rode his bike on the sidewalk, headed my way. Immediately in front of me I could see a man bending down to pick up something. On his back, in some kind of quiver, he was carrying what looked to be three swords. In hindsight, that would seem a significant — perhaps even alarming — detail. But Miami is so strange. Already that morning I'd passed a leathery old man in a cowboy hat and a guayabera, his eyes shielded behind swimming goggles, his feet on the pedals of a tiny pink bicycle with a picture of Barbie glued to its white wicker basket.

The new bicyclist was my biggest threat, I deduced. The kid was coming toward me, peddling fast. He could knock me off the sidewalk, which would drop me into traffic. I was so focused on him I never even saw what hit my leg. I felt only a smarting. I was aware that I'd been struck, probably by something solid and metal. It hit my left knee just below the cap. It hurt no more than a slash from a hockey stick in the recreational games I played once a week, which meant it didn't hurt much. I didn't feel compelled to stop running. I did not even turn around; in the city, you try to avoid confrontation.

Pain emerged about a block later. Just a little, but enough to win my attention. When I glanced down, I saw a few splotches of blood on my knee and my shin. That's not even considered an injury in hockey, so I kept running. I had a to-do list to tackle. I wanted to be a success. When I got back to my apartment I'd rinse the wound with hydrogen peroxide, slap on a few Band-Aids, then get down to work. Yet at a quarter mile, blood spurted from my knee. I still don't know how this was possible, as I'd been struck in the kneecap. Any arteries are located on the back of the knee, right? Yet blood cascaded out, flowing in a red stream. My sock turned red, as did my Nike shoe.

I kept running. There still wasn't much pain. And what's a

little blood? Or even a lot of blood? That I could bleed so much without agony made me proud in a way. It was a testament to my newfound resolve. I'm the kind of guy who accomplishes what he sets out to do, no matter what. I'm a badass. Haitian dockworkers stopped loading a freighter to stare at my leg, giving me street cred on a tough street.

I reached the Fifth Street Bridge, the halfway point of my little run. By now my knee was disgorging thick ropes of blood, gooey and sticky like mucus. Just over the bridge, a sharp shock vibrated from my lower back, up my spine, to the base of my neck. The pain was as severe as it was sudden. It felt a little like being shot, I imagine. I don't know much about physiology, but I interpreted that, yes, the cut on my knee might be something serious. I immediately stopped running. I looked down, really for the first time. My lower left leg was bright, vibrant red. Oxygen flooded my blood cells. Placing my hand on the wound did not stop the flow.

I ended up in the emergency room at Jackson Memorial Hospital. X-rays revealed no ligament damage. A physician's assistant sealed the suture with seven stitches. He said I'd been sliced with a blade of some sort, surgically sharp. The blade had cut through my skin down to the tendons. I was lucky to not be seriously wounded.

I've since replayed the scene in my head more times than the Warren Commission watched the Zapruder film. It probably was an accident. I assume the guy with three swords on his back, whom I never really did look at, held a fourth sword in his hand. The blade from that sword must have grazed my knee as I passed. It had to have been an accident. It had to have been. If he'd really wanted to hurt me, he could have sliced my leg clean off.

A friend drove me home from the hospital. After swinging by

a Walgreen's to pick up antibiotics, she dropped me off at my apartment. I'd ducked into it before my trip to the hospital, just to pick up my wallet. I returned to find blood splattered all over the place: on the rug, on my furniture, on the cold tiles of my bathroom floor. The place looked as though it had been redecorated by Charles Manson.

Aside from the blood, my apartment was clean. Spotless even. No dust. No dishes in the sink. All my books proper on their shelves, my bed made and the two throw pillows on the couch fluffed and positioned. My to-do list sat where I'd left it, atop my empty dining table. A pen lay next to it, waiting for me to check off items as I progressed through my productive day. I hobbled over to the table on my new aluminum crutches, pulling out a chair and slowly sitting down, careful not to bend my left leg. I looked at the list. Call this person, call that person, write this and pick up that. Red ink indicted that at four o'clock, right around the time I was getting x-rayed, I was to make a phone call to a radio producer.

"Very Important!" I'd indicated next to the appointment. At the bottom of the list, I'd left a reminder to be productive.

"This is the only life I've got," I noted. "Work it." I uncapped the pen and positioned it in my writing hand. I had to stop running for a while, of course. It took several months for my knee to return to something close to normal. My weight rose to a lifetime high of 225. All those other ambitions I conjured on my birthday fell to the wayside, as I — as anyone — could have predicted. (I never got around to earning a medical degree, for instance.) Yet that first evening, home from the hospital, I scanned the list. At the top, I put an X next to the first item. I'd only made it through half my route, but I gave myself credit for the effort. It was the only thing I could mark off for the day.

So like I said, I have run before.

9

YODA CALLS ME at 5:45 in the morning.

"Are you up?" he asks. It is important to arrive at the workout with a clear head, he says. Before I even get out to Neva Road, the dusty patch north of town where we've started running long on Saturday mornings, I should visualize the day's route in my mind, all fifteen miles of it. Where am I going to stop for water breaks? How fast am I going to run miles four through eight, the most important miles of the workout? How long will it take me to finish? A real runner needs to know these things in advance.

I say I will try.

"Don't try, do!" Rich barks, and hangs up.

&

I'm running five days a week now, about forty miles total. I cross-train on Mondays, stretch lightly on Fridays, and practice yoga most Wednesday nights. I've lost a lot of weight. Thirty pounds already. My T-shirts drape my shoulders and chest. My jeans hang baggy and lose. The shorts I wore all last summer in Miami fall off my hips unless I cinch them with a belt.

"People are starting to notice," Carl tells me after a long run, when we've stopped for coffee at a place off Twenty-Eighth Street. "It's a good start."

My running is improving. Undeniably. On a Thursday-morning workout I hang on to the lead group for the very first time, keeping in stride with the best runners in the club.

"The only way to run faster is to run faster," Rich advises.

It's an endurance workout, seven-minute intervals "at pace," pretty much flat out. We splash through puddles and dodge cows and I simply never fall behind the group. Every time I start to fade, Carl pulls alongside with encouragement. Keep your jaw loose. Find a rhythm. Breathe easy, steady. Rich even calls me into the lead for one of the intervals. Everyone else must follow my tempo, meaning that if I dog it, their workouts will suffer. I feel a lot of pressure. I feel like vomiting, actually. When we finish at the cow gate, Rich is beaming. He raises his right hand for me to slap him five.

"You became a runner today," he says back at the Flatiron gym. I'm icing down my knees. He tosses me a PowerBar, reminding me to eat within fifteen minutes of every workout. Then he turns to his second wife, Patti, who is stretching on the floor near me.

"Robert became a runner today."

❧

Spring yields to summer much quicker than I expect. Temperatures climb into the nineties. The sky is clear and sunny, and little white flowers spring up everywhere. Students float down the creek on inner tubes they rent at a gas station at Broadway and Arapahoe. Our Sunday recovery runs start an hour earlier now to beat the heat, but I still must swallow as many as seven cups of Accelerade to rehydrate afterward. My landlord increases his visits to the Coop, bringing his kids and/or his wife and/or his in-laws with him. They climb atop the Coop's slanted roof to admire the view they'll enjoy after he tears the place down. On Sunday afternoons, I've started hiking with Valentine deep into the Rockies.

When not running or hiking or still trying to find some writing work, I try to check out Boulder. I watch *A Midsummer Night's Dream* at the university's outdoor theater, sitting on a stone bench and sipping a pint of "Bard's Brew." Naropa, the counter-culture college, holds a marathon reading of Jack Kerouac's *On the Road*. I walk into the school's small auditorium during chapter two. Onstage, the woman who founded the school breathes from an oxygen tank as Sal Paradise hitchhikes to Denver. A man accompanies her on the piano, his chest hosting a nest of feathered necklaces. Another man plays the bongos. In the audience sit tattoos and sarongs and tie-dies worn without irony.

Late in the spring, vendors' tents rise on College Avenue like at a street fair. Green balloons float. Frisbees fly. The line at Abo's Pizza stretches out the door. Everyone, clearly, is stoned. Like, really stoned. The whole point of the holiday is to toke up at exactly 4:20 p.m. on the university's Norlin Quad. When I leave the Coop in the afternoon, the students from the other apartments populate the picnic table and exercise their octobong. It's a little after two o'clock.

"Starting a bit early," I note.

One of the guys wants to reply, but first he needs to hold his breath for a few more seconds. He eventually exhales a stream of white smoke.

"Just getting in some practice."

On Memorial Day weekend I stroll the Boulder Creek Fest, a

cross between a standard art fair and a farmer's market. Winding through a maze of white tents, I am offered massages, alternative energy healing, and macrobiotic dog food for Valentine, who walks with me. One woman hands me a flyer for an organic fast-food place, noting the restaurant is "locally owned, wind-powered, and zero energy waste, so that's cool."

In June, I celebrate a birthday. I always try to take the day off on my birthday, which I will admit can appear redundant. No work, of course. But also no gym, no dieting, no nothing. Around dinnertime I walk down to Pearl Street. Fluffy white dandelion seeds float in the air like summer snowflakes. I eat a whole pizza and drink a couple of pints of Avery's and read a book on a bench until the sun slips behind Flagstaff Mountain.

EVERYBODY WINS WITH CAPITALISM, declares the sign of the panhandler sitting on a bench across from me. Two street musicians serenade us with a pan flute rendition of "Dust in the Wind." On my cell phone, I reread a birthday e-mail from Mrs. Wisconsin. She's figured out that I'm in Boulder. She still thinks about me every day and no matter what I might think of her she did love me and she loves me still and she will love me always. The pan flautists move on to their next classic-rock standard. I debate a reply.

"Talk talk talk, blah blah blah."

Or: "Go fuck yourself. No, go fuck your husband."

Or one that might really get to her: "I love you and I miss you and I know you love me so I'm waiting for you to wake up and drop your charade of a life so we can be happy together." That would freak her out the most. That's not one she actually wants to get, no matter what she writes in a birthday e-mail. She likes everything exactly as it is, I believe. Whenever things get a little boring in her marriage she can daydream about her tragic lost love. And the rest of the time, when things are going great, she can enjoy her two boys and her husband and their SUV and their flat-screen liquid-crystal TV.

"Go fuck yourself." That works best.

"Talk talk talk, blah blah blah." Back to that one. She was never anything but talk. That's the one I'd send if I had the guts. Which I don't.

On the Fourth of July I walk down to the football stadium to watch Ralphie's Independence Day Blast, the city's official firework display. I arrive early enough to see the whole show. Ralphie the buffalo romps around the field twice. Trained dogs catch Frisbees, which is more entertaining than I'd expected. A glee choir tries to get everyone to sing "You're a Grand Old Flag" but the lousy sound system makes it hard to follow along. In time, the sky fades so dark I can no longer see the Flatirons. The stadium really fills up. It's mostly families: two parents with teams of kids holding small plastic flags. There are also high school students coupled up boy-girl. Just before the fireworks launch, I notice a ring has formed around me in the bleachers. No one is sitting within twenty feet of me in any direction. I feel like such an outcast. Being single, struggling, and middle-aged in Boulder is like being gay in Cheyenne. There aren't many of your kind around and the culture is against you. I'm surprised I haven't had to register with the city.

∾

I date a woman for a while. A runner, of course. She's from Iowa, she's in her thirties, and she's one of the few Boulder Road Runners not yet retired; she works at the university. We don't last long. She wants stability above all else, like most women I know. I live in a chicken coop. There isn't much for either of us to build on, but I still say, when we break up, that I don't think she really gave us a chance.

"I gave us a chance," she replies. "I knew you didn't have a 401(k) and I dated you anyway."

I started that Independence Day watching her participate in a short race, one mile through the nearby town of Superior. It was casual, a fun run. Pancakes were served afterward in the community center. The guy who came in third broke four minutes.

I've run a few races, too. Nothing serious. Following Rich's advice, I am just trying to familiarize myself with the process, with the racing experience. On Memorial Day I ran the Bolder Boulder 10K. I've also finished that series of Dash 'n' Dine 5Ks at the rez. My first real race is scheduled for August, in the Illinois town where I attended high school and where my parents still live. The Hog Jog 5K it's called, a bit longer than three miles. I signed up for the Hog Jog on a whim, mostly as an excuse to visit my parents and my younger sister and even my brother, who will be visiting from Seattle with his wife and their new baby. But Rich has dialed in on it. He says the race will be an important marker of our progress.

At the end of July, two weeks before the Hog Jog, I run a small community race in Boulder, three kilometers, or just under two miles. Nothing. It is held in the west end of Pearl Street. Two loops around a simple course starting at the *Daily Camera,* proceeding west up eight blocks of shade trees and restored Victorian houses, then back. Nothing to it. Exercise, really. A chance to break in the new shoes I plan to wear in Illinois: bright yellow Brooks racing flats, ninety bucks at the Boulder Running Company and light as a dry sponge.

Even though it is a small field and just a weeknight community event, the runners separate into four different heats: "Kids," "Friends and Family," "Women," and finally "Men." The kids race is largely adorable, though most of the kids are fast and fo-cused, and the first-place finisher, a boy without an upper torso —just two long legs and a head, or so it seems—can definitely beat me. A parade of foreign exchange babies brings up the rear, a miniature United Nations adopted from Cambodia and China and Vietnam.

A Ukrainian Olympian wins the women's race, edging out an Olympian from Japan. I enter the men's race rather than the friends and family, thinking it's the label that fits me best, and thinking my improving workouts on Tuesdays and Thursdays have me in position to be somewhat competitive. This notion is quickly discredited. There are about fifty men at the starting line, all of them jumping around and stretching and wearing Oakley sunglasses. These guys are obviously elite, even world-class— the guy who ends up winning is on the Australian Olympic team. I can tell I don't belong just from my outfit of a baggy T-shirt and long nylon shorts that touch my knees. I feel conspicuous. I half expect a race official to step in and pull me from the scrum. I half want that to happen, too.

"You have to be humble to train in Boulder," I once heard a guy say at the Flatiron gym. I am humbled at the West End 3K. Completely. I run much of the race all by myself, the lead-ers beyond my field of vision. Volunteers from the Boulder Road Runners manning the barricades don't have to raise their voices to communicate encouragement. Usually it isn't even encourage-ment as much as acknowledgment. One woman from the club doesn't bother saying my name, or "Go!" or "Way to Go!" or anything like that. As I pass and we make eye contact, she says, simply, "Hi."

At some point in the second and last lap of the race, I find com-pany. For half a mile I run about even with this one guy, Bobby. I know his name because his friends along the course keep calling out to him as we pass. I'll say this about Bobby: he has lots of friends. He looks about ten years older than I am. Wavy gray hair and a compact torso tucked into a red tank top indicating allegiance to one of Rich Castro's coaching competitors. In the home stretch, as we close in on the *Daily Camera* building and the finish line, I pull ahead of him. Nothing personal, Bobby. I've been training. I've been making progress. Have you not noticed my feet, the way they're wrapped in bright yellow racing flats? Are you looking at my shoes now, as I pull away? Actually I'm not thinking anything like that. I'm just running, trying to finish strong. We are the back of the pack, the guys with brooms that trail the elephants in the circus parade.

I notice a backlog of runners crowding just over the finish line, waiting to have small timing chips snipped off their shoes. To avoid crashing into these people, I slow, right at the end. Bobby sees his chance. He lunges forward, almost tumbling onto the asphalt. In the official final results posted online later in the evening, he beats me by four-tenths of a second. Congratulations, Bobby. You finished fourth from last.

∞

I pull into to the gravel parking lot off Neva Road just before seven a.m., the normal starting time for the Saturday long run. The parking lot sits at the head of the Lefthand Trail, a dusty path about five miles north of town. A soft, hot wind flows down the foothills, rustling tumbleweeds as it whooshes across the grasses that weed northern Colorado's high desert. On the long ride from the Coop, on Rich's instruction, I tried to visualize the run ahead of me. Fifteen miles in a row, a personal record. Four miles of warm-up. Lefthand Creek, Haystack Mountain, then to Lookout Mountain, which isn't anything close to a mountain though it is an important weather observatory overseen by the US Department of the Interior. Twice around a four-mile loop, then back to the parking lot along an undulating dirt road. Stop four times to drink the water Rich places along the course for me. Swallow an energy goo after eight miles. Swallow another one at mile twelve. A serious run.

I prepared like I am supposed to. I went to bed early. I ate the same thing for dinner I now eat every Friday night: chicken parmesan, lots of water, and one bottle of Shiner Bock beer. Yet even with my wake-up call from Rich, I get to the trailhead at the very last minute. I open my car door cautiously, steeled for a reprimand. I needn't have worried. Rich and Carl Mohr and a dozen other runners all stand at one end of the lot, their arms crossed at the chest, their eyes watching seven students from the university wind down a rave. Techno music thumps from a Ford Escort. Black clothes that probably looked cool at three a.m. no longer seem so appropriate in the rising sun. Up and down the students dance, up and down, bouncing with energy I'd like to borrow for a few hours.

"You see this a lot in Boulder, this contrast between super-healthy living and the drug culture," Carl offers as we start our warm-up. My GPS watch takes a while to find a satellite. When it does, I fall into an easy groove behind Rich, who tells me to monitor my shadow to make sure I'm running in good form. Someone mentions a foreign runner who died just after crossing the finish line of a marathon. He'd just set a PR in his race. Everyone thinks that's so cool, dying right after setting a personal record. Someone else brings up the bond market and then the Tour de France and then a bit about the poor organization of the West End 3K, which had started almost an hour later than scheduled.

"Hey, you were looking pretty speedy out there Thursday," says a guy named Chuck, a retired school teacher. He's referring to the West End race. I hadn't seen him on Pearl Street that evening, which means he probably looked up my finishing time online. There are no secrets in the Boulder running community. I thank him for mocking me.

"No, seriously, 12:32, that's good," adds Carl, who not only looked up my time but memorized it as well. "That's really good."

We take our first water break four miles in. Then I continue. No one in the group intends to run nearly as long as my planned route, so I am alone for most of the morning. I listen to myself breathe. I listen to the slap of my shoes on the hard dirt. I analyze my form in the shadow stretching from my feet. *Don't bounce, glide!* In a classic case of last-song-in-the-car syndrome, my mental jukebox loops a Toby Keith tune I can't shake. I'm inside my head for two and a half hours. I want to stop. I won't stop.

"I hate to run!" I shout, twice. I focus on my coming reward for not stopping: a McDonald's Quarter Pounder value meal, which I eat for lunch every Saturday now, the one day I'm allowed to cheat on my diet. It's cool, I gotta admit, to be making progress. My third-from-last finish in the West End 3K — however humiliating in theory — has earned me respect from club runners like Carl, who may be my biggest doubter. They've noticed my weight loss and they approve. I'll enjoy that cheat-day Quarter Pounder because I've earned it. Fifteen miles. In a row. That's more than twice as far as I'd ever run before I got here.

By the time I return to the parking lot, the ravers have packed up and left. So have all the runners save Rich. Actually, Rich has already driven home, soaked his legs in ice water, showered, changed his clothes, eaten a small snack, and returned to witness my finish.

"Looking good!" he says when I reach his parked SUV. He wraps my thumb in a soul grip, saying I've put in a solid run.

"Tuesdays and Thursdays are for speed work. Saturdays are for putting in time on the legs." From inside his vehicle he produces a jug of ice water, which he dumps over my head. He also gives me a bottle of Accelerade to drink. You really should eat a banana, he says. I can't stand bananas so I eat a PowerBar instead, which he deems an okay substitute. I say the heat made things difficult. I say I ran really slowly. Oprah slow.

"Your time today isn't important," Rich replies, handing me a few ice cubes to drop into my Accelerade bottle. "Next week is what really matters. Your first real race. We'll see if you're on track or not."

10

ITEM: A LARGE cardboard box sitting in my parents' house, in the middle of my old room, which my mom now uses as an office. A label on the box: "ROBERT'S OLD STUFF."

❧

The Hog Jog 5K is sponsored by St. Mary's of the Annunciation, the Catholic church where I was confirmed, where both my sisters were married, and where my parents have attended five o'clock mass on Saturday nights for more than twenty-five years. Afterward they go for Mexican food. Today is Saturday, the early afternoon. I am down in their living room reading *The Right Stuff* when my dad asks if I want to join him at church. I waffle, asking if my presence will mean anything.

"You're forty years old," he replies. "You can make your own decisions by now."

I don't want to go to church. I never do. Church is boring. It seems so mindless, a mumbling of Hail Marys and Lord's Prayers and the small tradition in every mass wherein the congregation is asked to shake hands in a show of peace. The priests ramble through dull sermons. In high school, when I was finally old enough to drive a car, my mom would allow my younger sister, Gretchen, and me to attend service on Sunday, by ourselves. We didn't go. I'd drive to the church parking lot, where Gretchen would run out and grab a bulletin, our proof we'd attended. Then she and I would spend an hour at a hot dog stand eating red hots. It remains the only time either of us can recall enjoying church.

"Would you like me to go?" I ask my dad.

"It would be nice," he says. So I go. After mass, driving out of that same parking lot where Gretchen and I pulled our great scam, we pass a shrine to the Ten Commandments erected alongside a green cornfield.

"I didn't get anything out of that," I say, referring to the Saturday-night service. The priest, a native Pole, spoke in a singsong monotone that might as well have been a lullaby. I have no idea what point the guy was trying to make.

"I don't think anyone gets anything out of that," my dad admits.

He hangs a right onto Fremont Township Road, then another right onto Midlothian. The GPS satellite map in his Cadillac draws a bead on his current favorite Mexican restaurant, a new place across from the post office. He usually listens to satellite radio in his car, almost always to a station featuring big band hits of the 1940s. In a small and unspoken kindness, he spins the dial to WXRT, "Chicago's Finest Rock," solely for my enjoyment.

"Then why do you go?"

He doesn't reply. That's typical and, in context, not rude. His silences are long and potent and I've come to understand them the way a Jewish scholar knows the Talmud. For instance, he and I golfed the morning after I arrived. We spent eighteen holes in the same cart, verbalizing little more than the weather (humid) and the Cubs (doomed) and the situational merits of a

5-iron over a 4-wood (I'd go with the wood). All of which meant he supports my new life in Colorado. He'd be more comfortable if I landed steady income. I need to flee the Chicken Coop, definitely, and it'd be nice if I found a wife and all. But he's encouraged by my new focus. I don't seem as depressed as I was in Miami. I'm losing weight, which proves to him the running thing isn't just a lark.

His silence on the Why Attend Church question signals a lack of introspection. I don't think he's ever contemplated *not* going to church. Taking a shower at four p.m. every Saturday, driving to church at four thirty, attending mass for forty-five minutes and then going for enchiladas with my mom is just what he does. I don't think he's introspective in general, which is so different from me. I question every action I take. What I'm doing right now, is it the right thing to do? Is there something I'd rather be doing? Or should be doing? Was my marriage a mistake? Was my mistake moving to Miami in the first place? Let's go way back: Should I have taken the SATs more seriously? If I'm conscious, I'm inside my head, a method actor starring in a dinner theater production of my own small life.

"Okay, my alarm just went off: What's my motivation to get out of bed?"

Entering the restaurant, all the Spanish I hear is encouraging: Mexicans eat here. My brother and his wife are already seated at a table, their new baby a credible excuse to skip church. (Note to self: get a baby.) My mom is here, too; she arrived in her own car because she had to run an errand. We all pour cerveza Carta Blanca into frozen mugs and dip fried tortilla chips into chunky red salsa. The baby rounds out the dinner party and sits center stage.

"What's the point?" my brother asks, referring to my marathon training. "When you finish will you feel a sense of accomplishment? Please let me know, because I don't understand. Why would anyone run twenty-six miles in a row, voluntarily? I just don't understand."

David and I are pretty different. He's a lawyer living as far away from the family as he can. He likes to talk while I'm more comfortable listening. I loved sports growing up, he was into the theater. We almost never call each other, I guess just because we're different. But sometimes, when we do talk and when he says something like this, it's obvious we're closely related. His questions are my questions exactly.

ॐ

Item: A blue textbook from Ripon College, *Philosophy of Film*.

ॐ

I wake up at six a.m. My mom has stocked the house with good food but I eat only a chocolate PowerBar and a Coke Zero, a slight variation of my normal prerun diet. I pull on a white Boulder Road Runner's singlet, which Rich gave me at the Tuesday training session just before I left Colorado. It's the first time I'll be wearing a singlet.

"This race is a big deal," Rich said as he handed me the lightweight nylon tank top. "It'll be your first real 5K, and a real measuring stick." Aim to break twenty minutes, he tells me.

My dad comes down to the kitchen wearing *his* racing uniform: black nylon shorts, a Bill Rodgers–brand mesh singlet, once white but now brownish and threadbare after thirty years of races. *Stick with what works!* His lime-green Nike racing flats look similarly worn-out; bare big toes stick out of both shoes. We get in the car and talk strategy. He doesn't have a time he's shooting for.

He doesn't warm up beforehand, either; he saves his energy for the race. That's cool. That's the way I've always felt it should be done. I am nervous. He is nervous, too, he tells me.

"You look like runners," says a woman at the starting line. My dad does, of course. In this crowd I do, too. There's only about a hundred of us huddled in the gray strip of road between a cemetery and the church. Whereas I cowered in embarrassment at the start of the West End 3K in Boulder, the field gathering here is mostly potbellied men and gangly teenagers and mothers pushing strollers. "T-shirt runners" Dan Skarda calls them, with disdain. Recreational joggers. Not the real deal, not like me. I've got my singlet. I've got my bright yellow racing flats. It's cloudy but I'm also wearing my race-day sunglasses, which I bought for eighty dollars at Fleet Feet. I'm solid. And I will finish in ninth place overall.

"GO GO GO GRANDPA AND UNCLE ROBERT!" cheer signs waved by Gretchen's young daughters. The girls stand at the starting line in flip flops and pink terry cloth shorts, and they constitute almost the entire crowd. The course is an out-and-back along a rural route lined with cornstalks ripe for harvesting. The turnaround, about a mile and a half in, is a traffic cone topped with a small plastic pig. The August humidity carries notes of wet hay and moist earth and perhaps a drop of diesel fuel. After the starting gun, I can't hear anything besides heavy breathing and running shoes falling on pavement.

A five-kilometer race is a relative sprint, a test of a long-distance runner's top speed. I finish the first mile in six and a half minutes, embarrassing in Boulder but really fast for me. I pass the turnaround in ten minutes total, which is encouraging. As I run back to the church I slow a bit, almost involuntarily. My lungs swim in the thick air. Two high school girls in pink tank tops catch up to me. One of the girls surges ahead with one mile until the finish.

"There's the first woman!" cheers my mom, who is working a water table. She'll later claim she didn't see me.

I confront the familiar temptation to quit. *I've done all I need to do in life. Fine with me if we stop for bagels.* That surging girl in pink remains in my sightline, just up ahead. I can grit my teeth and maybe chase her down like that Bobby guy who clipped me in Boulder. But why? She seems nice enough. She never did anything to me. If I finish in front of her, I'll merely beat the first woman, and it's not like they give awards for that. I focus on Rich's instructions. I try to keep my shoulders down. I try to keep my pace steady. I finish right behind her.

I don't break twenty minutes as Rich had hoped, and I don't come close to my dad's personal best in a 5K, which is some ridiculously fast time. But my twenty-one-and-change did beat my dad *today*. By three minutes. It is the first time I've beaten him in a race. According to my calculations, it is the first time I've beaten him at anything ever, Scrabble excepted.

I grab a Gatorade from a feeding trough filled with ice. My sister hands me my official Hog Jog T-shirt, which reveals that the race was sponsored, perhaps appropriately, by two different funeral homes. My dad asks if there's water and I hand him my half-finished Gatorade bottle. He looks spent. He finished thirty-third overall. I came in second in my age group, and am called up to collect a small silver medal.

"Ooooh!" other runners gasp when my Boulder address is announced. That's right, people: I'm a ringer.

My dad also steps forward to collect his first-place medal in the over-seventy division. He has so many medals he makes a habit of writing the date and his time on the back of them to track how they were acquired. He skips back with today's medal draped around his neck.

"That's the way you win!" he cheers. I'm pretty sure he's joking; no one else his age entered the race. I need to log some more miles for the day, so I hand my dad my medal and T-shirt, then head out for a six-mile run back home. This impresses him more than anything.

❧

Item: A note from my dad.

> It was good to see you and be with you last week. Just remember that the time is fast running out on your undergraduate education. It's now time to make your move to whatever you decide to do next.
>
> Keep me posted.

❧

We celebrate at Giordano's, another small kindness to me. I love Chicago-style pizza and have never found the real thing outside the city. With my brother and my younger sister and their kids, we bring into the restaurant four children under the age of seven, one of them a baby. It is a zoo. My dad sits at the table but outside the group, watching. He fetches toys and silverware off the floor.

"That was the slowest race I've run in my life" is the only thing he really says.

After dinner, back home, he pours himself a light beer then settles onto the couch to watch both the Cubs game and the White Sox game at the same time. They have a system, he and my mom. He drives the remote, switching from one pitch to the other. A called strike on the Cubs game then over to the Sox game, where the pitcher removes his hat and runs a forearm over his sweaty hairline. Wait. The announcers fill the air with statistics. Wait. The pitcher finally winds up, then throws. A ball and quick back to the Cubs game. If both games are in commercials, he steers to the Food Channel or, if forced by still another commercial break, to the Home and Garden network.

My brother and his wife also sit in the room. He tries, for a while, to talk about parenthood and Seattle and his work. But the whole purpose of baseball, at least in our house, is to zone out; nobody need say anything to anyone. I refresh my dad's beer, grabbing an Old Milwaukee Light from a built-in bar that came with the house, and which he's personalized with cans collected over years of business trips. My mom sips a rum and Coke poured into a tumbler etched with a helmet of the Chicago Bears. This is their routine.

I like to zone out as much as anyone, baseball on the TV and beer coursing through my bloodstream. But I have a job to do. My mom has asked me to go through a box she found in my old bedroom. Keep anything I want, she says. The rest gets thrown out.

The bedrooms occupy the top floor. My parents' room at the head of the stairs, big and yellow with a bed and a TV and an easy chair and in the bathroom a sunken tub that never gets used. A picture window overlooks the lake. Down a hall sit the two bedrooms my sisters occupied, a linen closet, the kids' bathroom, and my old bedroom. (David slept in the basement, by choice.) My mom took over my room when I left for college. Entering, I see her computer and a folder of church bulletins and some paperwork from the library board she presides over. I also find a large brown box on the floor.

℮

Item: A tight bundle of love letters from my wife.

❧

I sit on a rocking chair and flip open the cardboard flaps. The time capsule seems to be from my college years, and a bit of my first grad school at the University of Chicago. There's a letter from a soccer player I studied with in my one semester abroad, in York, England. There's a blue theme book from a drama class, in which I critiqued a Sam Shepard play in blocky print letters. There's a notebook full of sine and cosine and graphs with wavy lines, which reminds me that, once I graduated, I never *did* have to deal with that stuff again. Ah, "Philosophy of Film," a class that met on Tuesday nights, and which our professor once abandoned, midlecture, because nobody would answer his questions.

"I'm sick and tired of the apathy amongst Ripon College students today!" he barked, then stormed out. We all waited a few minutes, maybe five, before we realized he wasn't coming back.

> *High Noon* is a film which makes many excellent statements. The one I feel it focuses primarily upon is: Man is inherently selfish. It is bad for a man to be selfish. If a man can rise above himself and be unselfish then he is good and will be rewarded. The film uses a number of scenes to convey this message.

No wonder he quit on us.

Journal entry, February 19, 1986:

I'm a bad student: I figured it out. Every teacher I ever had said I was a super smart genius. I've never been able to get good grades, though. I always allot plenty of time for my studies. My friends know I never go out on weekdays to do anything. I stay home and do homework. But really what I do is sit in my room and waste time. I just fool around and read stuff that doesn't mean anything. I get poor grades as a result. I don't know if I can bear down and pass college. I'm doomed.

There's a receipt for stereo speakers purchased my junior year. And a note to incoming freshmen from the cocaptain of the ice hockey team I joined. There's a team picture of the Boston Red Sox from the summer we moved to Chicago, the year Bucky Dent of the Yankees hit an improbable home run to end the Boston season. I was about to start the fifth grade. Back to the college years — there's a note from my mom's mother, widowed and retired in Koontz Lake, Indiana, where my mom told me she grew so depressed after the deaths of both my grandpa and their son Bob that she refused to eat until she died of starvation.

> Dear Robert
> Well here it is Halloween. Are you going trick or treating?
> Just kidding.
> So are you studying hard or are you taking it easy?
> But you better study because before you know it will be graduation day. Just think only 7 months more.
> Well I don't know anything else. Everything is the same out here.
> So take care of yourself.
> I love you.
> Excuse the writing.
>
> Grandma

There's a letter from my freshman-year roommate, a guy who married his college girlfriend (like I did) and who chose to stay friends with my ex-wife instead of me. There's a letter from another college friend, another guy who married his college girlfriend and therefore another guy I lost in the divorce. There's a floppy disk from the first-generation computer I used back then. There's also a letter from the city attorney of Ripon, Wisconsin, notifying me of my options should I care to contest my citation for underage drinking.

Everything is tossed in the trash, like old news, like our life in Canada, where we lived until I was five. Like our life in New Hampshire, like the old family name. The box is almost empty save for a neat stack of about twenty letters wrapped in a madras ribbon that my wife used to wear in her hair. Seeing the letters makes my heart feel dented and hard like a crushed soda can. I untie the ribbon, then open the first envelope, which contains a Valentine's Day card.

> I want you
> I need you
> I love you
> Besides, no one kisses half as good as you.

And then the second envelope, a card:

> I know that this is short but it gets my point across. Thank you for being a best friend.

And then:

> Thank you for all that you've done and given me. It goes much deeper than the material sense. Believe me, returning love back to you is one of my greatest pleasures!

It takes me an hour to read through the twenty letters. The first was sent the summer we started seeing each other, which was just before my senior year. The last letter arrived at my mailbox in Hyde Park, the year I studied social work while she finished up her undergrad in Wisconsin. In the letters she relays her struggle with her classes, the stupidity of her sorority, and her faith in me. Reading the letters makes me feel dead. I feel depressed. I feel worse than my grandma.

"How goes the trip down memory lane?" my sister-in-law, Sachia, asks. She's come up to check on the baby. I'm embarrassed to be crying.

It's all there in the letters, I say, my voice warbling. The way she felt grateful to have me in her life, the way she thought about me all the time. The way she looked forward to being with me and felt blessed to know me and how she told me, in one letter, that her love kept growing bigger every day.

Sachia sits down on the small sofa that has replaced my old bed. Her face is blank, like a therapist's. My tears are embarrassing but I can't stop. When I left my wife I didn't let myself feel pain. I felt guilt, yes, but I responded to that guilt with resolve. Divorce was for the best. I needed to do this for both of us (which I still think is true). She called me but I wouldn't pick up the phone. She sent letters I wouldn't read. I pushed her so far out of my life that when she left for Europe I didn't even know about it. Sachia is cool, but she doesn't know what to do or say. It's awkward for both of us.

❧

The next morning, my dad drives me to Midway in his cream-colored Cadillac. We have to leave early because I booked a seat on the first flight of the day, a tip he passed on from his decades of frequent flying. It's too dark to see anything out the window. There's zero traffic. The GPS map glows out a guide to the airport my dad doesn't need to consult. We talk running. He is encouraged by my performance in the Hog Jog.

"There isn't ten percent of the country who could do what

you've already done," he says. It's unsettling to collect a straight compliment from him, but I take it, as I suppose I've earned it. My next race will be a half marathon in Philadelphia. He envisions me breaking 1:30, which would be fantastic, and which is a time even Rich is afraid to predict. I stay quiet, enjoying the respect he's doling out.

At the terminal, he shakes my hand then pulls out a check to cover the airfare. It's a routine exchange, very common, but it always startles me. My dad still pays for my plane tickets. I'd turn him down on principle, except I can't afford to. The check is enough money to spring my dog from the kennel where I've boarded her. I can buy gas for my car and a week's worth of groceries. I take it. I thank him and then I leave for Colorado, where, thanks to Rich, the Boulder Road Runners have already heard about the Hog Jog and my time and my top-ten finish, and have already christened me "the Rocket."

11

SEPTEMBER. STUDENTS RETURN to campus. I sit at a table outside the Sink restaurant, watching incoming freshmen take University Hill, walking either a step ahead or a step behind people they'd like everyone to believe are not their parents. Before the semester starts, the students in the Chicken Coop move out. One goes to Denver with a business degree and dreams of becoming a professional snowboarder. Another, a film major, drops out after finishing only his sophomore year, not wanting to put on hold his dreams of becoming, yes, a professional snowboarder. (That kid, horribly, will die within six months, killed on a half-pipe attempting a tricky twist.)

New neighbors, a young married couple from Arizona, move in. Sarit is a midwife, studying Spanish. Aaron, the husband, is a massage therapist working toward a master's in cognitive therapy at Naropa. It doesn't surprise me that Aaron has never seen a football game. I promise to take him to one. In turn, he takes me to his "contemplative movement" practice.

We drive to Naropa's Paramita campus, located in a corporate office park off Thirtieth Street near the bank where Rich starts the Sunday runs. We slip off our shoes and enter a dance studio.

Painted blue waves cascade across the walls. A mermaid surfaces on a dry-erase board. Aaron hands me a flyer.

> Contemplative movement practice brings together the discipline of sitting meditation with free movement investigations and the practice of improvisation. It is an opportunity to integrate our outer and inner worlds, alone and together.

Six other people arrive, including the instructor. There are four men and four women. One of the men is ninety-two years old, with long hair and a hearing problem.

We all introduce ourselves before walking to our mats for meditation. I'm uncomfortable, out of my element, but I'm game. I sit with my legs crossed, my palms up and resting on my knees. Then I notice a woman across the room lying on her back. That looks more relaxing. The leader, Sara, lights incense, which sends one guy running out to the hall. Asthma.

A chime sounds, the signal to leave our mats for "personal body-mind awareness practice." Aaron throws a sweatshirt over his head, raises his arms in front of his chest, and wanders around the studio like a blind Frankenstein's monster. A guy wearing wristbands launches into solo Tai Chi. Sara commences baldly sexual grunts. She goes on for a while. I wait for her to orgasm. Aaron removes the sweatshirt from his face, crouches down in a squat and begins hopping his way across the floor, grunting with each small leap.

I find myself frozen, unable to participate. I debate walking out onto the floor and perhaps waving my arms. Maybe I'll hoot like an owl. I don't think anyone will ridicule my performance, not with Aaron acting out a mobile bowel movement. But — and this cannot be helped — I just don't want to act like an owl. Or a zombie, or to orgasm in public.

Eventually we break. Meeting in the middle of the room, Sara advises us to shed our linear thinking. She looks right at me. This class is "freeing." It is time to interact. We're supposed to bow each time we enter the arena, or space. Everyone is encouraged to enter at least once. Again she looks straight at me.

I don't enter the arena. Instead, immobilized by a combination of fear and amazement, I watch the "delightful group practice called 'open space,'" in which things ratchet up a notch. Aaron, off again on his zombie walking, stumbles into the Tai Chi guy, prompting the two of them to tap each other on their chests, back and forth. Sara bends into a handstand. She flips up and starts flexing her arms. She turns to offer her pipes to the old hippie guy, who palms a bicep. It is again erotic, the way she presents her body to him. It is a little creepy, too, like watching an old man touch a stripper.

"At my age you don't get many tastes of ecstasy," he will tell me afterward.

Sara switches to a Sugar Ray Robinson impression.

"Put 'em up!" she keeps saying. "Put 'em up!" Aaron wraps his chest in one of the padded blue mats, making him look like a baseball umpire. He confronts Sara, who punches him. Still on my mat, I believe I am in a safe space apart from the proceedings. A woman walks over to me anyway. She leans over my body, her hands resting on the blue wall. Then she starts writhing. And grunting.

"She was saying she deliberately went over to you and was drawing an aura from you and you were gaining something from her whether you wanted to or not," Aaron will tell me after class. Aaron comes up behind her as she squirms over me. He dry humps her.

A chime sounds. We meet again in the middle of the room. Sara, the instructor, reports that words can't capture what she feels. Aaron says the class has been good for him because making relationships with others is his big issue; these exercises give him the freedom to make those relationships. Sara looks at me. It is my turn to speak.

"I feel like I just witnessed my first orgy," I say.

❧

Back at the Coop after class, Aaron asks me to help him with one of his Naropa assignments. I wonder if I'll have to act like a gorilla or something, but it turns out to be no big deal. He just needs to tape an interview for a behavioral therapy class. The assignment involves empathic listening. We meet at his side of the Coop, in an apartment with hardwood floors, a kitchen, a full bath with a tub, two bedrooms, and a mudroom featuring a washer and dryer. Still, the place is cramped and emits the same aura as my hovel: chickens used to live here. We sit in one of the bedrooms, me on a daybed resting against pillows, he on a chair opposite a computer. He presses a red button on his tape recorder.

"Why did you move to Boulder?" he asks.

"Boulder seemed like the best place for me to train," I answer.

"What are you training for?"

"I'm trying to qualify for the Boston Marathon."

"Why do you want to qualify for the Boston Marathon?"

"Because it was something my dad pulled off when he was my age."

"Why is that important to you?"

"I want to see if I can replicate his feat."

"Why do you want to replicate his feat?"

"Because, um . . ." I don't know what to say. I stare at Aaron for maybe thirty seconds, which feels like two minutes. He doesn't say anything. He doesn't look down at his notebook or at the tape recorder. I wait for him to ask another question, preferably one with a yes or no answer, but he just stares at me, as he was no doubt instructed.

∞

When I was freshman in high school I developed a shoplifting habit. It got pretty out of hand. On weekends I'd go to the mall, usually with a friend or two, and we'd take anything we could possibly take. My bedroom became a stockpile of new golf balls and blank Maxell cassette tapes. I swiped a tennis racquet, too. And a new camera.

"Where did you get the money for all this stuff?" my dad would ask me, his eyes surveying my crowded room.

"There was a big sale," I'd lie.

I was no master thief. I'd loiter in the record store for a half an hour, pawing some cassettes nervously, or maybe a Walkman. I'd glance at the clerk again and then again as I waited for him to look away, waited for the right moment to stuff everything into my Windbreaker. The clerk would eventually tire. He'd come over and say, generously, "All right, little man. Just put everything down and leave, okay?"

The motivation behind my crime spree was easy to determine. I was skinny and shy at age fifteen. I didn't feel I had much to offer the world. So I was buying friendships, or trying to. Most everything I managed to steal I'd distribute on Monday mornings like I was Santa Claus, handing presents to classmates I deemed worthy of my beneficence. I bestowed a stolen video game cartridge upon a neighbor named Mark Kweller. To someone else I gifted an entire game system, worth more than $200. I'd just walked into Sears, picked up an Intellivision and walked out, storing it first in a locker near a bank of pay phones. Word of my largesse reached my sister, a senior at the same school. She tried to get me to quit. I couldn't. I felt popular when I handed out presents. I stopped only after I was finally busted, for stealing about ten dollars' worth of candy from a K-mart. My dad had to come into the store to pick me up.

"You're in so much trouble," he said when we left the little office in the back. The security guard noted I had enough money in my pocket to pay for the candy. So why steal it? It was the excitement, I would have said if I'd felt it was wise to open my mouth. It's fun to break the law. I like giving stuff to my friends. I feel a need to buy friends because I'm intimidated by the new school I'm attending. My dad looked embarrassed. Humiliated.

"Do you realize no one will ever hire you now?" he continued as he dragged me to his car. "You're never going to be able to get a job. Ever." I was fifteen years old. The store hadn't even called the cops.

When we got home, my dad pulled me up to my room, took off his belt, bent me over my bed, and whipped me. I can't recall the number of times he struck me. I can't recall if he said anything while he swung the belt. I do recall the first strike didn't really hurt, but the second strike did kind of hurt, and from then on there was real pain.

I doubt he realized I liked the pain in a way, was grateful for it. I knew, the whole time I was grabbing cassette tapes and video games and candy, that it was wrong to steal. I knew when I got caught I deserved to be punished. I knew I deserved to be punished even if I *didn't* get caught. When he whipped me, a tough penalty for a major offense, I felt I was getting what was coming to me. It was satisfying.

This was the role he played in my youth. The disciplinarian. A mysterious, little-known, little-seen man who brought home the money and who kept us in clothes and schools and food and who chopped wood on Saturday afternoons and who went to church on Saturday nights and who, for a while, changed in the parking lot after church to run seven miles home. A man who traveled all week on business, returning home to punish us for whatever crimes we'd committed in his absence. I don't know if he ever whipped my brother — for what? — and I doubt he ever touched my sisters, though Jennifer went through her age of insubordination. I don't know if his dad hit *him*, an only child. I just know that to this day, whenever I screw up, I'm waiting for him to come at me with his belt.

He would be mad if he saw me squandering my time, my chances. If he saw me plain old fucking up like I was doing back in Miami. I want him to see me fuck up, then I want him to punish me. I want my American sin of sloth out in the open, for once he knows about it, for once that belt slaps my ass, the problem vanishes. I never shoplifted again, or thought about it, or was tempted.

When my father finished whipping me he gave me a choice. I still remember the exact words he said; they struck me as absurd.

"You can either go see a therapist or you can have no further punishment." That's a trick question so loaded it's not even a trick anymore. No punishment was clearly the wrong option, an answer that would lead directly to more punishment, probably via a leather belt. Um, I'll take the therapist? The guy he and my mom sent me to, that I supposedly chose to go to, almost never asked me a question. He just sat there in the room, waiting for me to talk. I never talked. It became a crazy game. After forty minutes of him staring at me, after forty minutes of my head swiveling this way and that way to avoid eye contact, he would finally speak.

"Well?" he'd say.

"Well what?" I'd respond. Ten minutes later the session would end and I'd hand him a check from my dad, a ritual that amused him and me both. This went on for four weeks before I was deemed cured by my parents, or actually punished enough to stop seeing the therapist.

❦

I think back to those sessions with that counselor as I sit on Aaron's daybed, my new neighbor looking straight at me and waiting for an answer. Obviously Aaron's been told to repeat every statement I make in the form of a question, and then to keep his mouth shut. The method, I must admit, is forcing me to state plainly an answer I haven't yet grappled with. I say the question again, aloud, since he won't repeat himself. Why is it important to repeat my father's feat?

"I guess I just want him to respect me."

12

THE PLANE APPROACHES Philadelphia. I look out my window at the coal piled along the Delaware. An oil refinery sprays orange flames into skies that seem as though they're about to drop acid rain. We pass a Boeing plant and an empty racetrack. Bright, airy Boulder brews optimism every day like a jar of sun tea. Philadelphia appears gray and dirty, cold and overcast with an incoming winter. I spy piles of junked cars and old washing machines and used tires. Two soccer teams dart around a brown field. A fat smokestack discharges ropes of ash, or maybe steam. Is it *that* cold?

"We're going to have great fall weather," my sister Jennifer had promised over the phone. Doesn't look that way. By the time we land, my mood is as depressed as the landscape.

My older sister went to Marquette University, same as our dad. She married her college boyfriend—a runner—and the two of them are raising two boys whom I love to death. I've always thought of Jennifer as a runner, too. She ran track and cross-country in high school. She earned eight varsity letters in the two sports. My dad likes to brag, when he gets the chance, that some of her times still stand as school records. She married a runner, and running was what brought them together, I've presumed. I also presumed running was something she loved.

"To this day I hate it," Jennifer says. "I wanted to play volley-ball but he wouldn't let me."

We're talking now in the lobby of the downtown Marriott. All around us, string beans in shiny sweat suits check in to the hotel, or walk out into the city for breakfast, or return from the nearby convention center with their race-day numbers and the electronic chips they'll fasten to their shoes to ensure they don't shortcut the course. Tomorrow will be my first half marathon, a major mile-stone in my training. It cost me a lot of money to fly here and book a hotel room and register for the race and board my dog and char-ter taxis and eat three days of restaurant food. It would have been much cheaper to run one of the half marathons held somewhere in Colorado every weekend. Rich's recommendation that I enter the Philadelphia Distance Run has filled me with expense anxiety, but I've been trying to focus on the upsides. Three world records have been set on its flat course with a "well-earned reputation for speed." It's at sea level; I'm curious if there's anything to this alti-tude training I've been doing. And I get to see my sister.

She drove down from Saratoga Springs with her husband and the boys, arriving late last night. Rich has instructed me to rest, to not walk around much before the race, but it is impossible not to, not with my nephews here with me. We walk to Independence Hall, passing through security to stand on a spot where Abraham Lincoln once gave a speech. We take pictures next to the Liberty Bell. As we stroll over to the Betsy Ross house, a quartet of run-ners in Bolder Boulder T-shirts sprint past us, swelling my new-found regional pride. Pennies sprinkle the white grave of Benja-min Franklin. We continue on down to the Delaware, where we sit on the river wall and watch boats motor past.

Back at the convention center, we check in at the race expo, picking up my number and the computer chip to fasten to my shoe. It's about lunchtime, so we proceed over to the Reading Terminal Market. The place is crowded and loud in a good way; for a sure tourist trap, the market somehow feels authentic. "Yo!"-shouting vendors hawk cheesesteaks. Amish women in one booth flip Pennsylvania Dutch apple pancakes, which my sister sets her eyes upon. As we wait in line, she turns to me with a question.

"Have you ever been to Philadelphia before?"

❧

"You're not coming are you? I knew it. I knew you were going to do this."

She was indignant. She was disappointed in me. I was the one who lacked guts. When I'd hesitated a bit, when I waffled on meeting her in Philadelphia, I'd already separated from my wife. I'd moved into an apartment largely so she — Mrs. Wisconsin — and I could talk on the phone, so we could be closer. I'd made moves. But when I expressed a little doubt, when I wondered if I could pull off a week with her at a neutral site, she went ballistic.

I had to pick which life I was living. I had to commit. Although we were both still sneaking around, I had to put my money where my mouth was and walk the talk and all that. And that was good. Ultimately I'm grateful for that. Yet on the day she yelled at me, she also posted an online review of a book on interior decorating. Mere hours after she bullied me to follow through on our adulterous affair, to prioritize her, she told the editors of Amazon .com that a book taught her how to tie her whole house together with color. Her house in Wisconsin. Over the phone, to me, she didn't say anything about painting or palette harmony. To me, she made no mention of the life she continued to build with her husband. She said only that I was a coward.

My wife had introduced me to her, first at a restaurant in their hometown, I guess before we'd even married. I would like her, I was told. I'd like her husband, too; we'd all have a lot in common. I don't remember what she looked like at that first meeting. I remember he was wearing a black leather jacket. He and I talked for a while at the bar while she and my wife gabbed in a booth. I don't recall much else.

I next met them both at a wedding. I know I was already married by then. She was wearing a long blue satin dress. She kept slipping outside to smoke with her friends, most of whom were also my wife's friends. I'd slip outside myself, hoping to talk to her. At one point she and I sat at a round table while everyone else danced. She seemed really interested in my stories, which flattered my vanity. I recall her dancing at one point, wearing that blue dress.

I *really* met her, it all *really* started, at a house party. It was Christmas, which makes me think the house party must have been only a few months after that wedding. It was those same mutual friends of theirs, all in their late twenties like me. I remember how the house looked fully adulted out with a dinette set and living room furniture no one is ever meant to sit in. It looked just like my in-laws' house. It looked just like my parents' house. The front door featured a small window, a half circle with five triangled panes resembling an orange slice. When she walked up to the front door, when she saw me through that window, she lit up. Remarkably so.

Years later she'd admit she arrived at the party looking to hook up with a different guy, someone with whom she'd been flirting. She spent the night talking to me instead. She remained interested in everything that came out of my mouth, just as she did at the wedding. I was interested in her, too, yes. Very much so. I won't deny it.

There is one specific point from that night I remember as well as anything that happened in the years afterward. Six of us had left the party and relocated to the basement of another house, one owned by the bride and groom from that earlier wedding. I sat on a couch with my wife. Mrs. Wisconsin sat in an old, swiveling recliner. The talk was of politics or something; I can't remember the topic. I remember her intelligence. She was opinionated and interesting and funny. I remember thinking to myself she was exactly the kind of woman I wished I was with. It's an ugly thought, I know. My interest spiked further when she walked upstairs to join a conversation with my wife and their mutual girlfriend, flashing a patch of black satin panty through a hole in her jeans.

I didn't do anything. I found her attractive, sure, but married men always find other women attractive. I didn't make plans for my life's unraveling. That night in the basement I kept quiet. I played darts with her husband. They'd married when she was twenty-three, he told me. They'd met in grad school. He was, and remains, nine years older than her and eight years older than me. I liked him a lot. I distinctly remember that fact. I remember telling her when she followed up a week later with a flirtatious e-mail that I did, indeed, like him a lot. I wrote back that I "had no intention of fucking with another man's life (insert Freudian slip here)."

She sent more e-mails. I was happy to receive them, I admit. They excited me. They made me feel attractive. We acknowledged we were drawn to each other. She had a crush on me, something she first told her husband after the wedding, and then again after that basement-darts-get-together thing. She said they could talk about stuff like that, she and her husband. She said their marriage was open and tolerant. Supposedly, she would have been fine — happy even — if she'd caught her husband in a closet making out with some random woman at that wedding. Flirting, she said, was fun. I told her I didn't want to flirt. I told her I wanted to fuck her, and because of that we probably shouldn't talk any more. By then I had started calling her toll-free work number.

I no longer have the e-mails she first sent. I don't have my journals from that time, either, as they were stolen, along with my passport, some cash, and all three of my computers when someone broke into my Miami apartment. She saved the e-mails. Apparently she printed them out and tucked them in a drawer of the house in Wisconsin she shared with her husband. When he found the e-mails he wasn't as open-minded as she'd claimed he would be. Of course, by then, we'd escalated way beyond flirting. By then Philadelphia was something already years in the past.

When I ponder why I killed my marriage, I land on stories I was told only after my wife and I separated. My sister, who loved my wife, said she knew all along we weren't right for each other. My brother apparently predicted at my wedding reception the marriage wouldn't last six months. My parents aren't particularly touchy-feely, yet they realized something physical was missing. They'd noticed that my wife and I didn't touch each other at the rehearsal dinner, not once all night.

When Mrs. Wisconsin started e-mailing me, I was vulnerable. I was open to her interest. At the time I'd already been flirting, cautiously, with a sales rep at my newspaper; I can't claim Mrs. Wisconsin dragged me into sin against my will. But I don't think I ever would have gotten there without her. She pursued me aggressively. She wanted something from me. As best I can reconstruct things, she was a bored wife. She'd married even younger than I had. Her life was very safe and very small, and she seemed to need some excitement, some danger. In her e-mails, she told me recklessness was the trait she most admired in a man. In hindsight, she'd just wanted a fling. I guess.

&

My flight from Miami landed before her connecting flight from Chicago. I waited for her in the Philadelphia airport. When she arrived, she looked uncomfortable, suddenly uncertain about what we were doing. She wore a white blouse. She was skinny in her way. She did not touch me or kiss me, and her smile looked sad. We sat far apart in the cab. At dinner in Chinatown, near her hotel, we talked uneasily. There were long silences. Neither of us knew what we were doing.

This initial awkwardness would grow familiar over the next few years, as we met more and more often. She developed a routine on her flights in to see me. When the captain announced the approach to Fort Lauderdale or Miami, she'd turn off her music or close her book and just sit back to reflect on us. She'd think about how much she liked me, about how much she wanted to be with me. She'd wonder for a bit if she would be as attracted to me in person as she was attracted to the idea of me that lived in her brain. There would be tension for about a day, starting when we'd meet in the airport terminal, as our mental imagery synced with reality.

In Philadelphia, we ended up having fun. We rode a bus to the art museum. We sampled cheesesteaks at the Reading Market. We walked around downtown. I don't recall exactly what time of year it was, but I guess it would have been summer. She wore a tight gray top attached to her shoulders with thin spaghetti straps.

"Guys like it when I show skin," she reported, absorbing eyeballs as we walked Arch Street to that LOVE sculpture. She was officially in Philadelphia to attend a conference. I walked around by myself when she had meetings. Returning from one walk, I found her sitting at the far end of our nonsmoking room, exhaling cigarette smoke out the window.

"Hey, baby," she said, smiling.

I used to have a picture of her walking near the hotel. I tossed the photo long ago, but the image has stayed in my mind. She's wearing stretchy black pants and a thin white sweater with long sleeves. I also owned another picture, of her sitting on a bench near the Swann Fountain. Tulips bloomed at her feet. The art museum lurked in the distance. She was wearing blue jeans and a purple cardigan. I remember things that weren't photographed, random memories I can't shake. At dinner one night, a shrimp slipped off her spoon and shot over the lip of her blouse into her cleavage. Very funny, like in a romantic comedy. At dinner another night, out a window, we saw a couple on the street dressed for swing dancing.

"I like dates that involve special outfits," she said. In the cab back to the airport, at the end of the trip, she sat on my lap. We kissed deeply. We told each other we were in love.

Eventually she would move to New York City. She'd take a new job, leaving her husband in Wisconsin. (Though, it turned out, never formally separating from him.) She moved to be with me, she said, and I believed her. I took the first steps toward moving to New York, too. I quit my job. I proceeded with my divorce, giving my wife the house.

Mrs. Wisconsin never became Miss New York. She stayed in Manhattan for barely six months before she fled back home, back to the Midwest. During those six months, when she'd fly down to see me in Miami, I'd steam-clean my carpet. I'd dust. I'd wash my car and my clothes and myself until my skin turned pink. Yet when I'd fly up to visit her in Manhattan, dirty dishes sat in her sink. She'd make no plans for what we'd do in the city. Every night before bed she'd order me out of the apartment so she could telephone her husband. I'd come back frozen cold, steaming hot at her continuing contact with him, angry she was still slinking around while I'd done what was necessary for us to be together. She'd be in bed naked, her eyes cast down submissively. I'm so sorry, she'd say. She didn't love him anymore. It was over between them. Honestly, baby. She'd drop the sheet, reach out to me with bare arms, and promise she would make it up to me.

I'd sleep with her. I'd still sleep with her even after she moved back with her husband, back into her house, back to her old job. She came down to Miami a few more times. I spent a long weekend in her state capital. We stayed in a room at the university's student union. We sat facing Lake Mendota on sherbet-colored deck chairs. At a shoe store, she tried on two pairs of black boots, asking me which ones I liked better. I told her it didn't matter, that I'd never get to see her wear the boots. She admitted that was probably true. She admitted she could never leave her husband. Yet, in the car, after the shoe store, as I drove her back to her real life, she said she felt like killing herself.

"There's your house," I replied, rolling to a stop. I pointed at a small bungalow. "There's the next twenty-five years of your life. Go. Your husband's waiting for you. He probably wants to hear all about your weekend."

It still didn't end. There was another trip, to Chicago. There was a second separation from her husband, brief as it was. There was yet another flight down to see me in Miami, a trip where she swore we would be together forever. By then I was trying to get something going with Miss Cable News. I was trying to move forward. Yet each time she came back, I couldn't ignore her. I vibrated when we walked down the street. Like a stupid little girl,

I felt safe when she held my hand. At the end of the day I wanted to be with her, and that's the simple truth.

Then she went to Hawaii with her husband. When she returned to the mainland I told her, finally, that it was finally, really over. Soon after that she got pregnant. And that, finally, was when it finally ended. Finally.

Sort of. Almost. She sent me pictures of her belly growing in silhouette. She sent pictures of the yellow walls of the baby's room, which her husband had decorated with a big hand-painted tree. She called me from the hospital. *She called me from the fucking hospital.* Mrs. Wisconsin called me from the maternity ward to tell me nothing had changed.

Three years after her son was born, she saw me one more time, in Miami. She was there on work. She'd called impulsively. She just happened to have a free day and was I just as free to get together? On the beach, she held my hand. On Lincoln Road she told me I was the greatest man in the world. We kissed some more. She said she wanted to fuck me, though there was no time. When she left, I reprised the part I'd played for seven years. I rolled around the floor of my apartment, tearing out my hair. Every connection to my old life was now gone. I felt unmoored, alone, scared.

Sometimes I like to think she really did want to be with me. Sometimes I feel confident and arrogant and I have self-esteem. At those times I think she would have been better off living with me. Her husband would have been better off, too. I think, at those times, that her relationship with me wasn't the problem. The affair was a symptom of problems in her relationship with her spouse. Exactly like my marriage.

Other times, I'm angry. I'm prosecutorial. I pore over evidence, looking for skullduggery. She said she loved me. She said she wanted to be with me. Clearly she didn't. She took the money a divorce would have cost her and sunk it into new Italian tile in her kitchen. And a new SUV. She wanted romantic love. She wanted sex. But she didn't want to give up anything to get those things. She said she loved recklessness. I've never seen the defendant do anything more reckless than pay her mortgage! She never made a move without a backup plan, and she never failed to cash in those backup plans.

"You're really bitter," she wrote in one of our last e-mails.

Yeah. I hate her guts when I get lonely. I hate that she's not here to solve my problems, which is a dynamic I resented in my wife, that I was supposed to solve *her* problems. When I flounder, I wish I had a teammate. I liked the way Mrs. Wisconsin made me feel safe. She was capable and confident. She could take care of me. She was, in a lot of ways, kind of like my dad, a weird thought I've never been able to shake. I try to talk myself out of loving her. I try to dismiss all that happened as a meaningless little fling, a trifle. I can make a pretty good case.

❧

I wake up at 5:40 a.m., worried. Do I have safety pins for my race number? I have no idea. Toilets flushing in other rooms signal that I'm not the only one up and getting ready. The elevator in the hall starts opening and closing frequently. I pull out my gear, realizing I should have done it last night. There are safety pins already attached to my race number. Good. My mouth is dry. My legs feel heavy and somehow sort of hollow. I eat my PowerBar and drink from a bottle of Diet Mountain Dew chilled overnight in an ice bucket. Is my flight home really at 4:00 p.m.? Or is it much earlier?

I pull on brand-new tiny red nylon shorts, the kind real runners wear. I pin my number to the new orange Boulder Road Runners singlet Rich gave me, first writing Rich's name and cell phone number on the back of the race number in case of emergency. Wait a minute; I should have put my sister's info on there instead. Ah, fuck it. My shoes remain bright yellow. I thread my timing chip through the laces of my left shoe, tie the laces, and then inspect my outfit in the mirror. Orange top, red shorts, yellow shoes. Yep, I'm a Skittle. I check the start time of the race: 7:45 a.m. It's 6:23. I'm fine. I'm awake and alert and trying to be as calm as Dale Earnhardt sleeping in his car before the start of the Daytona 500. Dale Earnhardt died at the Daytona 500, didn't he? Ignore that. Ignore how my back suddenly hurts, a dull pain from my spine up to my neck, to a spot where I slipped a disk ten years ago. Why is it hurting now? I go over the route one last time. Start at the art museum. Loop through downtown for four miles, then back to the museum. From there, four and a half miles up the Schuylkill. The same distance back down, again back to the art museum and the finish line. I tuck a packet of goo into the key pocket of my racing shorts. I pull on the old black University of Colorado intramural sports T-shirt Rich gave me to toss aside at the starting line. Again, when is my flight home? Four o'clock. Okay. It's go time.

Light seeps into the city. Workers in hard hats amble to a skyscraper rising two blocks from my hotel. I see a few runners, then a few more as I turn toward the art museum. By the time I reach the "Rocky" steps, we're a zombie march 25,000 strong, all of us dressed in nylon and Spandex with sunglasses perched atop mesh caps. I urinate in a bush outside the Rodin museum. I urinate again at the art museum, and then I suck down my goo. I take my position at the starting line. We're segregated by our estimated finishing time, which places me in corral six. Rich advised me to avoid the pack by standing to the far left of the corral and to push my way to the front. I pull off the T-shirt he gave me. One last time, in my head, I go over Rich's advice. I'm visualizing the opening four-mile loop. I need to piss yet again.

My bloodstream is fueled by last night's baked ziti with veal and chicken. We ate at this neighborhood restaurant in South Philly, a hole-in-the-wall located in the Italian market, which isn't in an Italian neighborhood anymore. To find the restaurant we passed Mexican butchers and Vietnamese bakeries and a store stocked with hair spray and eye shadow that was appropriately named "Yo! Beauty Supply." They really do say that word a lot around here. I said the word, too — "Yo!" — when I raised my one glass of beer for a toast. One glass of beer? I know alcohol is a diuretic, but I shouldn't be urinating this much. Should I?

I make it back from a porta potty moments before the starting gun. We sing the national anthem. We clap when the first air horn blast releases the wheelchairs onto the course. We clap again when the air horn squeals the start of our wave. It takes a while to roll through the five corrals in front of us. When we do finally slip under the yellow banners at the starting line, loudspeakers blare the theme from *Rocky,* a song the locals must be absolutely sick of. I click a button on my watch.

Go easy. Go easy. Don't start out too fast. Stay off to the side to avoid the rubes who don't know what they're doing; they'll burn themselves out before they reach the river. Power through the first few miles. I'll feel like quitting, Rich told me, correctly. My lungs scream and my legs hurt and I can't believe I have to keep up this pace for twelve more miles. Now eleven miles. Now ten miles. Power through. I've passed city hall and the convention center and my sister and the boys who cheered on "Team Boulder" from a light post at the end of the first loop, back near city hall once again. There's the art museum. Four miles done and I'm finding my groove just as Rich prophesied.

"I like your shoes!" a woman calls out to me. Nice. Spectators six bodies deep jangle cowbells and hold signs to encourage their friends. I smell pretzels warming in a cart parked just off the course. The pack has thinned out. The stragglers have been dropped and the really good runners have all sprinted on ahead. Most everyone running alongside me holds my same pace. No, to be honest, I seem to be slowly passing almost everyone.

A two-person rock band plays at mile six. We cruise up the Sooeykill? The Psychill? That river with that name I can't pronounce correctly. Leafy trees shade the sun. There's a strong headwind I'd like to block by running behind some big guy, but I can't find a big guy running fast enough. Goo waits for us at mile eight, right before the only small hill on the course. We cross a silver-painted bridge to the north riverbank, where we turn our bodies toward the finish line.

"Almost there!" shouts a spectator.

"Bullshit," mutters a man laboring next to me. "Four miles to go ain't exactly almost there."

I'm not thinking about the four miles left. Instead I focus on finishing the next mile, which will give me ten in total. It's a trick I learned on our Tuesday and Thursday workouts. On those tempo runs, we might knock off four five-minute sprints in a row, a task that can stagger me. I've learned to focus just on the next sprint, which will leave me with only one more to go until I'm half done, and when I'm half done, there's only two sprints left and I can do two more, right? In Philly, a tailwind pushes us past the red-painted structures along Boathouse Row. The art museum is visible up ahead through the trees. I make it to mile ten. Okay, just three more. I can run three more miles, right?

I can. There's none of the fatigue I've been expecting. It's hard and I'm straining and I'm not exactly flying like an Olympian, but I still have gas in my tank. I can finish strong. A runner tries to pass me — Bobby? — but I find another gear and hold him off. The crowd hugging the curb thickens. We're nearing the end.

"Almost there!" cries another spectator, and this time I know she's right. I've already visualized the course in my mind. Gently curve to the left. There's the museum. Now curve to the right for a quarter mile before turning sharply onto the home stretch. It's a straight five hundred yards. I see the clock ticking over the finish line. Good lord, it's doable. Pick up the pace. Pick up the pace!

I have this memory of my dad at an early point in his running career. We're in New Hampshire. It's a sunny summer morning. My dad has already finished his race, first in his age group as always, and we're standing together near the finish watching the rest of the runners cross the line. Most of the runners aren't really running anymore. They're merely jogging, almost walking. But one man coming into view flies. He's going all out, sprinting, which impresses me but which earns my dad's scorn.

"If you finish that strong then you didn't run your best race," my dad practically spits.

Well fuck that. I'm sprinting. I am running as fast as I can, as fast as I've run since I played soccer in college. A second blinks on the clock, then another and another. I'm still going to make it, I calculate. I lunge across the finish line, look up at the clock and then down at my wristwatch. I think I did it. I think I just made it. When the official times are posted later in the day, I did indeed accomplish my goal. I finished in 1:37:59. Double that time and I'd qualify for Boston with exactly one second to spare.

❧

"That was a lot of fun," Jennifer says. She'd been waiting with the boys at the art museum. "As long as I wasn't the one running it."

Pain and soreness flare as soon as I stop. I can't bend down to cut the electronic chip off my shoe, which a loudspeaker is ordering me to do. A very large blister stings the ball of my left foot. A stiffness in my knee increases with each step I take to collect the free plastic sandals we all get, and to grab my big clunky medal hung on a yellow ribbon. I pull a bottle of sports drink from a tub of ice but pass on the free soy milk. Slowly, my sister and the boys and I climb to the top of Sylvester Stallone's steps. She instructs me to pose with my arms over my head, victorious.

I was beaten by a guy with a tutu, the boys tell me. While they waited for me to finish, they heard the names of several Boulder runners who also finished in front of me, probably the same people we'd seen warming up the day before. My sister asks about the next race I'm going to run. Maybe she and the boys will fly down to Tucson in December, if that's the marathon Rich picks out for me. Or maybe Sacramento in January, if Rich recommends I run my qualifier on that famously fast, almost entirely downhill course. Boston is for sure. She'll take the day off work and the boys will take the day off school (her husband's a kindergarten teacher). We'll stay in the same hotel and after the race we'll go out for lobster and beer. She's really looking forward to Boston.

"I hope you beat his time," she says.

13

A FEW MONTHS BEFORE I left Miami, my parents flew down for a visit. It was Thanksgiving. They took a room in the hotel where I was living. My bedroom faced the parking lot. Because I knew my dad would end his morning runs in the lot, I tried to crawl out of bed and open my blinds before he returned. I wanted him to look at my windows and see that I'm up, that I'm busy in my bedroom office, that I'm engaged with the workforce and life and all that. This ruse didn't work as well as I'd hoped. On the Wednesday before the holiday, right after I wrapped up one little project I did indeed have on my plate — *See? I'm working!* — I emerged from my bedroom to join my parents in my small living room.

"That's it," I declared. "From here on in I'm on vacation."

"Your whole life," my dad grumbled, "is a vacation."

Thanksgiving is usually a big deal with us. If we'd been in Chicago, my mom would have cooked turkey and stuffing and a fluffy cheesecake baked from a recipe inherited from Grandma Pawlowski. I'd get to play with Gretchen's kids, and sometimes, if they could fly in, also with the offspring of my two other siblings. That last Thanksgiving, isolated in Florida from the rest of the family, my parents and I spent the holiday untraditionally, tailgating at a Miami Hurricanes football game. There was turkey deep fried in oil, and cranberry sauce, and plenty of Presidente beer from the Dominican Republic. A student came around our tailgate before kickoff, soliciting money for some school-related charity. A ten-dollar donation earned an orange-and-green hat adorned with the football team's *U* logo. It was a little cold that evening (by Miami standards), and I liked the hat, so I made a donation using some of my dad's money left over from our beer run on the drive to the stadium.

"You bought a hat!" my dad cheered when I pulled the toque over my ears.

"No," I corrected, "you did."

My dad turned to a tailgate neighbor and said, not without humor, "Story of my life."

He was born in 1936. That much I know for sure. I've seen his birth certificate so I know he was born in Milwaukee, the child of Bernard Pawlowski and Rosella Toth Pawlowski. As I understand it, my grandfather was a boilermaker, working enough years for Wisconsin Electric that he received a watch upon his retirement. Later he took a job at the Pabst brewery, in part for the weekly case of beer included in his compensation. What did my grandmother do? Her father worked as a janitor at Harley-Davidson, I've been told. She sold beer at Milwaukee Braves baseball games. I think. I don't really know for sure.

It's hard to assemble a history in my family. I'm a journalist. I like to think I've got some ability as an investigator. But when it comes to our family I'm in the dark. Once, when I asked my mother why my dad changed his last name to the one I was born with, she replied: "Why do you want to know?" At the time I was thirty-six years old. I've heard my dad referred to as the miracle baby. I've heard that his mother miscarried five times before she finally gave birth to her only child. My brother must have told me that, or maybe it was my older sister. The one time I asked my dad about his miraculous conception he didn't know what I was talking about.

He grew up in Milwaukee. That is well documented. He lived first on the north side, then in a small, square brick house on the south side, near the airport, among most of the city's Polish population. When we'd drive up from Illinois to visit his mother we'd pass the golden dome of his church, where he also attended high school. I've seen a picture of him as a newborn, bare butt in the air, posed on a furry white rug. I've seen a yellowed picture of his mother in a swimsuit sitting on a lakefront beach, her miracle baby splashing in the water between her legs.

I don't know much more than that, what I've seen in pictures. He was drafted into the army in a time of peace between Korea and Vietnam. Neither of his parents graduated from high school, and it is well known that he finished in the bottom five of *his* high school class, yet he went on to earn master's degrees from Marquette and from Loyola of Chicago. He and my mom raised four kids, of whom I am the third. My brother and older sister were born in Indiana. Because of my dad's work, the family moved on to three cities in Canada (I was born in Winnipeg), then to New Hampshire, then to the final stop outside of Chicago, to that big house on that small lake. He changed jobs when we moved to Illinois. He ran his third and last Boston Marathon six months after the move, training in Central Park on his then-weekly business trips to New York.

Anything more than that, I just don't know. The stories conflict or, more often, there are no stories at all.

⚮

My parents fly out to Boulder soon after I return from Philadelphia. They arrive on a beautiful fall afternoon, a Wednesday, so I take them straight to the farmers' market. My mom ducks her head inside the Dushanbe Teahouse. A guitar player fingerpicks a Bach sonata while a vendor talks about the pumpkin patch he's about to open up. My dad and I walk up the creek path to the football stadium and the Frank Shorter statue. The first yellow leaves of the season fall from the trees. A hundred runners pass us and we both feel anxious, like we should be running, too.

They rent a cottage at Chautauqua. They're only staying for three days so I must be an efficient tour guide. One afternoon at the Celestial Seasonings tea factory, the next morning a drive to Rocky Mountain National Park, where the elks are bugling. A beer at Mountain Sun on Friday evening, then out to Pearl Street to watch the university's football team and marching band parade past. I'd encouraged my parents to stay through Saturday, when the Buffaloes are hosting Oklahoma. My parents like football, and I'm willing to pay for the tickets, but they elected to fly home early on Saturday morning solely to make it to Saturday evening mass at their church, as always.

When my parents visit I eat well. Dinner their first night in Boulder at Radda Trattoria, an upscale Italian place located in a strip mall near my Laundromat. For breakfast, huevos rancheros at the Chautauqua dining hall one morning, Cajun eggs Benedict and deep-fried beignets at Lucile's the next. One afternoon, my dad and I walk down the Hill to Glacier for chocolate milk shakes, our afternoon snack. That night, my dad selects spare rib risotto at Jill's, in the St. James Hotel. I have the filet mignon. When you're dieting, I'm learning, every good meal stands out.

We all like the Chop House, a masculine chain restaurant crowded on our visit with Oklahoma football boosters. My dad and I order the exact same thing: buffalo prime rib, a side of cheese potatoes, and a salad with creamy Italian dressing. My mom and I sip martinis, then red wine. My dad asks for a "local beer," and after the waiter runs though a list of excellent Colorado microbrews my dad chooses a Coors Light. The liquor loosens us up, as it usually does, and we talk easily about lots of things. Somehow we get to how they came to adopt my younger sister, who joined the family when we lived in Toronto. That got my dad reminiscing about his career at that time, and about a coworker who had already adopted a child. Then he just started talking about his career.

He never talked about work at the dinner table when I was a kid. What he did with his time, on those business trips or in that office of his, was his world alone. In newspaper stories written about my dad when he qualified for Boston he was described as a "manager of industrial relations." What the hell is that? He's been my dad my whole life. He's been working that whole time, up until only about a year ago. And I still don't really know what he did for money. Or how he got into it, or what made him so good at it.

I've picked up details over the years, almost by osmosis. I know his job had to do with unions, or did once we moved to Illinois. There was a documentary film released around the time I graduated from college, about a labor strike at a meatpacking plant in Austin, Minnesota. I saw it, and when I asked my dad about it he knew everybody in the film, on both sides. I spent a few Christmas vacations in his office, tabulating surveys of "worker satisfaction," filing newspaper clippings about unions and strikes and AFL-CIO meetings. We'd get there at seven a.m. He'd disappear for hours into his office, where I could see him writing on a yellow legal pad, using a ruler to keep his sentences in neat lines. When I was really young, my younger sister and I would drink free Coke from the office fountain until we were giddy, then we'd sneak downstairs to the building's candy machine. The subsequent sugar highs are what I remember most about my dad's work.

Now at the Chop House, cheap beer and rich food have him feeling comfortable and expansive. He's talking about way back, volunteering details from our time in Toronto when he worked at Moore Business Forms, in human resources. I listen with interest. Not about the work, which sounds boring, frankly, all exit interviews and business suits and forms in triplicate. What fascinates me is his confidence. How certain he has always been that no one in the world can do his job better than he can. There is no bluffing here. I know he's telling the truth, that he really was good at what he did. I suck on the salty last olive from my martini, listening, absorbing it all, until finally I must interrupt.

"What makes you so confident you had the answers, that you were so valuable?"

"Because I know the answers. I was the best human resources person around."

That kills me. I don't know where he gets that confidence. I spend all day, every day, cataloging my faults. I'm too old for my profession. I'm balding. I'm lazy. I'm intellectually soft. I'm easily distracted. I'm a loner, obviously, and bad with money. I'm divorced, I'm a failure. I'm a failure. I'm a failure. Could he have somehow taught me his confidence? Or how about this: Did he hold his kids back by competing with us, by reflexively, probably subconsciously, striving to crush us? He's no Bull Meacham, but still, has he read *The Great Santini* or what?

"How come you were so certain you were good?"

"Because I *am* that good," he says.

14

FRANK SHORTER'S SEEN this video a thousand times by
now, maybe more. There he is, as always, a twenty-eight-
year-old running the best marathon of his life. He's up
there on-screen, wearing blue nylon shorts and a skinny red singlet embossed with the letters *U, S,* and *A.* The mustache he'd
sported four years earlier, when he won the Olympic marathon
in Munich, in 1972, has been shaved. His thick black hair glistens
from rain and, at this point in the race, from twenty miles of per-
spiration. On the screen two runners splash through the streets
of Montreal, battling for the gold medal in the Olympic marathon of 1976. As his opponent pulls away on the monitor, Shorter
shakes his head. His eyes haven't blinked in more than a minute.

"It's just so obvious," he'll tell me later. "It's just so very obvious."

Shorter's watching the video off to the side of the narrow vault
that is the Boulder Fleet Feet running store. He's standing by
himself. He's so absorbed in the video that he hasn't noticed me
watching him, or that a small crowd is waiting for him to start
speaking. It's a Wednesday night in October, the first night of the
World Series. The local baseball team is making an unscheduled
appearance in the series, but Boulder is so much the running

town that about twenty of us have still turned out to hear Shorter speak. Specifically, he's here to break down the upcoming Olympic men's marathon trials, in New York City, in Central Park.

The owner of the running store has set out brie and crackers. Bottles of imported beer chill in a tub of ice. Shorter often starts his speeches with a video of the Munich race, which he won. The store owner, presumably unaware of the wound he'd open, has instead looped the Montreal race on a television. Before Shorter starts talking, and while the video continues to play, his eyes monitor the race like the lawyer he is. *That surge by Waldemar Cierpinski at the twenty-mile mark? That's unnatural. Cierpinski's running stride is smooth and efficient, yes, but he clearly doesn't know much about racing strategy. He doesn't have to, right? Just look at how effortlessly he pulls ahead at mile twenty-four. Cierpinski—an East German!—just has more in the tank. Suspiciously more, right?*

Shorter manages to smile when he's introduced. He's tan and slim, dressed in a long-sleeved running shirt and sweatpants. When he starts his speech, he does talk about the marathon trials, a bit. The Central Park course is hilly and twisty and will pose a challenge for the runners. Mostly what he talks about is steroids.

"I hate to segue back into drugs all the time," he says before comparing drug cheats to computer hackers. There's a community of cheats out there who want to one-up their cheating friends, he says. He talks about the sprinter Florence Griffith Joyner, a world-record holder who died at age thirty-eight after an epileptic seizure, a premature death long suspected to have stemmed from steroid abuse.

"Not to dwell on the drug thing," he says before talking about the downfall of the Olympic sprinter Marion Jones. Her conviction for lying in a steroids investigation is so very satisfying, the karma of it all. When someone asks about China, the host of the then-upcoming summer games, Shorter talks about what a Wild West that nation is when it comes to steroids and blood doping and EPO and human growth hormone. There is no enforcement there, he says. He talks about getting the Justice Department involved in catching drug cheats here in the US. He talks about getting the FBI involved, too, and most importantly the IRS.

"It's like catching bank robbers," he says to a question about the seeming futility of trying to stay ahead of the cheaters. "We can't catch them all, but does that mean we shouldn't try to catch any of them?"

Even when the formal speech ends, Shorter stays on his message, a message that has nothing to do with the 134 elite American runners preparing for the marathon trials. He moves to the front of the store, closer to the cheese platter. Trailed by most of the audience, Shorter grabs a bottle of Red Stripe, opens it, and then sits on the plastic seat of a folding chair. Someone brings up the World Series and how turnout at the store might have been higher had the Colorado Rockies not been playing the Red Sox that night.

"You know about Josh Beckett, right?" Shorter asks. The Red Sox starting pitcher, he says, a World Series MVP, was busted for steroid use in the minor leagues and was never punished for it. "Not to segue back to the drugs all the time," he adds. He takes another swig of beer.

It's the first time I've seen Shorter speak. Except for that one time I passed him on the trail near his house, it's the first time I've seen him at all. The *Daily Camera* running columnist Mike Sandrock introduces me, but Shorter spends most of his time talking to a woman who looks to be about twenty years old. He made a beeline for her as soon as his speech ended, and he's been chatting her up for the past ten minutes. Eventually she walks off and he asks if anyone can give him a ride back to his house. Despite my enthusiasm ("Me! Me! Pick me!"), I lose out to another guy and end up driving home alone. As I make my way down Broadway, past the mural of Shorter painted on the side of a bank, I think about his speech. All that drug talk. Steroids, steroids, steroids! It's like he's obsessed. It's like everything I've heard about Frank Shorter is true.

❧

Thirty years after he last achieved anything of note, Frank Shorter still dominates the Boulder running scene. His résumé has been memorized by almost every athlete and even every recreational jogger plodding through an early-morning workout. The Olympic gold and silver, of course. A five-time national champion in the 10,000 meters. A four-time winner of the Fukuoka Marathon in Japan. The 1972 winner of the Sullivan Award as America's outstanding amateur athlete. From 2000 through 2003, he served as the founding chairman of the United States Anti-Doping Agency (USADA), the quasi-governmental body responsible for screening Olympic-level American athletes.

I began to wonder if he even existed as an actual flesh-and-blood person, though. I saw him that one time on the trail near his house, but I never saw him at any of the monthly running socials, never saw him at the track or out on the trails, and never saw him even hanging around one of the races held in town almost every weekend. At one running social, as I sipped from a pint of Buffalo Gold beer, I asked Tera Moody about her interactions with Shorter. Moody has lived in Boulder for ten years, won a national cross-country championship at the university, and would go on to finish fifth in the Olympic marathon trials. She told me she'd never met Shorter, though she said she would like to. The banker

Steve Bosley founded the Bolder Boulder 10K with Shorter and has been a key business partner and advisor of his for more than thirty-five years. Bosley is an unabashed Shorter fan, the booster behind both the statue and the mural. Yet when I asked him how often he sees his longtime friend, Bosley said only about once a year.

I came to think of Shorter as Boulder's Boo Radley. Although his legend lives in everyone's psyche, concrete proof of his presence comes mostly via newspaper quotes. In interviews conducted at his house off Wonderland Lake, Shorter throws barbs at the Kenyans who train here, saying they don't follow as strict a drug testing regimen as the American athletes do. He's criticized Uta Pippig, the former East German who has been linked to blood doping and who has lived in Boulder for years. Through USADA, he's also taken on Tyler Hamilton, an Olympic gold-medal-winning cyclist who served a two-year suspension for blood doping, and who also lives in Boulder. In that *New York Times* article on the Boulder running scene, the one that inspired me to move out here, Shorter "raised a general concern that foreign athletes went to Boulder to dodge testing."

When I ask about Shorter, I hear stories about his divorce from his first wife, then from his second wife. He's standoffish, I'm told, aloof, isolated in that house of his. "Frank is all about Frank" is a quote I don't need to attribute, as at least thirty people have said it to me. Almost every one of those people has a story about how they'd see Shorter somewhere in town, maybe at the grocery store, and he'd be warm and friendly. And then a week later, crossing paths again, Shorter wouldn't give the time of day.

"He is bizarre," says Steve Jones, the former marathon world record holder who's lived in the same neighborhood as Shorter for twenty years. "I go out of my way to avoid Frank if I can.

I've seen him at airports and I've ducked around the corner. He's walked on airplanes and I've ducked my head behind a newspaper because I don't want to be the one that's being ignored."

"I think it ruined his life," adds Dan Skarda. He's referring to Shorter's silver medal in Montreal. "It ruined his life. I really think it did."

The idea that Shorter still obsesses about his silver medal seems preposterous. He already has a *gold* medal. His long-ago win in Munich gave him a sinecure, a ticket to a life of prosperity. Even all these years later he still earns good money conducting running clinics and speaking about his gold-medal win. He is America's long-distance running hero. I can't think of any way his life would be different if he had a second gold medal. How could he possibly be worked up about it? Why won't he just let it go?

"That's easy to say if you're not the person that's been cheated," explains Don Kardong, who finished fourth in Montreal. I reach Kardong at his work number in Spokane, where he's the race director of the Bloomsday 12K. "I think on the one hand, just for your own or my own mental health, you have to do that, let it go. But then again, when I start thinking about it, again, it's not right. It was so enormous. It's not something that can be just sort of shrugged off, even if it happened a long time ago."

❧

The more I learn about Frank Shorter the more I want to know. In a city where everyone seems to have his act together, Shorter's the most complex person around. Two divorces, a DUI down in Colorado Springs, his isolation from even people who consider themselves his good friends. Still, he inspired my dad. He remains a big deal, a legend. The owner of Fleet Feet, after the speech, expressed disappointment that more people hadn't shown up at the store.

"I mean, c'mon," the owner told me, "it's Frank fucking Shorter."

I'm most intrigued by Shorter's obsession with the drug stuff. It seems to be taking him down. I can't relate anything in my life to drug cheating on the Olympic level. Obsession, though: I can identify more than a bit with that.

One morning about a week after the speech, and after I put in my miles for the day, I walk to the Carnegie Branch of the public library, located on Pine Street north of Pearl and just up Broadway from the giant mural of Frank Shorter. The building served as the city's original book repository. Now that a modern main library has opened down by the creek, the Carnegie branch specializes in historical archives, and has few visitors. I have my choice of long, brown tables. Sitting at one of them, I spend a few hours flipping through three folders bulging with newspaper articles about Boulder's most famous citizen.

The clippings date back to Shorter's arrival in Boulder, and focus mostly on his running career. There are photos of his first wife managing Frank Shorter Sports, his former running store on Pearl Street and one of Shorter's first attempts to cash in on his running success. The store is described as a tourist desti-nation, a place people visit just to connect in some small way with the great runner. The wife in the picture, Louise, divorced Shorter in 1984, the store closing soon after. In the files, there's an announcement of Shorter's second marriage, which ended in divorce in 1999. The slow wind-down of his athletic career is covered in detail. He failed to make the Olympic team in 1980, finishing eighty-fifth at the marathon trials.

"Maybe my time is past," he said then. By 1984 there was no doubt; he failed to make the team again that year. "I have to find other ways to get ultimate satisfaction," he surmised. Two years later, in 1986, came the first article I found in which Shorter mentions steroids.

Drug and doping talk had been in the air for a while by then. The former University of Colorado standout Mary Decker, in an article published by the *Daily Camera* in 1980, mentioned her coach's insistence that she lift weights.

"He's got me doing that instead of taking steroids like the East German people — I won't call them women," she told a young staff sportswriter named Rick Reilly. (Decker would later be sanctioned for blood doping.) Shorter initially kept out of the fray. Immediately after the '76 games, in an interview conducted at his in-laws' house in Kansas, Shorter said he'd tried his best to win the marathon, but he'd had a bad day. His disappointment was not something he planned to dwell on forever. In his 1984 autobiography, *Olympic Gold,* he showers the marathon winner, Waldemar Cierpinski, with only respect.

Then things started to change. In the 1986 article in which he first mentions steroids, Shorter calls for stricter blood testing. By 2002, every article in the file makes reference to Cierpinski the cheater who stole a gold medal. Shorter grew explicit in his condemnation. In testimony before Congress in 2005, Shorter said this: "I can tell you what it's like to have your dream compromised by the drug use of another."

East Germany was a relatively small country. The communist nation collected twenty-five total medals at the Mexico City Olympics, in 1968. Eight years later in Montreal, the East Germans somehow collected *ninety* total medals, more than twice as many as more-populous West Germany. It was long suspected that East Germany's government fueled its athletic machine with steroids, as Mary Decker vocalized. When the Berlin Wall fell, those suspicions were substantiated. Files found in the offices of the Stasi revealed systemic doping, with the illegal drug use orchestrated by the highest levels of government.

In 1997, Shorter contacted a German biologist, Werner Franke, who was working his way through the Stasi files. He also met with Franke in Colorado Springs. The materials Shorter received have been well documented by other reporters. There was a column of numbers corresponding to 143 athletes, many of whom were proven steroid users. Cierpinski was on the list, number 62.

"This indicates that several middle and long distance runners already in the '70s were part of the doping program of the GDR and that Cierpinski was already on androgenic steroids in 1976," Franke wrote in a letter to Shorter.

When Shorter shared the Stasi files with Don Kardong, the fourth-place finisher, Kardong promptly contacted an American Olympic official and asked him to "drop everything and get me my medal!"

"The more I thought about it the angrier I would get," Kardong tells me. "Initially my response was more like, 'You're kidding? He was on that list?' Then you start to process it, how that might have helped him. Then you start wondering, If he hadn't done that, where would he have placed? Then I can see myself getting a medal and then it just starts to get to you."

Shorter's running career effectively ended in Montreal. Chronic foot and back injuries kept him from ever again contending on the international level. He won the Bolder Boulder 10K once, in 1981. His last victory, anywhere, came in 1983, when he was thirty-five. Just before he approached age forty, in an interview with the *Daily Camera*, he said he was again training seriously and hoped to become competitive at the master's level. Nothing really came of that. His clothing company dissolved in a flurry of lawsuits. An exercise-for-business-executives seminar thing never got off the ground. He never took up law. Shorter floated a trial balloon of maybe running for the United States Senate, but he never launched a campaign. For several years, he analyzed track and field for NBC, but he claims his TV work dried up because of his antidoping crusade. In one article I found at the library he said that, since his running days were behind him, he hoped to start coaching other runners. He never got around to it. Several athletes who used to run for the University of Colorado have relocated to Eugene, Oregon, to work with Alberto Salazar, a former top marathoner who followed through on his coaching ambitions.

That leaves Shorter with the antidoping stuff. That's his thing. That's what he's up to. There's a very old article in the clippings in which he's asked about his failure to win the race in Montreal. He replies that winning one gold medal is enough. I certainly would have thought so. I would have believed him, too, if every runner in Boulder hadn't told me about his obsession. And if I hadn't gone to Fleet Feet to hear him speak. I got to witness his obsession for myself, plain as day.

Oh, and one other thing I find in the clip file: Frank Shorter hates his father. I mean, *hates* him.

15

I'M HAVING DOUBTS about Rich. My running is going well, yes. I'm faster than ever. I'm logging as many as fifteen miles in a row on my Saturday-morning workouts. My scale reports I'm closing in on forty lost pounds. Yet a question nags at me: can I run even better?

When I started in Boulder, everyone volunteered training advice. The advice differed radically. Long miles, short miles, speed work, hills, diet, everything. I had to choose a path, and for better or worse I chose to follow the one blazed by Rich Castro. Yet long after I made that decision, dissenting opinions keep coming. Rich was a sprinter, what does he know about marathoning? You're only logging forty miles a week? And you want to run a 3:15 this year? No chance. Even friends in the running club, *in Rich Castro's running club,* volunteer criticism. One friend strongly disagrees with my slow, long Saturday workouts, runs where, as Rich often explains, I'm just putting in time on my legs.

"If you want to go fast you have to work on your speed first," says this friend. Another friend in the club says Rich isn't working with me individually as much as he should be.

The doubts — so incessant! — start to stick in my head. Rich *isn't* working with me enough, is he? He said he was going to wake me every morning with a phone call at five thirty. He did that twice, then just stopped. He said he was going to draft a workout plan for the weight room. He said he was going to send me up and down the Sanitas trail wearing a backpack full of rocks, a training idea swiped from a cheesy movie about the Boston Marathon called *Saint Ralph*. He never followed up. He was going to put me on a diet of soy nuts and cranberries, which I would have gone on—as horrible as it sounds—but he never followed through. While my doubts grow, the name of one man keeps coming up.

"The great coach Bobby McGee says, 'When a bad idea floats into your head, you have to say thank you for coming, thank you for visiting, now get out of here.'" That was said by Tom LeMire, a member of the Boulder Road Runners trying to buck me up after a tough training run.

I'd seen the Great Coach Bobby McGee once, the day before the Bolder Boulder 10K. I was with the running club at the Harvest House, a major hotel that backs onto the Creek path. Because of the upcoming race, we'd moved our normal Sunday run over to the hotel, and had downgraded to an easy jog of no more than two miles, something simply to keep the legs loose. It was after that jog, when I was taking sun on the hotel's wide back lawn, that I saw him. He sported short gray hair and a gray beard of matching length. He spoke in accented South African English. He was addressing a group clad in nylon shorts, tank tops, and running shoes. The people he was talking to, apparently, were his clients.

"His fastest training group runs seven-minute miles," snickered a member of the Boulder Road Runners sunbathing on the lawn next to me. "Yet they pay him up to ninety dollars an hour."

Seven-minute miles are solid, and if I could maintain that pace for a marathon I'd qualify for Boston easily. But they're not great.

For a 10K, which is obviously a lot easier than a marathon, seven-minute miles are almost pedestrian, the stuff of a recreational runner. Boulder, my friend and I agreed, is full of hucksters.

There's a training club called F4 that works out at the rez. Members of another training group wear red tank tops to advertise their allegiance to a coach named Ric Rojas. Even the people who organize the Bolder Boulder 10K offer group training. All of these services cost real money. In the case of the Bolder Boulder training groups, and of the clients I saw Bobby McGee addressing before the race, I don't get it. Why would someone hire a coach to train for a mere ten-kilometer run? How important can it be to score a decent time in a race that short?

Coaching, I've come to understand, is part of the culture in Boulder. There are coaches for everything in this town. The bulletin board at my Laundromat advertises gurus in Zen meditation, Osho meditation, and something called "golden light meditation with Oceana." The leader of my yoga class on Wednesdays is also a life coach. "Let Laura Kupperman show you the way," cheers her website. Before one trip out of town, I boarded Valentine with a woman who in addition to taking care of dogs tells me she, too, also does some life coaching. One day a few months after I arrived in town, I shared lunch at Leaf vegetarian restaurant with Scott Sharp Armstrong, the proprietor of the Boulder Coaching Academy.

Armstrong's calling card is an e-book, self-published and entitled *Boston or Bust*. It's his story of qualifying for the Boston Marathon after twelve years of trying. The topic interested me, obviously, and that's why I asked him to lunch. But his e-book is unimpressive. It lifts egregiously from self-help books by established brands such as Tony Robbins, Zig Ziglar, and, most blatantly, from the personal-success pioneer Napoleon Hill. ("Cherish your visions and your dreams, as they are the children of your soul, the blueprints of your ultimate achievement.") *Boston or Bust* is not much more than a string of quotes from these authors, seemingly aimed at fourth graders; it reads like a *Power of Now* excerpt in *Highlights* magazine. During our lunch, Armstrong told me he has clients whom he charges a thousand bucks an hour.

I pay for coaching, I'm aware. But why so many other people in Boulder do, too, is beyond me. Is it simply so affluent a community? Has everyone here already paid off their house and cars and their vacations and their kids' tuitions, with money left over to hire a coach for something as inconsequential as a local ten-kilometer race? Or for something as vague and all-encompassing as "life"? Is it because so many Boulderites are engineers and scientists working at Google and NCAR and IBM? They're trying to perfect the machine, perhaps. Do engineer types believe expert guidance is a necessary cost of any project? Is that it?

Whatever the reason, the demand for coaches in Boulder is a godsend to the professional athletes living here. Just about every coach — from the personal trainers at the Flatiron gym to the cyclists leading Saturday-morning climbs to the swim specialists working with triathletes — is hustling to continue in his or her chosen sport. All of them aspire, at least professionally, to be the Great Coach Bobby McGee, the man at the top of the pyramid. He's marketed himself so successfully that coaching is his sole business. That's rare. That's desirable. The coach and former world-record-holding marathoner Steve Jones still needs to paint houses for income. The Great Coach Bobby McGee does not.

I'd checked out McGee back in April, back when I first considered hired help. I pulled up his website, saw he charges those ninety bucks an hour for group training, and immediately terminated his candidacy. (I pay Rich Castro money, but it's a token amount, about a nickel an hour. Rich has more than paid that back in free Nike gear alone: shoes, hats, long-sleeved shirts, short-sleeved shirts, and racing singlets. He's also given me boxes of chocolate PowerBars, boxes of goo packets, and tubs of Accelerade energy drink. And fantastic Mexican meals at his house more than once.) But now, by October, the money McGee charges is looking less prohibitive. How much money have I already spent moving here? How much am I spending on my training all together? How important is it to get to Boston? Maybe it's time to give him a chance, if he's so great and all. Maybe I should thank Rich for getting me this far, but it's time to graduate to the next level.

I call McGee's phone number and ask for a quote. A personal session will cost a lot of money. A *ton* of money. Four hundred dollars for ninety minutes one-on-one. Ridiculous. No way. I wouldn't pay that much in a million years. Or maybe in a week — for seven days later I agree to a one-time coaching session with the great man. Clandestinely, behind Rich Castro's back.

We meet up at Tom Watson Park, a small rectangle of green wedged between the reservoir and the main campus of IBM. (Tom Watson, in this park's case, refers to the computer company's founder, not the golfer.) When I pull into the parking lot, the Great Coach Bobby McGee is already there, talking on his phone. He hangs up as soon as he sees me. He gives me his full attention. He asks me to write out a check. That is the first task. He is very happy to receive the four hundred dollars, gazing at the digits I've written on the draft as if they please him immensely. He tucks the payment into a portfolio and we go to work. Quickly. Who am I? Uh huh, yes. Okay. Three-fifteen in one year of training? Okay. Your father was a runner? Okay. I'd filled out two forms in advance, e-mailing them to his assistant, who I believe is his wife. Question: what is your serum ferritin level and general range? Answer: I have no idea.

"Let's check you out on the exercise mat first," Bobby McGee says. In the park, near a squadron of picnic benches, he unfurls a rectangle of squishy blue foam. On his command, on the foam, I squeeze out a few push-ups. I then lie on my hips, lifting legs skyward in scissors kicks. I'm imbalanced, he determines. Okay? My left side is weaker than my right side. Okay? He scribbles on a piece of paper. He says I am bowlegged.

It is a warm day for late October. Bright sun. A guy without a shirt slaps a handball against a concrete wall covered on one side by autumn-red vines. Moving fast, the Great Coach Bobby McGee directs me to that path over there, parallel to North Sixty-Third Street. Let's see you run, he calls out in his South African accent, which makes me think of a dingo eating a baby. Just run the way you normally run. Down to that tree. Okay, and back again.

"You're bouncing. You bounce—up and down like you're jogging on the moon."

He tells me to lean forward. Leaning forward will give me momentum. I'm supposed to lean almost to the point where I'll fall over, which will naturally make my legs rush to catch up to my torso. I should cock my arms, too, okay, like this, hands in fists swinging up so high it appears with every step I'm trying to punch myself in the face. My arms now seem extraneous, like the tiny and useless appendages on a tyrannosaurus rex. He films me running on the path. Both ways, my normal natural bounce and the new forward lean. We move over to a basketball court. He tells me to take off my shirt and run to the far basket and back. Run both ways again, the natural bounce and the new lean. He takes a few photos. We're done.

That's it. He rolls up his exercise mat, pockets his camera, and speed walks with me to the parking lot. Take smaller steps, he says. Consider buying a metronome to increase the number of strides I take per minute. He shakes my hand and steps into his car. It is ninety minutes from the moment I signed over the check until the end of session. I had his complete attention for each paid minute. He made me feel good, important, like I was getting something for my money. Then our time ran out and he's gone. I watch his tires kick up pebbles as he peels out of the parking lot. I feel as though I've just visited my first prostitute.

Bobby McGee drives to the bank, where my check to him will clear that afternoon. I cross Sixty-Third Street to the reservoir. I am dressed and it is sunny and I figure I'll put in a full workout. I head down one of the dusty paths that snake around the reservoir. I try to implement what the Great Coach has just taught me. I try to lean. I try to hold my arms up high and tight like a boxer cornered against the ropes. I can't do it. Or perhaps I can, but it feels completely unnatural. As soon as I taste the slightest fatigue I revert back to my old familiar bounce, springing around the rez like it's the Sea of Tranquility. A friend tells me it's difficult to change a running form. Very difficult. If it can be done at all, it might take a year or more to implement successfully.

❧

About a month after my session with Bobby McGee, he sends me a small package in the mail. Inside are descriptions of two exercises he recommends I perform: "single-leg compass squats, essential for stability of the runner's knee" and "the side plank" to keep my "knee from dropping while in swing phase." He reports I have slight scoliosis in my left shoulder. Countering that, my "transverse abs [are] firing well and nicely symmetrical."

There is a DVD included in the package, which I download onto my computer: thirty-two photos of shirtless me jogging on the basketball court, and three short videos, thirty seconds each, of me running along the footpath near Sixty-Third Street. I can tell from the videos that the form he advises me to adopt—leaning forward, short steps, arms up and almost punching my face—really is better than my natural lazy bounce.

"I appreciate your business & it was fun to work with you," the Great Coach concludes. "I hope the information keeps you on track to that 3:15-in-a-year goal. You have some real talent; nurture it. I look forward to working with you in the future."

I don't work with McGee in the future. We never talk or e-mail or see each other again, and I never manage to fully implement his suggestions. I stay on with Rich. People continue to criticize him. I no longer care. Rich isn't the one getting me to Boston, or failing to get me there if things don't work out. Paying top dollar to another coach won't affect my destiny, either. The responsibility is mine alone. Rich is a tool. His advice, if sometimes scattershot, is generally solid. It would be nice to turn over full responsibility to him, to show up where he says I should show up and do what he says I should do and have the goal just sort of achieve itself. But that's infantile, isn't it? That's the behavior of a child. A main objective of this whole project, I recognize, is to grow up. To be a man. As I go forward, I'm going with Rich. Fuck it. The guy's fine.

16

SIX MILES. OKAY. Each lap around the parking lot is about a quarter mile according to my GPS watch. Okay. That's twenty-four laps. I can do twenty-four laps. I lace up my shoes, click on my chronometer, and run. It's six a.m. It's completely dark. I'm in Irving, Texas, circling the parking lot of the Ramada Inn Airport hotel. Weeds sprout from cracks in the asphalt. A shuttle bus idles outside the lobby. The first flights of the day take off, their red taillights glowing as they rumble above me. As I count down the laps, as I compulsively check off my daily running assignment, I acknowledge that I have now, officially, in a way no one in my family would dispute, become my father.

This is what he does, or used to do for a quarter century: travel the country on business, stay at chain hotels, and run in the morning to start his day. I did it with him exactly once, four years ago. He had business in Orlando. I had something to do in Orlando, too, so I drove up from Miami and crashed with him at his hotel on the strip-mall fringe of the city. It was a chance to see the life: Dinner at a Carrabba's Italian Grill, where he knew the waitress from the night before. Chocolate chip cookies upon our return to the hotel, a perk for frequent guests. Two bottles of light beer each as we lie on our beds, watching college basketball on the TV. Lights out at nine, like clockwork. At 5:00 a.m. sharp he awoke without an alarm. He dressed, slipping on his shorts, his T-shirt, and his trainers, which he'd placed by the door before bed. I got up, too, dressed in a panic, and rode down with him in the elevator. By 5:06 a.m. we were running at full speed from the Hilton parking lot down to a Burlington Coat Factory, up and around an anonymous office park, then back to the hotel for a second loop. He ran ahead of me, much faster. By the time I finished, he was already cranking out one hundred sit-ups and thirty push-ups in the hotel's small exercise room. He showered, shaved, and pulled on his suit, and then we ate breakfast together as the sun rose. He went off to his consulting gig. I went back to bed for two more hours.

Now here I am in Irving, Texas, living his life. I'm supposed to be in Mexico, actually. Rich and a core group of Boulder Road Runners fly down every November to run the Media Maratón de Puerto Vallarta. I decided to join them this year because

1) I can use another half-marathon training race.
2) It's just money, right? Flights to Philadelphia, trips to the Pacific coast of Mexico, what does it matter? Put it on my credit card. It's all part of my training. I can justify all of this. Right?

Fall in Boulder has been so enjoyable, for so long, I wondered why we're leaving it for a week. Driving home from the Laundromat on Sundays, I'll count the growing number of trees with yellow leaves. Herds of deer wander down the foothills into the city, spooking Valentine when we take our morning walks. Temperatures park in the seventies, inspiring me to spend several afternoons reading books in the grassy meadow that fronts Chautauqua. Then, late in the month, I pull open the blinds to find that the snow that already covers the Arapahoe Basin has drifted down to University Hill. Okay. I'll take seven days in the sun.

I flew to Texas the day after Halloween, my blood sugar spiked by Twix bars because no tiny vampire or ghost had the guts to haunt the Chicken Coop. I sat next to a hematologist who pulled from me my running history and who could tell "just from looking in [my] eyes" that I'm going to qualify for Boston. "I can also tell you have father issues," she added. The airline overbooked my connection to Puerto Vallarta. I was traveling alone, and the fleshy neon tourists boarding the plane so startled me I was in no hurry to join them. I collected a $500 travel voucher, spent the night watching cable TV in the hotel, and got my run in this morning. Now, just before finally boarding a plane to Mexico, I send my dad an e-mail letting him know how I started my day.

"You'll go far with that pattern," he replies, all Benjamin fucking Franklin, certain the only way he's ever lived is indeed the one right way to go.

❧

Leafy green foothills hover over Puerto Vallarta like a tropical version of the Flatirons. I room with Carl Mohr, the fifty-eight-year-old who serves as vice president of the Boulder Road Runners, number two behind Rich. The guy who scoffed at my Boston goal back at that first beer social at the Walnut Brewery. Carl's a former software engineer for NCAR, retired at the age of forty. *Forty!* Now he helps his wife manage her wine shop near my Laundromat. He also runs Boulder Traffic Control, a small company that erects barricades for parades and road races along Pearl Street or up on University Hill. We're the oddest of couples, but we try to make the best of it by acclimating to sea level with a jog through Old Town. Exhaust from four-stroke engines hangs in a toxic cloud. We pass a Hooters and a Hard Rock Café and a Señor Frog's, a stretch of storefronts that I believe constitutes Puerto Vallarta's arts district. Cobblestones massage our feet. I taste salt in the oily air, warm and humid but not as sticky as I'd expected. We pass a Mexican naval museum on the sad little *malecón*. Footbridges span dry riverbeds that drain into the Pacific.

"Let's do a couple of strides," Carl suggests. "Okay, twenty steps at pace, go!"

When we finish our workout, I walk along the beach behind our hotel. I scan for good-looking women. No dice. Not one. I breach the security at some of the larger resorts, strolling around their pools. I find a lot of Americans, mostly old, all drinking beer and reading paperbacks. Back at our hotel, I go with the flow by sharing chips and salsa and dark Leon beer in Rich's room. There's Carl, retired for eighteen years. There's Rich. There's Tom LeMire, a retired restaurant health inspector. At the tin-roofed shack where we go for dinner, they discuss time-shares at a resort up the road. They talk about how dental work is so much cheaper down here. At another table of two, a man and a woman both wear those black wraparound cataract sunglasses. There's no one my age here, I tell Carl.

"That's because they're all working," he replies.

❧

There was a brief period, several years ago, that for classification purposes I like to call the best week of my life. I spent much of it in New York City, visiting on business. My book was about to be published. Miss Cable News expected a lot from the book. When we'd drive to Miami Beach on the MacArthur Causeway, when we'd pass the multimillion dollar mansions on Star and Palm islands, she'd joke that we'd be living in one of those houses soon, right after the book drops. On that trip to New York, during the best week of my life, it seemed like her bet was going to pay off. I met with my publisher. I shared dinner with my literary agent. An editor at *Sports Illustrated* invited me to lunch.

"Look around," the editor said when we took our seats. "The most important people in the industry are all sitting in this same room with you." The head of recruiting at the *New York Times,* the newspaper my girlfriend and I both saw myself working for, took me to lunch, too. I felt valuable, in demand. Miss Cable News called me every day that I was in the city, several times each day. When I got back to Miami, I found a bouquet leaning against my apartment door.

"Can a woman give a man flowers?" she asked in the note. "I think I'm in love with you."

Then the book fizzled. Then I wasn't offered a job at the *Times,* or anywhere else. Then I went into a depression. Paralyzed, I'd lay in bed, not knowing what to do with myself and knowing my girlfriend would soon place her bet on someone else. It took a while for things to shake out, but she eventually ended up with a doctor. I eventually ended up, for a while, in Mexico.

∞

"I'm worried about you," says my *New York Times* editor, the one who believes in me, the one who gives me almost enough work to stay afloat. Almost. She's the only one who knows I'm down here. I called to check in on a story, maybe the last story I'll ever write for her. "You're in dangerous midlife crisis territory. You'll never come back from down there. You'll work on a screenplay or something. We won't see you for ten years."

Fine with me. I'd been on assignment in Los Angeles. I'd always felt like a big cheese on those assignments, being flown across the country. That last story was something about football and star quarterbacks training together. I was the only reporter allowed to cover the training camp, and I got to cover it only because I represented a famous newspaper. The paper flew me out. Its editors put me up in an oceanfront hotel, then paid for my meals and drinks and the sunblock I smeared on my face every afternoon. My association with a big, important institution gave my parents something to brag about. My dad, flipping through the paper on an airplane, would come across an article of mine and marvel.

"I never thought I'd see my son in the *New York Times*."

I'd been working for the *Times* for three years, ever since their head of recruiting had called me out of the blue, the kind of call I'd never even fantasized about receiving. He flew me to New York, where he introduced me to the editors, and those editors started throwing me work. Good work. I'd be washing my clothes in Miami when I'd get a call asking me to drop everything and fly to Shreveport, Louisiana. Same for an assignment in Chicago. Or in Milwaukee, where the president of Marquette University — my dad's alma mater — cleared his schedule just to talk to me.

I made the *Times* my top priority. I fantasized. I let myself think it was going somewhere, that I could become a yuppie with a stable, impressive job that pays good money. I could buy a house again and marry another woman (probably Miss Cable News) and raise kids and drive a relatively new car. I daydreamed about my return to the standard-issue life track for quite a while, stopping only when I realized I was losing a bit of cash on every story. I was getting older and the paper almost never hires people above a certain age. Even though they had been the ones to call me, I suspected my window was closing. In Los Angeles I was informed it had already closed.

"We think you're great," stated the editor who believed in me, in an e-mail. "But we'd never hire someone like you."

She spelled it out. I came up through alternative weekly newspapers, a track that carries zero cachet with the mainstream media. I've never covered a beat like most sportswriters, say, following the Miami Dolphins for a season or two. I'm a white male in a professional niche overloaded with white males. The *Times*, like most newsrooms, is desperate to hire people who don't look like me, a position I understand and even endorse. I felt like a good fit at the paper, but it wasn't going to happen. My editor made it clear.

I was supposed to stay in Los Angeles for four days. I got her e-mail early on day two. I wrapped up my work abruptly, turned in what I'd finished so far, checked out of the hotel and drove to the airport. I could have flown back to Miami. Instead, I hopped on the next plane to Mexico.

"Going to Cabo? Excuse me, señor, going to Cabo? Would you like a Corona hat?"

Of course I would. I'll take a Pacifico T-shirt, too, since you're handing them out. Girls seated a few rows behind me laugh so hard they snort. One of them is getting married, and this is the start of her bachelorette party. The woman next to me, in the middle seat, sports lime-colored sandals. Her toes are painted bronze.

When we land, at the tip of the Baja Peninsula, nobody checks my papers. I follow flip-flopped women in flouncy white skirts and flip-flopped men in board shorts and beer T-shirts. I just keep walking, and before I know it I'm in the parking lot being asked if I want a cab, or a beer. I opt for one of each, head into town, and take a room at a cheap hotel near the bullring. My accommodations feature a twirling overhead fan, a tile floor, and some kind of folk art on the wall. A small desk waits in the bedroom. The mini-kitchen includes a refrigerator and a microwave. I feel like I've lucked out. I turn on the TV. Onscreen, on a Spanish-language variety show, two girls in hot pants jump rope.

∞

My shoulders burn from too much paddling. My lips are rimmed with salt like a margarita glass. I'm dehydrated and sunburned. The pores of my skin have constricted, shriveling shut as though they've been splashed with lime juice. I feel a little seasick, too. I ride to the very edge of the beach, swerving at the last second. The nose of my fiberglass board shoots toward the sky and I fall backward into the water. It's shallow here, and rocky. My bare feet slip on the slime that covers stones as smooth and round and large as volleyballs. I touch lightly, gingerly, exploring for jagged edges.

It's time for lunch. All morning I've been surfing — or trying to. I forgot to wear a rash guard, so the insides of my arms are dotted with red blood splotches. I've jammed a toe on my left foot. My right nipple feels as if it's been razored clean off. Waves laden with small stones have sandblasted my thighs. A bruise rises on one shin just below the knee.

"I've got sand on my balls," Christian says when he climbs out of the water. Christian is my new friend. He's twenty-three. He has two boys, one three years old and one just a month into life. He lives in nearby San José with his girlfriend, in a small house owned by his mother. I've got sand on my balls, too. And on my ass, and embedded in my chin. Lather-rinse-repeat won't come close to removing the granules from my hair.

We meet around nine most mornings, on a vast crescent of

sand where the peach hills and pine trees slip into the Sea of Cortez. We don't really surf together. He surfs. I float around on my longboard, riding waves straight in a line. When I look back from the shore, I can see him cutting and juking like a water bug, gliding on a moving sheet of energy. We surf until noon or so, then drive to a shack near his house to lunch on shrimp and fish tacos. I pile my tacos with enough vegetables to resemble a Chicago red hot. He squirts mayonnaise on his shrimp, and salts his cucumbers.

Christian and I have decided to be friends because we both play soccer, *fútbol*. He's been to the States, to Oregon where his father now lives. The name of his hometown, Mazatlán, is tattooed on his back. Winnie the Pooh clings to his right shoulder, a tattoo in honor of his first child. He's turned me on to the authentic Mexican bars in Cabo "where there are crazy drunk *chicas*," and they only play salsa music and "none of that *Americano* crap" you hear at Cabo Wabo or El Squid Roe.

"Do you like Mexican chicas?" he asked me soon after we started surfing together. I like all chicas, I tell him. I do. It's the truth.

After lunch, Christian heads to a hotel on the tourist corridor, where he works as a waiter. If it's a full moon, a tidal draw that generates great waves, he'll be back on the beach to ride after work, too. In the water he is smooth. He is beautiful out there on the waves. Athletic, graceful, elegant. I don't mind saying so. That's the way I feel. I like to watch him surf.

❧

I did not like Cabo when I first got there. How could I? It's Domino's Pizza and Dunkin' Donuts and bands covering Van Halen covering the Kinks for an audience visiting from Southern California. Or from Ohio. Drunk, married women flirt while wearing straw cowboy hats adorned with seashells arranged to look like starfish. "Want some blow, amigo?" is the most Spanish I initially heard.

But now I like this place, I've decided. Now that I've drifted away from El Squid Roe and the Ruth's Chris steak house, Cabo seems more like real Mexico. I've begun tossing around the idea of staying on. This doesn't have to end. Christian can set me up. I can get a job in the tourist corridor, under the table. Or I can work a fishing boat trolling for tarpon. *¡Hola, turistas!* Welcome to *Meh-he-coe*, amigos! I can learn to dive for oysters. I'll move into Christian's mom's old concrete house with the rebar sprouting from the roof. I'll play soccer on his team. I'll marry a Mexican woman in the church in San José. I'll eat huevos rancheros every morning!

My funds are low, yes. There are fewer green twenties in my wallet and more of the pink and blue bills I've received in change. Mexican coins are piling up, weighing down the pockets of my shorts like sandbags on a hot air balloon. The coins jingle and clink as I walk at night, around town. I pass El Tucan and its accordion music and its Mexican girls painted with makeup and propped atop tall cork heels. A man tells me I can pay for companionship if I'd like. His women, he says, are almost virgins. I pass a T-shirt shop. FBI: FEDERAL BODY INSPECTOR, PSYCHO BITCH MAGNET, and knockoff Harley-Davidson tees. Two words are embossed on the chest of one black T-shirt: DIE TRYING.

I skip the bars and climb a hill overlooking the city. I scale concrete steps that give way to a narrow path, about as wide as a curb. My heart strains from the ascent. Black cockroaches scurry away from my shoes. I reach a perfectly flat cube of concrete, which I guess is a water basin. I hoist myself onto the cube and stare out at the city. It is still light, though the sun has set. The mountains stand in relief, jagged and one-dimensional, as if they were made of overlapping pieces of purple construction paper. A string of red taillights crawls up the tourist corridor, reminding me of the old news zipper in Times Square. There is an electric hum. I hear motorcycle engines revving. I hear a dog bark, then another dog respond. Two staccato taps indicate a police vehicle is trying to get somewhere. Someone is in trouble.

I lie back on the concrete and stare at the sky. The Big Dipper shines directly overhead. It's beautiful up here. Peaceful. I now understand why rich people build houses on hills. I can stay here all night. I can sleep on this concrete cube. Nobody will see me. Nobody will care.

❦

From the sky, flying in, the ocean looked blue. Up close, actually in the surf, the waves are a deep and translucent green, like a Heineken bottle. The water is warm, almost hot. It hits my legs, spraying my shins. I wade in deeper. The undertow, racing back to sea, pulls sand from beneath my feet, massaging my soles with countless tiny pebbles. I wade in deeper. The waves pelt my stomach, splashing up to my shoulders, misting my face with saltwater. I hold my wallet aloft. I am protecting my identity. I'm keeping dry the last of my $20 bills. The money will run out soon. I don't know what I will do then. I don't know anything.

I was supposed to meet Christian at nine a.m., as usual. By the time I show up, he's already in the water. I'm wearing my trunks. Sunscreen protects my skin, but I don't surf. I'd rather just watch. Out beyond the break, Christian's friends dive for oysters, throwing their craggy treasure into nets wrapped around inner tubes. Christian carves long, elegant lines of surf. Each cutback to the crest is followed by a quick turn of his knees and ankles. I expect slippage but there isn't any. There's no hesitation, either. His shortboard is an extension of his body, an appendage sewn to his feet.

The waves start picking up. Their crashes grow louder, more resonant. Each crash is followed by the rush of thousands of pebbles tumbling over each other in the race to reload the next wave. I know I could stay. A couple of collect calls on a Telmex pay phone and I'm all set.

I've already checked out of my little hotel.

I watch Christian surf for about an hour. Then I get into my rental car and drive to the airport. I board a plane to Dallas, where I will take another plane back to South Florida. I will try to win back Miss Cable News, telling her I've changed and I don't love Mrs. Wisconsin anymore and even if I don't have a job I'll make something of myself, I swear. I'll write for the *Times* for a few more years, still losing money with every assignment. I'll come to feel like a mistress to the *Times,* a booty call. Yet I leave Mexico feeling optimistic. I will go back to Miami, I tell myself. I will keep going. Or, at least, I will die trying.

❧

Appropriately, the Puerto Vallarta Half Marathon is in Spanish. The thin red T-shirts handed to us at the finish line feature logos for Telmex and Comcel. The countdown at the start, near a temporary tent city erected in the central park, falls from *diez* to *uno.* On the course, instead of cups of water or sports drink, we're handed long, thin balloons. We must bite a corner off the balloon to get the liquid, and naturally I choke on a plastic triangle the first time I try to suck out a sip. I am alone on the course the whole time. Left foot, right foot, breathe in through the *nariz*, out through the *boca.*

Puerto Vallarta's industrial underbelly unspools like hieroglyphics on a Mayan scroll: the airport, ramshackle gas stations, a Corona distributor, abandoned condominiums, and a few scrawny palm trees. Carl takes off so fast I don't see him until the turnaround, at a Home Depot. No crowds cheer us on like in Philadelphia. There aren't many runners, either, and most are locals, black-haired little guys with stocky chests, square hips, and thick, stubby legs. They look vulnerable. Yet most of them motor past me with ease.

I guess I've cultivated some arrogance in Boulder, a feeling like, Hey, this running thing is a big deal in my life. I make it a priority. I've flown thirteen hundred miles just to run this dinky race in your dingy *turista* trap. I'm a Boulderite just like Colleen de Rueck, an Olympian who wins the woman's title, as she does every year. I'm a Boulderite just like Dave Dooley, a seriously skeletal guy in his sixties who often sets records for his age group. I'm just like Carl, who picks up a few free pesos for finishing third in his age group. I figured I would kick ass just because I'm from Boulder. But I don't kick ass. Not at all. I finish six minutes slower than I did in Philadelphia.

It might have been the heat, which has simmered from the moment the sun broached the foothills. Maybe it was the guy outside our hotel room window late the night before shouting out his hatred for Americans and how he's going to kill the first one he sees. It might have been the shots of vanilla-smooth tequila we downed at dinner, telling ourselves they'd aid digestion and help us sleep better. I'm pretty sure the biggest problem was a tossed-off little line Rich told me at that dinner. This was to be a training run, he advised. Unlike in Philly, my time in Mexico won't matter much. So toward the end of the race, when I began laboring, when there was pain and stress and I began contemplating just how important it is to me, personally, to complete the stupid race, I eased up. I didn't push it. I faded, returning from the Home Depot much more slowly than I'd run out there. I'd been given permission to go slow and I took it, which is so just like me.

Still, mission accomplished. That's what Rich tells me at the finish line. That's what Carl tells me later when we sit in Señor Frog's and watch the Green Bay Packers beat the Kansas City Chiefs at *fútbol Americano*. Carl pays for our beers with his winnings. He wears his medal around his neck, telling me that's the protocol: you wear the thing around town the day of the race, then never again, tossing it atop the rest of your collection when you get home. I nurse my beers and an unshakable melancholy. I have to work, I think. I can't coast my way into Boston. I can't just show up.

It's always easy to second-guess after a race, or even after a long training run. After the hops and barley and the fat from a cheeseburger calm my sore muscles, I wonder why I didn't push harder. It's not enough to live in Boulder. It's not enough even to train with Rich and the Boulder Road Runners. I have to want to press on when the going gets tough. And that's the question, isn't it? How bad do I want this thing? How important is it to me, really? I take a sip of beer. I acknowledge, yet again, the open secret: I don't like to run. I can't pretend I do. I don't much like pain, really. At the end of the day, at the end of the race or whatever, that's my bottom line, the question I'm asking myself: Why am I volunteering to be in pain? What's the upside? What am I trying to prove? I know the answer to that, so maybe I should phrase it another way: Who am I trying to kid? Maybe it's time to stop running away from reality, to give up on this stupid Boston thing and go get a job, get to work, go join the people my age, none of whom are in Puerto Vallarta right now.

"You know what, buddy?" Carl asks, squeezing a lime into a

fresh bottle. "You've made a believer out of me and I was about as big a skeptic as there could be."

¿Cómo? Praise? For me? Can't you see I'm wallowing in self-pity over here? It's my natural impulse to dismiss Carl's encouragement, but the guy is serious. He volunteers to train with me from here on in. He's going to join me on my Saturday long runs, making sure I maintain my pace, helping me ramp up my workouts. He even says he'll run my qualifier with me. That's fantastic. That's a gift, *un regalo*. Not incidentally, that makes this money-sucking trip to Mexico totally worth it.

Why is he helping me? Why is he on board all of a sudden, right when I feel it might be time to shut down the whole project? I pull a mouthful of beer from my bottle. On television the Packers score a touchdown. Because I'm not quitting? Because I'm trying?

17

I GO OUT IN the morning with Carl, my new training partner. For the past several weeks we've been meeting on Saturdays at Neva Road, just before seven thirty in the morning. We park our cars in a gravel lot at the head of the Lefthand Trail. Four or five other runners often start with us, Rich included. I usually show up at the very last second, still sleepy but ready to run. I always stay in the previous night, going to bed early after eating that one same meal: chicken parmesan, lots of water, and a bottle of Shiner Bock. Routine. Live like a clock.

It's late November, a Saturday. Carl and I run alone, setting out on two loops of the Neva Road course and then back, sixteen miles in all. On our first loop, when we turn south at the yellow barn that guards US 36, we can see Pikes Peak in the distance, some ninety miles away. Powdered sugar dusts the foothills in front of us. The sun shines. A woman jogs past us, heading in the other direction.

"It doesn't get any better than this!" Carl shouts out to her.

"This weather is great!" she replies.

Good lord. What's with you people? Great weather? It's not even twenty degrees out. I'm sheathed in three layers of spandex and nylon, hatted and gloved. The cold air constricts my lungs, making me wheeze. The view to Pikes Peak is indeed something, but my eyes stay trained on Carl's feet as I try to match the quick cadence of his pace. Sixteen miles is an incredibly long distance for me, the longest I've ever run. I am grinding, really struggling to keep up, and we still have more than ten miles to go.

"The air! The mountains!" Carl cries as we power on. "I gotta tell you, there's nothing I'd rather be doing than this."

Please. I spend the rest of the run exploring *everything* I'd rather be doing. I'd rather be doing my laundry. I'd rather be watching chocolate chip cookies rise in an oven. I'd rather be in bed, first off. A warm bed. We have so many miles left that I am able to fine-tune my vision to *exactly* what I'd rather be doing. I'd rather be in a warm bed with a beautiful woman who has just walked my dog. There's a TV playing out a long day of college football. We've got a stack of *New Yorker* magazines nearby. There's a deep dish Chicago-style pizza bubbling up in the kitchen. Over the aroma of cheese and tomatoes and garlic and oregano, I can still detect the sweeter, chocolate notes from a tray of brownies cooling on a countertop. I'm probably drinking a beer. I am not running. Nowhere in this vision is there a sixteen mile run in the freezing cold.

"You looked good," Rich says over the phone when we finally make it back to our cars, and after Carl calls him with a debriefing. "You hit your marks just fine. You're running stronger than we expected. We should go ahead and carefully dial it up."

ℒ

My first sensation is comfort. I am very comfortable. I can lay here all day, curled in the fetal position, warm water caressing my shoulders and legs and scalp.

"Dude, you all right?" Some guy is talking.

"Hey man!" shouts another voice. "Yo, yo, yo, yo!" I try to focus, which takes some effort — I'm so comfortable. Squinting, I see red and gray tiles on the walls. My hand rubs the surface of the floor, a grippy, tactile rubber. The water splashing off my torso falls into a metal drain visible an inch from my nose. Naked men, several of them, run around all crazy like.

"Someone call 911!" a man shouts. Uh-oh. Another voice: "I saw him, like, clawing at the wall, or pawing it, and I could tell something was going to happen. And then I just heard this *thunk*. BOOM! Down! Like a tree!"

Carl and I were to run our first-ever twenty miler today. We talked about it all week. It's a big deal, a real test of my progress. By this morning I was wired. I woke up at five thirty, hitting snooze only until almost six, which was still early. I sat on the couch and listened to *Morning Edition* on the radio. I slathered ibuprofen cream on my knees. I made my bed, pulled on four layers of clothes, and headed outside. *What the?!?* My Mazda was covered in ice, the whole car coated like a candy shell on a translucent M&M. I had to chisel my way into the driver's side door, then warm up the engine block for half an hour before I could even scrape off the windshield. It was cold. A strong wind blew snow across Rose Hill Drive and the slippery streets out to Neva.

"Try to land flat on your foot," Carl advised when we started to run. "Try not to push off with your toes." The visibility was so bad I couldn't make out Haystack Mountain, which stands not a quarter mile off the road. Sunglasses shielded my eyes from a stinging frozen mist, but every other step I had to wipe condensation from the inside of the lenses with my polar-fleece fingers. By the time we reached the Plateau Road water stop, Carl decided to abort.

"I hate to have to tell you this, buddy, but today's not the day to do a twenty miler." After just one lap around the loop instead of three, he commanded us to head back. "Let's take this home and get our two hours in."

I didn't protest. I wanted to stick to the schedule but we *were* slipping on the ice, and we didn't want any of the cars sliding off the road to slide over us.

"You know what would feel really good right about now?" Carl asked when we finished up at the trailhead. "A hot tub. You should go over to the gym and take a dip in the hot tub."

Has there ever been a better idea? Normally, I'd ice my legs after a long run. I might wade into the freezing Boulder Creek, squatting for fifteen minutes on a submerged rock. Or, back at the Coop, I might fill a garbage can with water and snow, then step inside. Ice contracts the blood vessels in muscles, making it easier for them to bounce back before the next workout. Heat does nothing positive, except maybe, on an icy cold morning, help me find my missing extremities.

"A hot tub sounds kinda completely perfect," I admitted. Carl's suggestion seemed even more attractive to me at the moment than a warm bed and a beautiful woman and college football. I headed back not to my apartment but to the Flatiron Athletic Club.

The hot tub felt good. Really good. I doubt I felt that good in the womb. There are several hot tubs in the club. I chose to use the one in the men's locker room, near the showers and the sauna and on the way to the indoor swimming pool. I sat back and luxuriated, flipping through a mental slideshow of the icy two hours I'd just endured. I put my legs up. When the safety timer expired, I leaned over and pressed it down, launching another fifteen-minute session. When it expired again, I pressed it down again. Other guys came into the tub and left. I stayed, bubbling like a lobster in a pot. Warming up. Feeling really good.

I know what happened. It's perfectly obvious. By the time I finally climbed out of the tub, at the *moment* I climbed out, I felt light-headed. Woozy. Very woozy. Cautiously, I clung onto the hot tub handrail. *Just make it to the shower and I'll be fine.* Next thing I know here I am on the floor, everyone all excited and running around and screaming.

Eventually someone drags me into the locker part of the locker room. I'm placed on my back on the carpeted floor. Random men grill me like they're CIA agents and I'm an al-Qaeda terrorist. How many fingers am I holding up? Three, I say, accurately, trying to act like it's no big deal. What day of the week is it? Saturday. What month is it? December. I know my full name. I know the name of the president, too. Now you're holding two fingers in front of my face. Dude, I'm sharp. I'm fine. A crowd gathers around me, the cyclists and swimmers and the Saturday weight lifters. A guy with a squash racquet pushes his way to the front of the scrum. His curiosity seems a little invasive. I want to say something to him but I don't quite have the energy. Someone hands me a glass of orange juice.

I will be taken to Boulder Community Hospital in an ambulance, at the strident insistence of the gym's owner. I know he has liability concerns and I am in a compliant disposition.

"Just let me walk out on my own," I plead. "No stretcher, please." It *is* dehydration, a paramedic reports in the ambulance, common in extreme athletes like me. Extreme athlete? Cool. "You have fantastic veins," he adds after sticking an IV into my forearm. Fantastic veins? Also cool. At the hospital a doctor glances at the abrasions on my forehead, shoulder, and left hip, then lets me go.

"Drink more water," he says. That advice, plus the ambulance ride, will end up costing me, out of pocket, more than three thousand dollars.

The abrasions on my forehead clear up quickly, as do the welts on my shoulder and hip. I'm running again the very next day. Even after the physical reminders vanish, something stays with me, a memory. I'm lying on the ground in the locker room. Strangers hover over me, staring at me. There's that one guy with the squash racquet. I want more orange juice. I'm answering questions in a calm monotone, trying to show I'm alert and sharp and all there. I'm trying to maintain my dignity. I'm also on my back, my legs splayed in a Y. And this whole time I've been answering these questions I've remained completely naked.

"Jesus Christ!" a man shouts. "Can somebody cover him with a towel?"

⚬

My runs in December are up and down. Morning temperatures often dip below zero, my enthusiasm dropping with the mercury. Snow falls several times, requiring me to strap on Yaktrax, a kind of snow chain for running shoes. Still, I manage to run a few workouts so well that I'm praised by the club.

"You were really good out there today."

"You were commanding."

"I'm impressed."

And then one Wednesday when Rich is out of town, I completely bail on what is supposed to be a three-hour cross-training workout. I don't have an excuse, except maybe that I got a very late start. I jog about two miles on the Creek Path on my way to the gym, then I just simply stop. I turn around and walk back home. When Rich calls later in the day, I tell him I ran seven miles. He is still disappointed. Everyone has bad days in the winter, he says, but in my case every day counts.

"I could have lied to you," I say, duplicitously. I then ask about his vacation in an attempt to distract him.

Overall, I suppose, things are pretty much on track. On the morning of Christmas Eve, at a bagel place near the Flatiron gym, Carl and I make a decision. We've been scouting potential Boston qualifiers. We want a flat course. We want the race at sea level so we can take advantage of our high-altitude training. We want a marathon that has been around a few years so any kinks in the organization will have been ironed out. And we need a marathon in mid-February, the latest we can qualify and still recover in time to run Boston itself.

"Myrtle Beach it is," Carl says, and we shake hands. The next day, Christmas Day, as four inches of snow fall on Boulder, I sign us both up for the Bi-Lo Myrtle Beach Marathon. February 19. One year to the day since I left Miami. It's also thirty years (minus just one day) since my dad ran the eleventh Silver Lake Dodge Washington's Birthday Marathon in Hopkinton, Massachusetts, qualifying for Boston in his first attempt.

18

E MILY WITT WAS one of the last people I saw before leaving Miami. On the night before I left, she dropped by my apartment with her boyfriend, a columnist at the *Miami Herald*. My furniture was gone by then. The lone painting on my wall had been shipped to my sister in New York. No books remained, or any pots or pans. Anything else that didn't fit into my car had been surrendered to two neighborhood scavengers, men who so quickly pulled my junk from the Dumpster that I eventually invited them inside to take whatever was left — refrigerator magnets, a white plastic trash can, a spool of dental floss I'd missed. I'll admit the place looked depressing.

"You realize you have the exact wrong body type for long-distance running," the boyfriend said, not breaking any news.

"Why is it important for you to do this thing?" asked Emily. Between the lines she seemed to mean "stupid thing," but I didn't take offense. She worked at the newspaper I'd quit several years earlier, the year my divorce was finalized, the last year I'd earned more money than I spent. We went out one night soon after she arrived in Miami, moving in a small pack of journalists from a bar near her South Beach studio to a nightclub over in the Design District. She was smart and interesting. I liked her.

"Let's be friends," I said, reclining on a couch in a courtyard outside the club.

"Definitely," she replied.

We'd go for tacos sometimes at Lime, on Alton Road. At a barbecue outside the American Legion hall, on the shore of Government Cut, she vented about what we called her common-law boyfriend, the *Herald* columnist who was into her and then wasn't into her and then was into her again. She'd eventually move from Miami to Mozambique on a fellowship, and from there to New York City and more school. I, of course, landed in Boulder, doing my stupid thing.

Emily's father, Leonard Witt, is a professor of journalism at Kennesaw State University in Georgia. Prior to academia, he edited *Minnesota Monthly* magazine and before that the *Minneapolis Star-Tribune Sunday Magazine*. He also worked in public radio. He started his journalism career in Durham, New Hampshire, where he earned a master's degree in nonfiction writing. When he sat in our kitchen in Dover, watching us eat a family dinner, he didn't share any of the salad or garlic bread or sip any of the soda pop we kids were allowed on Sundays. He barely said a word. He just sat in the corner, away from the table, taking notes.

"You sure you don't want any of this?" my dad asked, pointing to a big bowl of spaghetti and meatballs.

"I'm sure," he answered. "Just pretend I'm not here."

I don't figure out Emily and Leonard are related until months after my move, and when I realize it I'm a bit freaked out. Small fucking world. I make the connection after I finally work up the courage to pull out the magazine story Leonard wrote about my dad. I unearth the story on a cold night. Snow whips against the Chicken Coop's thin walls, the wind howling so loud Valentine hides under the table. I'd swiped the magazine from my dad's office back in Illinois, on my drive out. I didn't read the story when I found it, and when I got to Boulder I buried the magazine on a shelf under papers and a cardboard box, as if I could pretend it wasn't there. I wanted to read it. I brought it with me. Yet I was scared of it at the same time.

New England, the magazine of the *Boston Sunday Globe.* March 12, 1978. The cover story is about androids, specifically about how soon — perhaps by the magical year 2000 — they will be trimming our hedges, teaching us French, serving hors d'oeuvres to our guests, vacuuming our floors, and monitoring both our children and our elderly parents. Current models feature a vocabulary of 250 words! My dad's story starts on page twenty-six.

"One man's marathon: After only a year of running — and at the age of 41 — Tom Powell made the 81st Boston classic."

The main photo shows my dad in his race uniform: tan nylon shorts, a blue cotton tank top with MARQUETTE embossed on the chest, the gold letters arched above my dad's folded arms. My dad's hair is black and wavy and a bit longer, in the 1970s style. He's almost smiling, though not quite. "Yeah, that's right, Boston," he seems to be thinking. "I made it to the Marathon in my first year of running."

"When Tom Powell approached his 40th birthday, he never thought about running or jogging. Just more than a year later at age 41, in 1977, he is walking into the Hopkinton, Mass., high school gym to pick up his official number for the 81st Boston Marathon."

The story — six pages long! — is structured around my dad's race-day experience. He's shown before the race in a high school gym, where "the smell of liniment permeates the air." He proceeds to pick up his number, 1262, which makes him happy. "A smile of accomplishment flashes across his face that still has the gaunt look of a collegiate wrestler.''

Leonard Witt gives a bit of backstory on how a bet with a family friend inspired my dad to take up running. How he won his age group in his first race, and how he qualified for Boston in his first marathon. "In the fifteen months or so that Powell has been running he has built up from just a few miles a week to about 60 miles a week of running . . . Of course, most people would not be able to do this.

"Dr. John Neff, a Dover [New Hampshire] physician and a friend of Powell's, is not at all surprised by Powell's feat. 'While others say, "I don't believe it,"' Dr. Neff says, 'when Tom sets his mind to do something, he does it.' Neff remembers when Powell was going to build an addition onto his house. Neff was sure it would be impossible. The plans Powell had outlined would require the skills of at least three specialized craftsmen. But Powell did what he set out to do and did it well."

My dad is described as physically short with blue eyes like the actor Paul Newman, and a frame so thin it shocks me: 135 pounds, a weight I passed by age fifteen.

"But I eat like a horse," he says in the article.

When the gun goes off in Hopkinton, I'm apparently standing near the starting line with my brother, my sisters, and my mom. After my dad departs, we dash to the car — my mom cutting her shin in the process — and drive to where Route 128 intersects the course. We fill two paper cups, one with Gatorade and the other with Coke, and we wait.

"The line of runners seems endless. Tom's 8-year-old son Robert sums it up, saying, 'There's still a million people.'

"'Dad didn't die?' Robert asks his mother.

"Before the race, Powell's wife jokingly told Tom, 'If you

drop dead running the race, someone is going to have to drag you across the finish line because you've made so many commitments to so many people.' Now it is not a joke. Forty-one-year-old men have died of heart attacks."

My dad finished, without dying. Leonard Witt tried to squeeze some drama from the possibility that my dad wouldn't make it — *41-year-old-men have died of heart attacks!* — but my siblings and my mother and I weren't worried at all. The guy's a bulldog. He remodeled his own house! When he sets his mind to do something he does it!

The story ends in a makeshift emergency room set up in the Prudential Center parking garage. My dad's right foot oozed blood. He had forgotten to turn his cotton socks inside out, and a stray thread, over the course of twenty-six miles, had torn his big toenail clear off.

The final paragraph:

"After a long rest, Powell gets up slowly and another runner takes his place on the cot. Powell slowly limps up the stairs and past the alarm bell. Out in the plaza of the Prudential Center are his wife, kids and friends. They congratulate him, they kiss him, they present him with a homemade laurel wreath and for 41-year-old Tom Powell the 81st Boston Marathon is over, as is the first year of his running career."

I've always remembered that last line. " . . . as is the first year of his running career." That line is the key passage in the story that lives in my head. He made it to Boston in one year. As I reread Leonard Witt's narrative of Gatorade and heat stroke concerns and my dad's eventual finish at the Prudential Center, my eyes catch on another line, a line I'd forgotten about or had never noticed. It's a tossed-off aside printed in a short section about my mom and her excitement on race day.

"She has tried running with Tom," Witt wrote, "but she can't keep up with him." That sentence sure rings true. That's the dad I recognize, out ahead of us, leaving us all behind.

∞

The way I remember it, they'd started running together, my mom and my dad. They'd both decided to exercise and lose some weight. Running was to be an activity they could do as a couple. But then my dad got so good so quickly my mom abandoned running to become the driver of the chase vehicle.

That's what I'd always understood, anyway. These stories float down to me and become my reality. Then, later, when I ask about them, I'm told I've got the story wrong. For instance, I once asked my mother if I was named after my Uncle Bob, her brother.

"No," she told me, "you were named after Robert Kennedy." The former US attorney general was shot eight days before I was born, and I was part of a boomlet of boys named in his honor. That made sense. That became the story of my name as I understood it. Yet a few years later, when I dropped a reference to being named after a Kennedy, my mom laughed. I wasn't named after Robert Kennedy, she insisted. How ridiculous!

So I often wonder if I ever get the real story, on anything. My mom must have told me at least once about jogging with my dad to lose weight; how else would that idea enter my head? As I read over the *Boston Globe* article, I realize there is another, official history that differs in key ways from mine. I take the details from the article and slip them into the story in my head, melding the two narratives into one new master draft.

Road races were common in the 1970s in New England, when we lived there. Regional stars like Bill Rodgers and Joan Benoit ran races from Connecticut up the seacoast into Maine. Dr. John

Neff, the man impressed by my dad's home-improvement project, ran Dover's ten-mile Independence Day Run every year. In 1975, his wife, Sylvia Neff, ran with him for the first time. Sylvia returned from the race crying. She'd been the last person on the course and was told to either speed it up or drop out, so she dropped out. My dad was one of several men at a party who promised to run with her the next year, a pledge he later insisted had been the beer talking.

My dad had never run before, at all. On a Saturday morning the next February, he laced up a pair of tennis shoes, threw on a sweatshirt, some old cotton sweatpants, and a red-and-blue hat topped with a pom-pom. He left our house, walked past a small stand of birch trees in our front yard, and stepped onto our street, which was called Country Club Estates in honor of the golf course. With my older sister and brother at his side, he took the first stride of his running career. About a minute later, after traveling only the distance between two telephone poles, he stopped. That was it . . . He was out of breath. He hadn't gone even a quarter of a mile.

Every day he'd try to run a little farther. Three telephone poles, then four telephone poles. Eventually he made it one full mile to a bridge spanning the Cocheco River. When he hit two and a half miles a day, Adolph, our curiously named dog, refused to run with him any more. My older brother, who tried to keep up in a pair of Chuck Taylors, dropped out after developing shin splints. My dad upgraded to these strange new Nikes, shoes with a tread that appeared to have been poured into a waffle iron. He ordered a subscription to *Runner's World*. He bought a book written by Jim Fixx.

Something clicked. The challenge of running became addictive. He started mapping out distances in his car. Could he make it three full miles without stopping? Okay, how about four? As the evenings started to warm, he worked up to a regular five-mile circuit. My older sister sometimes accompanied him on her small blue bike, zooming up ahead on a tree-lined road and waiting for him to catch up. Back at the house, he'd let her take a few sips of the chocolate milk shake he poured himself after every run. He ran a little longer on Saturdays. Sundays were his day off. All the other guys who had said they were going to run on the Fourth of July with Mrs. Neff claimed injury or illness or some other reason that they couldn't enter the race.

Independence Day 1976. The United States turned two hundred years old. My dad was forty. It was sunny, as you hope the Fourth of July will be. I specifically recall standing against a tree and watching the parade, for some reason reminding myself I was eight years old on the bicentennial and never to forget it. The race? I don't remember it at all. Or maybe I do. In my mind I can conjure up a finish line of triangular plastic flags in patriotic red, white, and blue. I see a teenage girl from the running club my dad would join, and I recall she was wearing tight briefs instead of the shorts that all the men were wearing. I remember those briefs.

As I understand it, the plan had been for my dad to run alongside Sylvia Neff. He was to keep her company in the back of the pack. But when the gun fired, he just couldn't restrain himself. It was a race. The goal of a race is to win. Sylvia Neff would later report that all she saw of my dad was his backside as he took off.

A bit past the nine-mile marker, my dad pulled up even with a kid who was really struggling. "How far to the finish?" the boy asked. Although my dad knew there was less than a mile left, he told the kid to hang in there, but there were still more than *two* miles to go. The kid, discouraged, quit on the spot. My dad breezed past him. One competitor down. One place higher in the standings. It's a race, kid, not a run. When my dad finished, he enjoyed all the attention. Another runner told him he was a natural.

He stuck with it. In addition to his nightly runs, he started training at lunch when possible, coming home to knock out as many as ten miles while we kids ate peanut butter sandwiches and drank grape Kool-Aid. After work he'd run five miles more. If there was a blizzard outside he'd circle our small basement for thirty minutes. Whatever problems he encountered during the day, personal or business, he was able to resolve during his run. It was just him, no other people around. No job. No kids, to be honest. No wife, either, to be even more honest. He told himself my mom appreciated her time alone, which wasn't really true.

He didn't talk about running with us. Or if he did, we weren't listening. We knew he ran. We saw him step outside in his shorts and Nikes and come back an hour or two later all sweaty. We could hear him up in his bedroom thumping out push-ups and sit-ups after every workout. And we went with him to his races, always sticking around until he collected his trophy. But it, the running, was his thing alone. None of us aspired to follow in his footsteps. None of us understood why he liked to run so much.

"If you're going to do something, do it well," my dad concluded midway through another ten-mile workout. The North Berwick, Maine, traffic circle lay ahead, his turnaround point. He stayed on the soft shoulder to avoid traffic. A rock rested in his palm should a stray dog cross his path. In his head, an ambitious idea bloomed. "And if you're going to run a marathon, run Boston."

19

M Y ANNIVERSARY. THE TWELFTH. In snowy Boulder, snippets of the wedding day flash in my mind. How excited I was, so amped that I sliced my lip shaving. How *right* it felt to be the center of attention. I recall my friend's toast as the best man. I recall after the reception, riding upstairs, the way the women in the elevator of Milwaukee's Pfister Hotel fawned over my wife's big white wedding dress.

"Oh, you got *married!* On *New Year's Eve!*" I remember what my mom shouted, just after midnight, as a sixteen-piece orchestra played "Auld Lang Syne" and four hundred guests tooted horns and twirled noisemakers: "You'll never forget your anniversary!" No. I never will.

A New Year, a fresh start and all that. I cancel a Netflix subscription, which was distracting me. I put all my notes from my different, uniformly stalled projects into their proper files. I go over my finances, vowing, as I always do on December 31, that next year *the spending will stop!* I take down the expired Walden Pond wall calendar hanging over my table, the one my mom gave me as a present last Christmas, and replace it with a new calendar featuring artistic photos of blown glass, her Christmas present this year. I set my New Year's resolutions, eschewing my usual aims for "better time management" and Tracy Flick-esque commands to "Be Happy!" There is no mention of love or its pursuit. There's nothing about career success, or charity or anything selfless. One goal stands at the top: qualify for the Boston Marathon. Below that: run the Boston Marathon. That's all I want to do. I am focused. That's all there is.

A local band called Rose Hill Drive is covering Aerosmith's "Toys in the Attic" in its entirety tonight at the Boulder Theater. I'd wanted to go, a bit, just for the synergy of it all. But I don't want to stay out late, and I don't want to pay New Year's Eve prices to see a band just because they were named after my street. *The spending will stop!* I was planning to hike up the Flatirons, maybe around eleven p.m., to sit on a rock overlooking the city and its streetlights, taking in the New Year in quiet contemplation. But the temperature has dropped to near zero. The wind howls so powerfully that highways have closed for fear of avalanches. I stay in.

"You're listening to *Toast of the Nation* on National Public Radio." Indeed I am. They're just getting going and for some reason they're in Amsterdam. That's gotta be on tape delay, right? Holland, where my wife lives now, I'm told. Where the masters of Dutch jazz are playing in the New Year. Wonder if she's there, at that club? I think of Milwaukee's lone jazz club, which we visited once before married. I think of a New Year's Eve we spent in Chicago marching down Michigan Avenue, stone frozen, searching for a cab. I think of the first New Year's Eve after I left her, a big milestone year, one everyone on the planet had been waiting for their entire lives. I recall rolling around the floor of my apartment, howling, alone, my fingernails gouging my scalp, my cries so deep I actually spit up a little blood. I recall the two of us standing in her church on our wedding day. Red poinsettias from

Christmas decorated the altar, a plant that reminds my mother of funerals. I recall my promise to my wife to never, ever leave her.

"Why don't you kill yourself?" she asked after the divorce, more than once. She'd call me on the phone, at night, for maybe a year after the paperwork went through. "You really should kill yourself. The only honorable option for you is to kill yourself. I don't understand why you haven't killed yourself."

That's what I think of when I'm alone and listening to jazz out of Amsterdam on our anniversary. Which, in the Netherlands, it no longer is. The countdown has shifted to the East Coast. Back to America, squarely into Miami's time zone. Bossa nova jazz bouncing around a club in Manhattan. "It's five minutes to midnight in New York. Five minutes to midnight. No more blues for the New Year here on *Toast of the Nation.*"

I recall Miss Cable News, back when it seemed we could make that work. We were on South Beach, on the beach itself. It was warm and humid at midnight. There were plenty of people near us, including, conspicuously, a guy stumbling around without pants. We stood in the sand, our hands on each other's backs, kissing as fireworks out-neoned the Art Deco hotels. I'm thinking of a year later, with her in New York City, how happy she seemed when she again kissed me at midnight. We were at Webster Hall, our trip to Manhattan funded by the *Times.* They'd flown me up for a second round of interviews, which took place the week after Christmas. Following the interviews, on New Year's Day, at the Algonquin Hotel with friends who know about Dorothy Parker and the Round Table, we toasted our future, everything seeming so promising for me, and thus for us.

"Hey, I saw your ex last night at a party," said a friend at a more recent New Year's Eve get-together, just a year ago. My friend had been at a party in my old Miami neighborhood, the place where I used to own a house. "She looked good. Really, really good." My friend was referring to Miss Cable News, since upgraded to her doctor. "Oh, and I saw your other ex, too!" my friend crowed, laughing, realizing that there were two at the same party. That would be my ex-wife, not yet the expatriate. "And she looked good, too."

I lost a lot of friends in the divorce. Everyone we both knew in college chose her over me, as did half the people we knew in Miami, which included several people from my work, my boss among them. I accepted the loss of these friends. It felt right, like something I deserved. There were still a few people from our circle who'd call me up for a beer on Lincoln Road, or invite me to their low-key New Year's Eve get-togethers. But these same friends also continued to party with my ex-wife. And then with my ex-girlfriend, too. My ex-girlfriend and my ex-wife party together! Miami grew so suffocating.

The radio show moves on, sonically soaring over the detritus of my Miami to land in the Central time zone. Frozen St. Paul, Minnesota. They have jazz there? Why not? I went to a wedding in St. Paul once. Went with my wife. I'd yet to meet Mrs. Wisconsin at that point. I'd yet to know myself capable of adultery.

I think back to another New Year's Eve, a year after the millennial one I spent rolling around the floor. She lived in New York then, Mrs. Wisconsin, supposedly separated from her husband. Supposedly there for me. I was in Miami, wrapping things up before joining her. My parents were in town for the holiday — they always seemed to visit Miami during winter for some reason — and we went to dinner at Norman's in Coral Gables. A big meal. Huge. A million courses, expensive wine. I paid for everything, which impressed my dad (and which, stubbornly, he later insisted on paying back, halting my protests by stuffing an already signed check in my shirt pocket). My mom and I got lit on martinis, my dad on his beer, then all of us on wine. I couldn't stop talking about Mrs. Wisconsin. On the phone, all the past week, she'd bemoaned our separation, how she hated having to travel to Wisconsin instead of ringing in the year down in Miami. She loved me, she said. She couldn't wait for us to be together. Her trip home would be horrible, she insisted. She was finally going to take that painful but necessary step.

Leaving out the leaving-the-husband part, that's what I told my parents. That she loved me. That I loved her. That I was going up to visit her, upon her return to Manhattan, in just three days. I couldn't wait, I said.

I later saw a picture of how she spent that night. In the picture it's midnight. She has her arm around some friends, other married couples who lived in their tiny Wisconsin town. In the picture, she's wearing a top I'd bought her in Miami on one of her visits. She looks good. Darn happy, as she might put it. When I took that trip to New York, she told me all about the improvements her husband had made to their house, how impressed she was. The place looked so much better than her cramped and expensive studio. She had to go to work the next day, but since she was now moving back to Wisconsin to be with her husband, and since she no longer wanted to be with me, she expected me out of the apartment — the one she'd soon abandon — by the time she returned from the office.

It's the regret of my life that I didn't throw away every single thing in there. All her clothes and medical records and bills and bank statements. The frozen pierogies she kept in the freezer and the pots stored under the sink. The books stacked by her bed, and the bed itself if I could somehow fit it in the trash chute down the hall. The Band-Aids in her medicine cabinet and her tweezers and her toothbrushes and the shower curtain and, what is this? Her fucking wedding ring! Sitting right there by the sink. (She always took it off when I visited.) I should have thrown that away, too, but I didn't. I didn't even leave a note of righteous anger. I left like a wimp. I left for the airport like a guy who thought he still had a chance, who still thought she loved me and still wanted to be with me and we were still perfect together and that she'd wake up the next morning realizing I wasn't just some extramarital fling, something to spice up her goddamn marriage. That I was indeed the love of her life. That I completed her and all that shit.

Fuck her. Fuck her husband, too. (Actually I take that last one back. I have no problem with the guy, and I still feel terrible I got messed up in his life.) It's now twenty minutes to my midnight and I can't stand it anymore. The radio people have relocated to some club in Denver. Denver? Wow, where? Ah, screw it; I don't care. I need to get out of the Chicken Coop. I need out now, damn Denver's jazz scene, damn the cold. I leash Valentine, pull on my winter coat, and head outside.

Whoa. It is *cold*. Those strong winds have blasted snowdrifts so smooth they look like fiberglass boat hulls. I can't hear the wind, though. I can't hear anything. There is no sound whatsoever. I can't hear gurgling brooks running down to the creek, as I usually can, nor do I hear cars on the road. I climb the icy pavement up Flagstaff Mountain. A white holiday star shines on the mountain, electrically powered by wind turbines, naturally, though people in Boulder still complain the star could use more-energy-efficient bulbs. I head toward the house line. One home displays a string of alternating blue and green lights. Another house shines all white, including the Christmas tree visible in a front window. There is *no sound*. I thought there might be parties on the block, people shouting and having fun. The only thing I can hear is the jingling of Valentine's chain and the scrape of my arms as they swing in my puffy blue coat.

We climb higher, up to Fifth Street, which turns into a dirt road. NO OUTLET. We take it anyway, then ascend the steep unpaved driveway of a new house I've watched rise since autumn, the highest house on Flagstaff. The weak beam of my flashlight reveals a three-story cube of glass and concrete. Very modern. Too modern for my taste, but what a view! In the light from the city and the stars I can read a keep out sign. We push inside anyway, through the space where someday there will be a front door. I see blocks of Styrofoam insulation and colorful strings of electrical wiring. There are no stairs yet. I tie Valentine to a post, then climb three flights of scaffolding to the top floor. Bare concrete and glass. This must be the future bedroom. That pit over there will be a fireplace, I bet. Someone's set out a green plastic lawn chair facing the mirrored windows. I walk over to it and take a seat, take in the view. To the south, red taillights climb the hill to Denver and, I guess, to its jazz clubs. Lyons lies somewhere in the darkness north. Straight ahead blink the lights of Longmont, and red radio towers, and the runway strip of the regional airport where small planes buzz over our Sunday runs. It's too dark to make out the university, though I know the football stadium is somewhere down there to my right. Just to the left there's Pearl Street all lit up, and the Boulder Theater where Rose Hill Drive must be done with "You See Me Crying" by now, completing their Aerosmith tribute.

The wind is stronger up here. I can hear it. I can finally hear something. The air carries the weak bleating of a party horn, the first faint note that this is a holiday. It must be close to midnight. In Miami, in Little Havana where I lived after the divorce, New Year's Eve is a reason to blare salsa from every apartment and every car parked on the street, doors open for aural impact. Immigrants from Honduras and Nicaragua offer grapes and wishes for *un prospero año*. It's still so quiet here in Boulder, even with the wind. I can hear Valentine shivering down below.

I pull a can of Coors from my coat and crack it open. Happy

New Year. I listen for a countdown. Nothing. I step through the missing back door to take a piss on the hill. When my boot hits the snow, a red burst illuminates the sky. Five glowing flares reveal everything: the brush and the snow and the orange plastic fence keeping the mountain lions away, hopefully. A second spray of fireworks, five more pops in all, blooms over Chautauqua. Even three floors up I can hear Valentine freaking out from the explosions, minor as they are. I scurry down the outside of the house on frozen mud, duck inside to untie my dog, then head home. I shine a flashlight on the road as we walk, careful to avoid patches of ice. When we get in view of the Coop I release her leash, letting her sprint to the apartment at top speed. Snow flies from her paws. She hates New Year's Eve, too.

Back inside, I pour my last can of Coors, the third of the night? Fourth? Too many for a guy drinking alone, but it's a holiday, and I tell myself it's all right because it's not like I'm lonely or depressed or anything. Public Radio has moved to San Francisco by now, somewhere in the Fillmore. I have no history on the West Coast. I've hurt nobody there. One minute till their midnight. One minute until my one in the morning. I turn off the radio. I brush my teeth, then head to bed with my dog and my toothpaste mouth and my little beer buzz. I need some sleep. I gotta run in the morning.

❧

The Boulder Road Runners meet at the Flatiron Athletic Club. The gym is open even on the holiday, which is so Boulder. It is sunny, clear, and cold. It was exactly a year earlier, in Miami, that I started my training with a two-mile jog along the Boardwalk, a run I struggled to finish. Today we're scheduled for seven miles, a distance I've begun regarding as "easy."

"Where's all the air?" asks a guy named Gavin, a member of the club for more than a decade. He's referring to the thick, rich oxygenated atmosphere at sea level, in Iowa, where he's spent the past month taking care of his elderly father. We run out to the golf course on icy roads they don't plow; in Boulder, the city clears the running paths but not the side streets, which is telling. Carl is here, and he grumbles when we pass a woman who doesn't return our Happy New Year greetings. Fortunately, the next woman we pass does wish us all a happy holiday, doing so while holding her arms out wide to signal a group hug.

"That's better," Carl says.

I jog cautiously, not wanting to slip on the ice. Even so, I have no trouble keeping up with the group. I have my lungs, as they say. I feel good. I should probably admit to being happy to be here, with my running friends, starting the day and the year constructively. Any moodiness from the night before disappears in the rhythms of our workout, in the small talk and the companionship. As we close in on Boulder Creek, Gavin catches up to me. He asks how my running is going, in general. Actually, he says he's heard my running is going good. I don't know, I reply. I can't tell how well I'm doing.

"That's right," Carl interjects, speaking to both Gavin and to me. "He doesn't know how well he's doing."

Rich pipes in: "I'll tell you how well he's doing. I don't sling shit, I tell the truth. And he's doing . . . fucking awesome."

Goodness. Fucking awesome. Fucking. Awesome. That gets my attention. That's a hell of an endorsement. I get so down when I'm left alone, when I'm by myself. Now here, back running again with this group, I feel better. I'm progressing toward my goal. After the run, when we disperse back at the gym parking lot, Rich tells me he's serious. I'm looking great. I still need to have some luck to qualify, but I'm looking really, really good.

20

I'M LEARNING A lot about chinook winds. Five days into
the New Year, I wake up to find Valentine in my bed, a place
she's not usually allowed to sleep. Her head is burrowed
into my armpit. All night she'd cowered as hot air rushed down
Flagstaff Mountain, rattling the Coop's blue asbestos shingles,
knocking down trees and melting the snow on the front lawn.
I check the weather before I dress: an unbelievable sixty-one
degrees outside, warm enough for shorts. Winds are gusting up
to fifty-five miles per hour. I step outside before sunrise to find
snowmelt from the Flatirons flowing down Rose Hill Drive. The
wind concerns me, but I can't afford to think about it. I've got to
hustle out to Neva Road to meet up with Carl. It is time for the
longest run of my life, 23.5 miles. It is the day I finally have my
breakthrough.

Carl and I have talked about today's long workout for two
weeks. Last night, as the winds rattled the Coop and as I ate my
chicken parmesan and drank my one bottle of Shiner Bock, I
went over the workout in my mind. The regular four-mile warm-
up, then four laps around a four-mile loop, then back home the
way we came. At least three hours, though hopefully not much

longer. Brutal, boring, and, because of the ongoing chinook winds, nothing at all like what actually happens.

It's like we're moonwalking. We lift up our feet to take the next step, and in that fraction of time when we're airborne the wind thrusts us backward. We're hit hardest when we run due west from La Grange toward the foothills. The chinooks are powerful, and it takes us forever to reach the yellow barn that marks the halfway point of the loop. Turning south onto US 36, we need to tilt into the wind, tilt forty-five ridiculous degrees like ski jumpers flying sideways. We try not to blow into a ditch or, worse, into traffic. Finally making it another mile down to Plateau Road, we turn east, the wind at our backs now shooting us forward as though we're bionic. We're scheduled to run the loop three more times, but that clearly isn't possible. If we can somehow run only east we can salvage the workout. But if we do run east for the sixteen remaining miles, we'll be halfway to Fort Collins with no way to get back home; I don't have any money on me, nor does Carl. Neither of us has a phone. I assume we have no choice but to pack it in, but I also know we absolutely need to log our miles. There is no wiggle room in our schedule. This long run, the longest run of our entire training, is too important to skip. When we reach the water stop at Lookout Mountain, I await Carl's decision. It looks bad.

"You boys need some help?"

It's Rich! Pulling up in his big black sport utility vehicle! He's bailed on his much more modest workout and is here to assist us. You want to run east? No problem.

So we head east, on a route I've never trafficked. We run past the upside-down funnel that is Haystack Mountain, and head down into the valley. It's farmland mostly, divided by soft dirt roads that give our steps a little bounce. Patches of snow lurk among fields of rich soil, the snow looking like marshmallows floating in acres of hot chocolate. There is no traffic at all, no cars, few sounds. Bare branches twist from trees stretching into gray sky. We pass a small cemetery flying an American flag. Every two or three miles we find Rich standing next to his SUV with water bottles in his hands.

It's a long run, and my mind wanders to everything. To a family meeting convened in New Hampshire when I was probably nine years old. It was all six of us. My mom opened new business with a report that dad had been to the doctor and had learned that all the cigarettes he'd smoked will likely shorten his life by ten years. That was the purpose of the meeting, to let us know he would die young. We all cried. We'd miss him. Then I think of Mrs. Wisconsin and a letter she sent me way late in the game. She was going back to NYC for a week of business and I should meet her at her hotel.

"This could be your ship coming in," she wrote. It wasn't a letter, actually. It was a PowerPoint presentation, her petition flashing and dissolving on my computer screen.

More than an hour after Rich joined our team, we're working a stretch of dirt road. It has been a long run already and we have eight miles still to go. This isn't just time on the legs, either. We're simulating marathon conditions, which means a consistent, punishing pace. I focus on my footwork. I try to tune everything out. No talk. Just my breath. Just Carl's breath. Just keep going. Rich pulls even with us in his big black SUV. He inserts a CD into the stereo system.

"The Future's So Bright I Gotta Wear Shades" is a dated, hokey song by a band I totally respect. Timbuk3 were a talented duo out of Wisconsin. They refused to sell the rights to their one hit even though McDonald's offered them a million dollars to use it in commercials. I never really liked the song, though. I thought of it as a novelty. The fact that Rich burned it onto a CD makes me smile at first — what a dork. But the song, I now discover, makes me smile in general. This is the first time in Boulder I've been allowed to run with music. Listening to it on Rich's stereo, out on the cold and remote high prairie, resets the song in a new context. It pumps me up. It pumps up Carl, too. We run a bit faster. Even better, the next track is "Satisfaction" by the Rolling Stones, a song I definitely like. The long dirt road dissolves into a brown river winding through the jungles of Vietnam. Laurence Fishburne dances as we water-ski behind Rich's truck. Rich taps his steering wheel. Carl inhales a second wind. I find my second wind, too.

"Have you had a runner's high yet?" People in the club ask me this all the time. No, I've never experienced transcendence during my training. Never once have I felt a rush of joy or a sensation of floating or anything like the phenomenon as it has been described to me. I *have* noticed how wonderful it is to *stop* running, to lounge the rest of the day, not worrying if I need to exercise or not. To this point, running's given me only a college-football-on-TV-watcher's high. But I can now say I've had a moment. I've had a moment where I've actually enjoyed running. I'm having it now as I bob along with my coach on my right and my running partner on my left, classic rock cutting through the crisp air as it generates movies in my head.

It's only a moment. Rich speeds ahead to prepare our next water stop. Carl and I climb a mild hill into Niwot, where automobile traffic will prevent Rich from again driving alongside us. Carl is a metronome, holding steady right at the pace we need to run. I start struggling to keep up with him.

"You have these stretches where it hurts or you're going slow and you just grit your teeth and power through and then pretty soon you feel better and you have a good stretch," Carl advises.

He tells me to find a rhythm, to relax and act like I'm riding a bike. Only an hour, an hour and fifteen minutes left and we're done, he adds. That's not exactly good news. That's a long time. But I keep going. I try to forget where I am. I think of a line that Frank Shorter said in the 1968 Olympic Trials, to his friend Kenny Moore after they'd been running for two hours already:

"Why couldn't Pheidippides have died here?"

We pass Niwot High School, home of the Cougars. Carl tells me there was this woman, a really gifted runner, who never reached her potential. Then one season she started winning races, posting her best times ever. People asked her how she made it happen. She said she went from the Mentality of Fear to the Mentality of Faith.

"That's what you've got to do now, Robert, switch to the Mentality of Faith."

The last water stop is about two miles from the finish. Rich stands alongside his truck, a bottle for each of us in his hands and two towels draped over his arm. I feel dizzy, a flashback to that hot tub morning. I swallow my last energy goo. Carl says something about dropping the hammer and gritting our teeth. I tell him to fuck off. I'm joking. I resume running.

We finish up just outside the town of Longmont, way out there. We can see the Flatirons, but they are tiny triangles far in the distance. Rich waits in his truck, at what he's determined will be today's finish line. Carl wants to keep going another two miles. His calculations are based on his stopwatch, but my GPS watch says 23.5 and that's our goal and seriously this time, Carl, fuck off. I stop. Immediately my head feels dizzy again. Rich hops out of his truck, runs over and grabs my shoulders. I clutch his gray CU sweatshirt for stability. I crouch down into a squat so that if I do faint I'll fall only a short distance.

I feel deep affection for Rich. I'm woozy, I recognize, but the dude has really come through. He's had ideas he's never followed up on, like that plan to have me run up and down the foothills carrying a backpack full of rocks. He is in no way perfect. But he gave up three and a half hours of his Saturday morning just to help us through this most important training run. He and Carl and I climb into the SUV for the long ride home. Rich's classic rock mix starts into "Born to Run" by Bruce Springsteen. I ask him to turn it up. With whatever strength I have left I pat him on the back. I thank him, several times.

"You did great," he says. "You did fucking great."

℞

I call my dad when I get home. I tell him I ran all 23.5 miles and I didn't quit and Rich and Carl were quite pleased.

"You're over the hump!" he cheers. I share with him the final numbers pulled off my GPS watch. It took us three hours and fifteen minutes to run the whole way. Too slow, I feel, but both Rich and Carl point out we're at altitude, we're wearing five pounds of extra clothing, and we're in the midst, as Carl puts it, "of some serious-ass training."

"Three-fifteen?" my dad asks. "When I was training I ran twenty miles in two hours. How come it took you so long?"

He's trying to be funny, I think. The phone call is light and upbeat and I know he's being supportive in general. But that so pisses me off. I can't take it as anything but a dig, probably subconscious on his part, an affirmation that he remains the alpha male.

"Because I'm not you, Dad," I tell him.

21

FRANK SHORTER ANSWERS the door of his house wearing blue nylon running pants and a gray sweatshirt from his alma mater, Yale. It's eight a.m. on a Monday. I was a little leery about knocking on his door. I've been told he can be ornery, or at least mercurial in his moods. You get him on the right day, I've been assured, and everything will be fine. Shorter seems fine. He is trim and tan. The gray in his hair in no way leavens a remarkable boyishness, though to see him in motion is to recognize his age. He has said the body really breaks down after fifty, and by the time I'm meeting him he's had a decade to test that theory. He's endured countless surgeries on his hips and feet and back. No cartilage remains in one knee. As we step, slowly, downstairs, Shorter leans his full weight onto the banister.

"As you can see, pets rule out here," he says, leading me into his living room. We sit on a couch covered with a blanket for protection from a pair of gray cats. Picture windows frame a panoramic view across Wonderland Lake to the Flatiron Mountains. On a side wall I notice a *Life* magazine cover of Shorter's win in Munich. A glass-topped end table holds what I presume are his medals. The room whispers Olympic champion sotto voce.

Mike Sandrock from the *Daily Camera* set up the meeting for me on Shorter's condition that I spend my time focused on the drug issue. That makes me the latest in a line of reporters to visit Shorter at his house, to sit on this couch, and to conduct the same basic interview. A well-written story published in Denver's *Westword* eight years earlier, about how Frank Shorter, who was robbed of his gold medal in 1976, is fighting to clean up sports, differs little from a story published in the *Rocky Mountain News* three days after my visit.

As mandated, we talk about drugs. Or I should say *he* talks about drugs, for almost three hours. Shorter talks about East Germany and Lance Armstrong and the disgraced American sprinter Marion Jones and how trying to catch drug cheats is like trying to catch bank robbers. Even if we can't catch them all, does that mean we shouldn't try to catch any of them?

It's the same stuff I heard him talk about back at Fleet Feet, and the same stuff I heard him say more recently when I followed him around in preparation for our interview. At the opening day of registration for the Bolder Boulder 10K, he told a woman who sought his autograph, when she casually mentioned Montreal, "You know the guy who beat me cheated. You know that, don't you?" He spoke later at the Chautauqua Community House on University Hill. The announced topic was in the same vein as his earlier speech at the Fleet Feet running store: "What to Look For at the Olympic Games."

Cheating. Again. Specifically, look at the Kenyans. They're probably cheating.

The interview in his living room lasts longer than it took Shorter to traverse the streets of Montreal. I take lots of notes. I'd share them here, but that doesn't seem necessary. The man is obsessed with performance-enhancing drugs and the athletes who surreptitiously use them. There's really not much more to add beyond that.

When our conversation wraps up, Shorter unfolds off the couch, standing up slowly. His right foot doesn't support his weight, making him step gingerly. I point to his small glass end table and ask if that's where he keeps his medals. It is.

"You want to see them?"

The white fur that lines the case storing the gold medal is blackened from thirty-six years of fingertips. Shorter unwraps a chain from the back of the case, then places the medal in my hand. MÜNCHEN 1972 on the obverse, Bauhaus nudes of Castor and Pollux on the back. The silver medal, which he pulls from a wooden box, is differentiated by color, of course, and by a simple laurel wreath on the reverse. The medals are oddly unmoving. I feel nothing except their weight. There's no emotional transfer of sweat. I can't sense the 140-mile weeks Shorter endured to earn them. My participant medal from the Hog Jog 5K feels about the same.

Frank Shorter won his gold medal in Munich, the city of his birth. The medal, when he holds it, evokes pleasure, and marvel.

"My God, how did I run that fast?"

He recalls his last lap around Olympic Stadium, the eighty thousand people, the glass canopies shaped to evoke the Alps. The stadium has since hosted a World Cup soccer final and even a cross-country ski championship. The October before I met with Shorter, the stadium served as the finish line of the Munich Marathon. The winner of that race broke the tape in the exact place in which Shorter ended his gold medal run in 1972. I ask Shorter if he's seen who won. He hasn't, which can be interpreted as a positive sign.

Falk Cierpinski, a German, first emerged internationally as a competitive triathlete. He eventually changed his focus to long-distance running, and he's showing enough potential as a marathoner to be named one of the top prospects in his homeland. It was Falk Cierpinski, son of Waldemar Cierpinski — the man who beat Frank Shorter in 1976 — who won the Munich Marathon.

"What was his time?" Shorter asks immediately. Two hours and twenty-five minutes, I tell him. Respectable, definitely, good enough to win a race, but not close to world class.

"If it was 2:25 then he probably was clean," Shorter says. "If it was 2:09, that would mean he was on drugs."

❧

There is one other thing to share from the interview, now that I think about it. I went to Frank Shorter's house to talk about drugs, and that's all Frank Shorter wanted to talk about, officially. But there was something else he absolutely wanted to talk about. It came up almost immediately, startling me when it did.

We were just ten minutes into our talk. We'd opened easy, chatting first, and briefly, about my two digital voice recorders chronicling our conversation. He shared general facts about what he does with his time: He spends about eighty days a year on the road speaking at races like the White Rock marathon in Dallas, the Indianapolis minimarathon and even the Miami Marathon. We talked a bit, naturally, about his racing career. About how he served as his own coach, and about how he was the first man to import track-style racing strategies to the long marathon race. We also discussed his victory in Munich, how satisfying it was to have his coaching decisions vindicated. And, then, for more than twenty minutes, we talked about his father.

I certainly didn't see the topic coming. From reading clips at the Carnegie Library, I was aware of Shorter's hate for his father, but I was in his house to discuss drugs, and my notebook was full of questions on only that topic. After Shorter finished talking about his Munich victory, I'd ad-libbed a question about his independent nature. He said this in reply:

"I was always that way, from the time I was a little kid. Because I had to be. I came from a family of ten, where there was physical, emotional, and sexual abuse."

In 1991, in a speech in Fort Lauderdale, Shorter said he was "physically and mentally abused" by his father, Samuel Shorter, a prominent doctor in Middletown, New York, the upstate hamlet in which Frank Shorter grew up. Frank Shorter told the *Sun-Sentinel* newspaper there was also "sexual abuse and other things" that he didn't want to talk about "because it was just awful."

Shorter was born in 1947, on Halloween, the second-oldest of what would be eight children. In *Olympic Gold*, Shorter wrote about his father respectfully. Samuel Shorter comes across as a tough man, not a monster, and certainly not abusive. Once when Frank was training around Taos, New Mexico, where his family had temporarily relocated, a car of "Indians" ran him off the road. When Samuel Shorter heard this, he got in his car with a gun and tried to find the men who had threatened Frank. In the story, in the book, Frank's father comes across like a decent man trying to protect his son.

"Oh, I think when he followed me with a gun it wasn't so much to protect me as it was hoping he had a reason to use it," Shorter told me in his living room, breaking into a rich peal of laughter that sounds not unlike that of the actor Tom Cruise. "Isn't that interesting that I could have that perspective?"

I said nothing. I didn't know what to say.

"There was a minority," he continued. "There was an Indian he actually did attack at one point when we were there. Because [my father] had a girl, a little girl who worked in his office who he was sleeping with and it turned out she was with this guy and he got jealous."

Seven years after the biography was published, in his speech in Fort Lauderdale, Frank Shorter said his entire family was abused.

"We were young children," he told the *Sun-Sentinel* after the speech. "My mother finally discovered after six months of taking what she thought was a weekly night out, we were being abused by my father who would stay home and take care of the kids. She had to stop going out because he would invariably discipline everybody by beating them up."

Shorter claimed to remember being physically abused at age three.

"You know the difference in discipline when a parent takes out a belt, then hits you a couple times with the belt," Shorter told the paper. "Then you have my parent that used the buckle rather than the strap. That sent a signal to me at an early age.

"There was mental abuse as well," Shorter continued in the newspaper article, and again, in so many words, to me in his living room. "My father is a very bright man. He knew how to practice verbal abuse."

Shorter said his father's abuse was alcohol-related. The *Sun-Sentinel* called Samuel Shorter for comment. The elder Shorter admitted to the newspaper he had a drinking problem.

"I see him each year from a distance but he hasn't communicated at all for several years with me," Samuel Shorter told the paper. "He has pretty much turned against a number of the family and his friends. I really don't know the reasons. I expect I am guilty of something. I don't know what I am being accused of.

"I don't know how to defend myself. I am sure he will say worse about me. It's all very sad."

Frank Shorter, in his living room during our interview, talked about everything covered in the article. He also told me his father would come home drunk and drag one of the kids into another room, usually a younger sibling of Frank's, "and beat 'em." Shorter said his father's behavior "was, like, really disgusting."

I was struck by how quickly and easily the abuse entered our conversation. At one point, after we'd talked about his father for a while, Shorter raised his hand to signal he needed a moment. I sat there, silently, as Frank Shorter choked back tears. Eventually he gave in and cried, for about a minute. Again, I didn't know what to say. I didn't know why Shorter was talking about it, to me, with my voice recorders running.*

&

Within six months of my interview with Shorter, the young Falk Cierpinski shaved ten minutes off his marathon time, down to 2:15, making him and Waldemar the fastest father-son combo in marathon history. Shorter returned to his hometown of Middletown, New York, where he ran the Classic 10K. Samuel Shorter fell gravely ill on race day, and two days after the race, while Frank was still in town, he died. In the local coverage of the death, Frank gave no comment. In an interview conducted with a Middletown newspaper before the race, and thus before the death, Frank Shorter floated another trial balloon: he'd like to become the head of the US Olympic Committee. It's obvious why he'd want that job. It's also obvious — *drugs!* — to the Olympic officials who might otherwise jump to have a gold-medal-winning Yale-educated lawyer steering their ship. So as before, as with many of Shorter's post-running-career plans, nothing came of it.

---

* Three years after our interview, Shorter went on the record about his father in a long article published in *Runner's World*.

As I prepare for my marathon qualifier, I continue to run on Wednesdays with the regular group. We continue to navigate a path near Shorter's house. His name still comes up frequently, as it has since I arrived in town. We'll be running along the foothills or perhaps finishing up a workout back atop Mapleton Hill. Someone will say they saw Shorter at the liquor store and he was as warm and friendly as can be. Someone else will say he saw Shorter somewhere else, perhaps at McGuckin Hardware, and Frank couldn't have been more of a jerk. Before I met with him, I'd come to see him the way many in Boulder see him: mysterious and difficult, a seemingly selfish man on a mockable crusade to win a gold medal to match the gold medal he already has. I'd grown certain that he was a miserable soul locked away in his house, the lonely long-distance runner stewing in demons of his own design.

Now I see him more softly. Now I recall the house. The living room's white walls and high ceilings that made every word he said bounce around like audible electrons. It was awfully intimate in his house. It was just Frank Shorter and me and those walls and that ceiling that magnified every sound. I sat there silently while Frank Shorter sat across from me, thinking about his father and crying.

22

I'VE STARTED RECEIVING massages. Once a week, for an hour and a half, at the hands of the same guy that both Rich and Carl also see once a week.

"It's the easiest thing you can do to go faster," Carl tells me. "You lie down, and when you get up you're faster."

In Boulder, if someone's not a life coach, he or she is probably a body worker. There are enough muscle manipulators in town to support four branches of a McDonald's-like chain called Massage Envy. A masseuse camps out at the Trident coffee shop, unkinking necks in ten-minute increments between sips of a latte. Even Chicken Coop Aaron, my Naropa neighbor, dabbles in professional massage when he's not attending movement therapy orgies.

Massage strikes me as an obscene luxury — when I tell my sister I'm headed to my weekly rubdown she cackles at my spa-day lifestyle. But runners in Boulder consider massage a fixed cost of the sport. Massage works the lactic acid out of worn muscles. It helps legs recover, leaving the whole body better prepared for the next hard run. In the ramp-up to Myrtle Beach, with my weekly mileage climbing, massage seems to be a cost I can't, or at least shouldn't, avoid. Besides, it's just money, right? I'm on permanent vacation, right? I'm retired, like Rich and Carl. Financially, like Rich and Carl and all these other runners in Boulder, I'm set for life. Right?

"Pain is unavoidable, suffering is optional," states a sign in Kevin Jordan's small studio, located in an office off Thirtieth Street near a dry cleaner and a doggie apothecary. Muscle charts hang on the walls. Pictures of his kids stand on a tiny desk next to a small stereo spinning a violin concerto. Kevin changes the cotton sheet on a padded table. He's telling me about a poster of Michael Jordan his daughter pinned over her bed, one in which the basketball player talks about all the shots he has missed and how ignoring those misses has helped him end up a winner.

Kevin leaves the room for a minute. I take off my clothes and lie facedown under a second sheet. I disagree, I say when he returns. Michael Jordan wins all the time so his perspective on losing, on rebounding from missed shots, is warped. It isn't the first time I've reflexively rejected an upbeat spin on things, and Kevin has endured just about enough of my negativity.

"You have to flex the gratitude muscle," he recommends. He rubs sanitizer into his hands. "All that negative talk is ego. It's all sabotaging. We're going to start with your right leg today."

He slathers my lower right leg in warm oil, then digs his fingers into the ropy muscle of my calf.

"Like a lot of people, you set up a perfectly reasonable and valid goal, then you sabotage it. Now flip over."

I flip over, onto my back. He works his thumb along my sartorius, near the groin, a little-known muscle that carries a big load on every step.

"You need to flex your gratitude muscle," he repeats. "Every time you start to sabotage yourself with a negative thought, you need to tell yourself five things you've accomplished, or that you've got going for you. You came out here, you joined a running club, you're getting massages, you've lost a lot of weight. You're doing it!"

I mumble something, knowing he's right but blanching at such Pollyannaish positive thinking. I recall the drive out to Boulder from Miami, when I stopped at my parents' house. "You've always been a martyr," said my mom before she punched me on the shoulder. "You're a crybaby." Kevin asks me to flip back over onto my stomach so he can address my left leg.

"This carries over into your attitude toward racing. The attitude you're bringing to Myrtle Beach mirrors the attitude you had in Philly: 'Let's just do this, let's just see how I run.' You've got to do better than that! You can't just slow down in the last two miles when it starts getting tough. You can't just *run*. Racing is a race! That's a good mind trick, by the way, remembering that it's a race. Any problems with your knee this week?"

He digs into a tight muscle in my right hamstring and continues dispensing tips. The difference between a jogger and a runner is an entry form — joggers jog, runners race. Everyone has some setbacks; it's all how you roll with it. Another mind trick? Run away from your fears.

"I've got a theory about your dad, too," he says. "If you want to hear it."

I lie there for a few seconds, back on my stomach again, my face pressed into a foam ring that leaves space for my nose, chin, and mouth. He pulls on my right foot, stretching out the tendons from my ankle up to my knee. Of course I want to hear it.

"From what you've told me, you're living too much in your father's shadow, worrying about what he'll think of you, when all you need to worry about is what you think of yourself. You can't measure up to what he thinks. Fathers have high standards. I don't know if anyone can measure up to their father's standards. It can't be done."

He leaves the room so I can get dressed.

"Now drink lots of water tonight," he says when he returns. "We'll do this again same time next week."

❧

We dial back our training in the last two weeks. "Tapering" is the technical running term. I catch a head cold and stay in bed all of one Monday morning, following an order from Rich to get at least ten hours of sleep. Snuggled up with Valentine against the February chill, I slip in and out of consciousness, dreaming I've won the Boston Marathon. I imagine I've run a world-class 2:05, but starting from the back of the pack. By the time I cross the finish line, some Kenyan already sports the winner's laurel. Yet I know that I've run the fastest. I motion to the nearest race official to check my number and my time.

"I'm number one," I tell him. "I'm the winner." Eventually, after looking up my time, and after verifying my feat with the many witnesses who saw me on the course, they give me the title, to much international acclaim.

Rich is excited for my upcoming qualifier. Maybe more so than I am. On the night before my flight to South Carolina, he sends me off with jambalaya and homemade pasta, served at his house. He has a whole evening worked out. After dinner we walk over to the big, beautiful new Sony television he bought with winnings from his unbreakable Thursday night poker game. I sink into the sofa, which kicks up a footrest like a La-Z-Boy recliner. Rich's second wife, Patti, places a heating pad around my neck to relax my muscles. She also throws an afghan over my legs. I sip water from a glass she hands me. Rich hits a button on the remote to start the show.

First we watch a bit from *Rocky*, a scene where the boxer and his girlfriend lie awake in bed the night before his big fight. All he wants to do, he says, is go the distance.

"Who am I kidding?" Sylvester Stallone asks.

"See?" Rich says, stopping the video. "He's freaking out. He's worried. All part of the process."

Next, for some reason, comes a scene from the poker movie *Rounders*, probably just to underscore how Rich acquired his sweet new TV.

"If you don't take a chance," says an actor playing a card shark, "life is one big grind." We watch scenes from *Top Gun* and *Tombstone* and then a scene from *Prefontaine* featuring a cameo by Frank Shorter. Finally, perhaps inevitably, we watch a large chunk of *Chariots of Fire*. The Vangelis theme as they run on the beach. Scenes in Scotland among the heather on the glen. I giggle, surprised I've gone so long in Boulder without watching this film. Rich fast-forwards to a scene near the end, after the main character has won an Olympic gold medal. The runner is closing a tavern with his coach. Both men are very drunk. The runner lifts his glass to toast.

"Pay attention to this part," Rich advises. Before I can, he stops the disk, stands up and acts out the scene, modifying the dialog for our purposes. "To Rich Castro, the greatest coach who ever lived!"

Rich will be in San Diego on race day, running in the cross-country nationals. Win or lose, I'll be done in Myrtle Beach before his competition starts.

"I've got it all set up already," he assures me. "They'll announce it over the PA. We'll be at the starting line and they'll come on the loudspeaker and they'll tell everyone that you qualified for Boston."

☙

Every Friday morning, if he doesn't have an appointment on his schedule, Kevin Jordan tries to run up Sanitas. My massage therapist parks his Outback in a small lot atop Mapleton Hill, near the hospital that replaced Kellogg's Sanitarium. He pulls on a Windbreaker and ties shoes specifically designed for trail running. He taps a button on his wristwatch, then starts his ascent up one of Boulder's most trafficked foothills. It's a speed hike, really, too steep at the start to jog. Kevin hurdles boulders and surmounts fallen tree trunks, sticking to a path worn smooth by countless hikers on countless previous ascents. It's only four-fifths of a mile to the peak, but 1,285 feet straight up. The one time I accompanied him we reached the summit in a little over seventeen minutes, which he said was solid.

On the Friday before the Myrtle Beach Marathon, Kevin climbs Sanitas with Clarence, a guy in my running group. Clarence owns a company that installs and refinishes hardwood floors. He used to be a professional snowshoe racer, which intimidates me even though I have no idea where or when anybody races on snowshoes, much less for money. The previous Saturday, Clarence had accompanied Carl and me on our last serious run before South Carolina.

Chinook winds blew strong that morning, a Saturday. We eased through the normal four-mile warm-up to the water bottles, then we ran comfortably for the mile north to La Grange, and easy still on the second mile west to the yellow barn that marks US 36. From the barn we broke into a sprint, or what felt like one. Carl led two miles "at pace," the 7:30 miles we intend to run the marathon. I struggled to keep up. I *wanted* to keep up, but my legs felt heavy, weighted down. My lungs wheezed audibly. Did I still have a head cold? I felt like I . . . couldn't . . . get . . . enough . . . air.

"That'll go away when we race," Carl said afterward, back on

Neva Road, back at our cars. I noticed what he didn't say. He didn't say "We're right on track," as he has in the past. He didn't say "There's nothing to worry about." He didn't squeeze me on my shoulders and tell me "we're going to pull it off" as he has on other Saturdays.

"Let's get out of this wind," is all he added.

Six days later, on Sanitas, at the top, Kevin Jordan takes in the high plains. In February there's little to appreciate. Winter has stripped the leaves from the trees and the green from the wild grass lining the hills. Clear out to Nebraska the palette is mud: auburn and brown and vanilla offset by gray mounds of snow. Kevin draws a cold breath into his lungs, then exhales.

"So tomorrow's the big day," he says to Clarence. "Robert's big run."

"He's not going to do it," Clarence responds, as Kevin will later tell me. Images from that last training session flash though Clarence's mind. He sees me lagging behind. He hears me wheezing. He knows the time I need and how unrealistic it seems. "I *know* he's not going to do it. He really struggled to keep up with us on Saturday, and I know for sure *I* couldn't run a 3:15."

Kevin Jordan doesn't defend me. Clarence doesn't turn from the view. To the south he can see downtown Denver. Immediately to his left, north, sit the driveways and bedrooms and hot tubs of the biggest houses in Boulder, ostentatious spaceships berthed in brush trafficked by deer, black bears, and mountain lions.

"He doesn't have a chance."

23

A FTER COLLEGE, WITH absolutely no idea what to do with my life, I decided I should embark on a career in which I could "do good." Social work seemed as do-goody as it gets. I applied to the University of Chicago and was accepted, in large part because my brother earned his under-graduate degree at Chicago, and in larger part because I'd ap-plied specifically to the school of social work and was one of the only men to do so.

I made a pretty big mistake going to Chicago, which I real-ized immediately. It was supposed to be the best school of social work in the country, yet in almost every class all we seemed to talk about was Oprah Winfrey, and who she had invited on her show the day before, and what we thought of the guest and the discussion topic and isn't Oprah just the best? For my fieldwork, I rode a bus to a nonprofit located near Comiskey Park. The agency's purpose, and my job specifically, was to reunite run-away teenage girls with their mothers (no fathers were ever in the picture). I tried. I'd invite the mothers and daughters to the of-fice. I'd lead them to a room where I'd instruct them to go ahead and talk things over. Yet no reunions were ever engineered. Even more discouraging, I couldn't help noticing that the social workers in the office, the career-track professionals, appeared completely burned-out. They looked morose. They shuffled papers and paid cursory attention to the clients they were supposedly managing. There were so many clients to manage and those clients turned over all the time and so many of the cases looked hopeless and, oh my god, is it four o'clock yet?

It was a two-year program to my degree. At the end of my first year, my mother came down to pick up some of my stuff from my Hyde Park apartment. I'd planned to spend the summer in Milwaukee with my sister, doing social work. At least, that's what I'd told my parents. At the Mellow Yellow restaurant, over lunch, my mom and I talked about my classes and how things went that first year and how she was born and raised on the South Side. Nothing out of the ordinary. We packed up her car and she drove home to the suburbs. I stayed in the apartment one more night, as planned. Just after dinner I phoned home. When my mom answered I told her there was one thing I'd neglected to mention at lunch: I'd dropped out. I'd quit. I wasn't coming back in the fall. I wasn't going to be a social worker.

"I don't even want to hear this," she snapped. "Talk to your father."

When he came on the line, he was livid. Very mad. There was all the money he'd just spent, for one. There was my aimlessness, too. I told him I'd probably go to Wisconsin and landscape again, my work for the past few summers.

"You just want to go up to Milwaukee so you can drink quarter beers!" he shouted.

As tense as the moment was, I struggled to suppress a laugh. I hadn't even thought about drinking beer. But I had once, sometime the previous summer, remarked that there were a lot of bars in Milwaukee, and it was nice to finally be of legal drinking age and that, yes, one of the bars in particular served twenty-five-cent plastic cups of beer on Thursday nights, which I thought was a pretty cool thing.

I use the quarter beer story, and how my dad had dredged up a small comment said in passing a year earlier, when I tell friends, usually with amusement, that my dad runs a police state. Anything I say to him can and will be used against me in the future. I bring this up because the police state remains in operation even now.

∞

Carl and I land in South Carolina on Thursday, Valentine's Day. Flying Delta through Atlanta, we connect with a tiny charter into Charleston, then drive up the Sweetgrass Highway to Myrtle Beach. Carl plays classic rock on the radio as we pass a series of old, round women with skin as black as tar. They lean back on plastic chairs alongside the highway, selling baskets woven from lowland reeds.

We check out the marathon expo as soon as we hit Myrtle Beach. In a conference room at the Sheraton we pick up our race bibs and T-shirts and four small safety pins each to attach our numbers to our singlets. We pick up a map of the course, too, which we follow as we drive 26.2 miles through town, familiarizing ourselves not with Heartbreak Hill or the Prudential Tower of Boston but with the landmarks of Myrtle Beach: a Sonic burger, a Target, a package store. T-shirt shops named Eagle and Wings alternate with miniature golf courses and a succession of chain restaurants: Carrabba's, TGI Fridays, and a Hooters with TRY OUR FRIED PICKLES on the marquee. Turn left at the KFC up there, okay? Ocean Boulevard is hotel row. Neon signs announce vacancies at the Atlantica, at the Driftwood Lodge, at the Yachtsman, and at a hundred other places. The Ferris wheel at the Family Kingdom amusement park appears arthritic, stuck motionless until tourist season resumes in April. No water splashes in the outdoor pool at our hotel, the Sea Mist.

Our room gives us an ocean view, such as it is. From the balcony we can see cold gray water, concrete clouds, and the slow arcs of metal detectors swung by men combing the empty beach. I lay out my race-day uniform of black shorts, my bright yellow racing flats, and the third new Boulder Road Runners singlet Rich gave me after dinner at his house, this singlet the color yellow. Carl and I step out for a quick three-mile jog. Easy. Just shaking the legs loose. Carl cheers the city's delicious flatness. I notice my late-stage training wheeze seems to have disappeared. On Ocean Boulevard, we pass an older woman standing outside a package store. A lit cigarette dangles from a gap in her teeth.

"Practicin'?" she asks.

"Yep."

"Aw right."

We jog a few steps further.

"Not every day you get to talk to the mayor," Carl says.

❧

My parents fly in on Thursday as well, and check into the same hotel. Their decision to join us for the race surprised me and, at first, elated me. They are interested in my life! They want to support me! There's no other reason to be here. The Bi-Lo Myrtle Beach Marathon isn't some destination race like the Honolulu Marathon or 26.2 miles winding around the redwood trees of Big Sur. It's not a big-deal competition, either. It sure ain't Boston. It's just a qualifier, a race that must be run in order to make it to Boston. Still, they're here. That's nice. That's unexpected. That's encouraging.

It's also terrifying. I take the good news of their presence and spin it into a worst-case scenario; it's the way I'm wired. I've been telling my dad about my training for a full year by now. I moved to Boulder, I signed on with Rich, I ran half marathons in Philadelphia and Puerto Vallarta. Just like I used to crow to him about the journalism assignments I'd landed, I've been selling a story of me as a serious runner. But I've never run a full marathon before. What if I blow it? What if I screw up like I screwed up those magazine stories? Then I'll have to face my dad. Then he'll be right here, standing witness. That scares me silent.

We meet up with my parents at the hotel, all piling into my dad's rental car for the drive down to the better restaurants along Murrells Inlet. It remains Valentine's Day. Inside Bovine's Steakhouse, candles flicker low, romantic light. Applause floats across the room as a young woman accepts the marriage proposal offered by her boyfriend. We are the only group of four seeking a table. The hostess seats us in a back booth upholstered in cowhide.

Our blood sugar levels are low. We got a little lost on the drive here, and we've been flying all day and Myrtle Beach isn't looking like the poshest place in the world with its T-shirt shops and ghost-town hotels, but Carl orders a bold zinfandel, my dad cracks open a few Bud Lights, and we settle in just fine, alcohol the wonder drug that it is. My dad tells his running stories to Carl, a rare interested audience. How he got into jogging, how he so enjoyed that first Fourth of July ten miler that he set his sights on Boston. How he didn't learn until just a few months before the marathon that he needed to qualify, and how he only qualified at the last second, in an obscure race in February, in Massachusetts. How it was snowing that day, and how he still pulled it off.

❧

Saturday morning, February 26, 1977. *Foster's Daily Democrat* newspaper, "Serving Southeastern New Hampshire and Southern Maine." Front page headlines: "Seacoast Welfare Rulings 'Illegal,'" and "Casino Opponents 'Elitists.'" There's a story on Secretary of State Cyrus Vance opposing US-Cuban ties. A local story details drug raids in Gilmanton, Sandown and Epping.

The top story, center of the page above the fold and just below the Olde English font of the masthead, frames a big picture of my dad. He's leaning back in an office chair, at work, shoes up on his desk. His tie is fat. His shirt puffs over his thin frame. He has long hair, parted on his left side. There are a few creases in the skin of his cheeks. He's the same age I am now.

His hands rest on his lap. His lips are parted slightly. He is not smiling. Instead he looks confident. Focused. Perhaps a bit like a badass. "Don't fuck with me, Southeastern New Hampshire and Southern Maine!" The headline, biggest on the page:

"At 40, Tom Powell is a Champ and Qualifying for the Marathon."

✃

"I really wish I was in shape to run the marathon with you guys," my dad admits after the waitress brings us our salads. "I like the marathon. That's my favorite."

"You've got a great kid here," Carl says, switching the focus to me while swirling wine in his glass. "He really tries hard. He never gave up. He's got a ton of guts. He follows what we ask and he's never pulled out."

My dad is warm with his beer.

"When he sets his mind on something," my dad replies, referring to me, "he really works."

Carl answers back: "And no matter how he does in the race he's really the most respected runner in Boulder right now."

Okay, I would normally say, that's enough. While it's nice to hear compliments from my dad — really nice — we're a results-oriented family. I haven't *earned* anything yet. But I'm liquored up, too. I'm caught up in the spirit of the evening. It's Valentine's Day! That couple over there is getting married! I like wine and Carl and my parents and this red pepper vinaigrette dressing the waitress recommended. I note aloud how Carl's really come around to my team. I remind him about our first meeting at the monthly beer social, just after I'd moved to Boulder. That night, when I told him I wanted to run Boston, he'd said "You? In one year?" He and I laugh now remembering it all.

I'm so caught up in the positive vibe of our dinner, in the adrenaline of finally being down here, finally getting to race, of sitting across from my parents who flew here just to be with me, of having grapes fermented in California pulsing through my bloodstream, that I don't even realize what I've said. I'm smiling and laughing and it's almost a minute, maybe two, before it occurs to me. I said the word *Boston*. I said it to my father. I said for the first time that my goal, from the day I moved to Boulder, was to qualify for Boston. Not to run Myrtle Beach or some rinky-dink race somewhere, not to check "marathon" off my life list. It is to run Boston. To qualify just like my dad did.

By the time I realize my gaffe — and what a gaffe! — the conversation has moved on to my parents' summer stay at Chautauqua, then to the fading health of CU's football team. I add a quip about the Buffaloes and Folsom Field but I can't help but notice what we're not saying. My dad isn't saying one thing about my now-public goal of making it to Boston. He sits there with his arms crossed, silent as Carl and my mom carry the conversation. I know what that means. I've placed the ammunition on the table, bullets he's discretely loaded into the chambers of his service revolver.

"Who does this boy think he is? Boston? In one try? Like I did? You've got to be good to make it to Boston, son. You can't just show up. You're trying to qualify for Boston? In your first-ever marathon? Who do you think you are?"

∞

There's a caption under the photo, that black-and-white shot of my dad at work with his feet up on his desk. "BOSTON MARATHON BOUND: A year ago Tom Powell, at 39, used his feet just for walking. Now he is a runner and they carry him more than 60 miles a week through Dover's streets as he prepares for his first Boston Marathon."

∞

My dad runs first, on Friday. A 5K race around a Myrtle Beach shopping mall parking lot.

GO TOM encourage the black letters on the white sign my mom prepared for the race. My dad prepared in his own way, all day, so focused he didn't stop to visit Carl and me as we lay about our hotel room, flipping between *SpongeBob* and the Weather Channel. We see him for the first time at dusk, at the mall, near the starting line. He wears his decades-old Bill Rodgers–brand windbreaker. Over his ears stretches a Puma-brand knit cap he must have found on the side of the road. I happily notice the new Nikes I bought him to replace the hole-y pair he wore at the Hog Jog. When he removes his jacket and slips into the starting scrum, I take in his shrinking frame. He is smaller than he used to be. And frail, though he would never admit it. It's been seven years since Gretchen's wedding, when we first noticed his stiffness on the dance floor, the first sign of his aging. The gun fires and he takes off, his elbows swinging in jerky, arrhythmic jolts. His torso lists to one side. His steps look strained, resembling only faintly — almost in parody — the smooth and nearly effortless shuffle of his prime. Twenty minutes later, though, that tough motherfucker still finishes in the top three for his age group.

❧

The Boston Herald American. *Monday, February 21, 1977:*
   "The most difficult of marathon conditions."
   "Blinding snow and slippery terrain."
   "An afternoon when the best way to get around was in a toboggan."

❧

Carl's watch beeps a four a.m. wake-up call. I don't think I slept for one second.
   "You need to sleep!" I'd scolded myself at one in the morning, and then again at two. I could hear the surf crashing on the beach, fourteen floors below.
   "Sleep! Go to sleep!" The head cold I've been battling for two weeks roared back full force, or seemed to. Text messages from friends vibrated my cell phone.
   "You've already done twenty miles nine weeks ago, then twenty miles six weeks ago, then twenty miles three weeks ago. You've already done it, and a third of those miles were at marathon race pace. You've done it before. You can do it."
   At the starting line, a half hour before the gun, the Coastal Car-

olina University marching band covers Metallica's "Enter Sand-man." A spotlight twirls, reminding me of a South Beach club opening. Carl and I wear black garbage bags at his suggestion, just our heads poking through and no holes for our arms. In our hands we hold waxy paper cups to fill with urine, clandestinely, under our black bags. At the national anthem, Carl discreetly tosses one of his cups into a receptacle. He returns stretched and ready. It's about fifty degrees, which is good. A light rain tinkles our faces. No big deal. Not a problem. A guy stretching near us sports a Boston Athletic Association Windbreaker, a reminder of why we're here; we aren't the only ones aiming beyond today. The guy takes off his jacket. We peel off our garbage bags and toss them aside. We shake hands and smile.

"This is it, buddy," Carl says. "Let's do this."

At the gun, in the dark, we start out strong. Carl takes off fast and steady, setting a pace I synchronize with my steps. Quick, light. Here's the first turn, at the pine trees, just like we went over. Up to the Goody's drugstore and now a right. Nothing we haven't already seen before. Adrenaline outmuscles the initial fear. *Oh my god this is fast!* Soon we settle into a groove. The first mile in seven and a half minutes. The second mile in a little-too-quick seven minutes. This is it. I'm racing. This is my race. After mile two, warmed up, we peel off our long-sleeved shirts, sacri-ficing them to the sidewalk. We tuck in behind a tall and athletic woman wearing virtually no clothes. I like the view and I'm hop-ing we'll run behind her the whole way but we're too quick; we drop her before mile three. Carl and I curve around the Home Depot parking lot, where we spot my parents for the first time standing in the grass and straining to make out faces in the dark.

"Hey, hey!" I shout to get their attention.

"They look pretty good!" I hear my mom announce to my dad.

Now we are on Ocean Boulevard, the concrete canyon, our first long straightaway. Six miles slightly downhill. I grab a cup of Powerade from a table and try to drink it. Sticky red sugar water splashes over my face and sunglasses and my singlet, very little falling into my mouth. I've kept my sunglasses on from the start, in the dark, out of habit. Now with light climbing over the hotels that line the waterfront, the glasses begin to serve their purpose. Through them I spy my parents again, just past the Sea Mist, around mile eight. My mom holds aloft a sheet of white poster board upon which she's scribbled, in black marker, GO ROBERT.

∞

The Boston Herald American. *Monday, February 21, 1977:*

Yesterday, just before the start of the 11th Silver Lake Dodge Washington's Birthday Marathon in Hopkinton, the temperature was around freezing and a fine, ominous snow was beginning to whip up ... [I]t became a run for survival through snow, slush, ice and a piercing cold.

... [T]he runners had to worry about snow plows, sand trucks and sliding cars. [T]he concern was frostbite ... Five miles to go [the leader] weaved off the course, leaned up against a light post and called it quits.

"The road is like ice," he said. "It felt like I was on a bicycle."

∞

Somewhere around mile nine, we pick up a runner.

"You guys look like you know what you're doing," she says as she pulls even with us. Her name is Ashley. She is from North Carolina. A tattooed Christian fish swims across her shoulder.

This is her second marathon, she says. Her first didn't go as well as she'd hoped. Now she's aiming for a 3:15. She wants to run negative splits, too, each of the twenty-six miles slightly faster than the mile before. She is impressed that we are from Boulder. When we tell her our goal time, same as hers, she smiles and says she'll run out the course in our company. Three miles later, we can't even see her anymore. She wanted to run those negative splits, she wanted to run faster each mile and we've been holding steady. Carl had decided even before we flew down that we had no margin of error. We need to keep our pace, seven and a half minutes every mile.

Whatever, Carl. Ashley's departure — her leaving us in the dust — scares me. My alarms sound. I didn't train enough! I'm not fit! I ate junk food all year; even fifty pounds lighter I'm still overweight. My chest feels heavy. No, that's not right. It feels too light. Hollow. I sense the molecules of oxygen slapping against the bronchioles of my lungs. Blood pools at my shoulders, never reaching my extremities. My legs are dead logs, my arms like sandbags. Bile settles in my stomach, or is it acid? I see my parents in the distance. They've cut up two blocks from their last station, knowing the course would loop back to the north. My mom again waves her sign.

"How you holding out? Carl asks.

"I'm fine," I tell him.

❧

By *LEONARD WITT*
Special to the *Democrat*

DOVER — Until the age of 39, Tom Powell of Dover never had an urge to run or jog. Now, at age 40, he is preparing to run in the Boston Marathon. All 26 miles and 385 yards of it.

Last year, Powell decided he might like to run in Dover's July Fourth [race], a mere 10 miles. He began training last February. Powell says, "When I began, I couldn't run more than a mile, and I was very stiff as a result of doing that. Now, I run an average of 50 or 60 miles a week."

That's right, the man said 50 or 60 miles a week. He said it while sitting at his office at the Moore Business Form Co. in Dover. He doesn't look 40 but swears he is. He looks much younger and is trim, weighing just 135 pounds. He smiles a lot, and says that since he began running he has never felt better.

Last week he felt better than ever about his running. He ran in the Silver Lake Marathon in Hopkinton, Mass. Like the Boston Marathon, the course measures 26 miles and 385 yards.

This marathon was a qualifier for the Boston Marathon scheduled for April 18. Of the 478 people who ran at Silver Lake, only 59 clocked times fast enough to qualify for the big one in Boston. Tom Powell was one of the qualifiers, and he has the fastest time in the Master's Class, which includes men 40 and above.

Remember that we are talking about a man who never ran before his 39th birthday. He did wrestle at Marquette College, but that was 20 years ago. Since then, he played some golf but wasn't involved in any strenuous sports.

But last week he accomplished the most strenuous of feats. He ran those 26 miles. His time was three hours, eight minutes and 31 seconds. That's about 20 minutes slower than he had hoped for, but, considering the weather, he did well.

∽

The course twists through Myrtle Beach in a big bow tie. That long loop down the waterfront hotels, then back up to the starting line on a strip of T-shirt shops, miniature golf courses, and liquor stores. Halfway done. Then again to the waterfront for a six-mile leg to the north. A turnaround, and once more back down to the finish line along a corridor of commercial kitsch. As we pass the midway point, the number of runners at our side drops dramatically. Almost everyone we jostled with at the starting line must have been running only the half marathon. Even with Carl beside me, it seems lonely now. It's harder to gauge our speed. I recall an e-mail I received last night from the *Camera*'s running columnist.

"Good luck," Mike Sandrock wished me. "Remember to stay strong through Mile 20. If you are tired and hurting at 13.1, then it's too late."

Carl slaps me on the back, saying "halfway done" and "right on schedule." Mentally, I'm hanging in there. Physically, though, I'm really struggling. I focus short-term, on that water station just up ahead.

"Pick up your feet, Powell!" shouts my dad. He and my mom have assumed their next position on the course, at the corner of Oak Street and Twenty-Ninth Avenue, right in front of the water station I've been concentrating on. I don't look so good. My dad tells me so in repeated, short cries. I toss him my thin gloves, which I don't need any more. I try to pick up my feet. It's the last time I'll see or hear them on the course. The last words to reach my ears, just before we turn up the waterfront: "Pick! Up! Your! Feet!"

❧

Foster's Daily Democrat. *February 26, 1977:*
    The Boston Globe described the weather as a "mini-Northeaster." The last 10 miles of the race were run in four inches of slush. Powell says, "I liken it to running in wet concrete."

He says his sweat suit was soaking wet, "literally like someone had dumped me in a lake."

The weather was awful, the hills were killers and a week before the marathon he had pulled a groin muscle, but he finished the race and won his class.

∞

We turn onto Ocean Boulevard for a four-mile stretch. The hotel high-rises give way to waterfront mansions, tasteful homes with palmetto trees sprouting from deep green front yards. The few spectators sitting on lawn chairs in their driveways are polite and encouraging and, because there are so few runners left on the course, give each of us individual attention.

"Hey! Boulder!" is the call when Carl passes in his running club singlet.

"C'mon, yellow!" is for me when I shuffle past one step later. "You can do it, yellow!"

Carl knows at mile fifteen. That's my first mile off pace, thirty full seconds too slow. Not a problem, I insist. I bring my pace back up on the next mile, hitting the target on the nose. I want nothing more than to stay on that target for the long waterfront stretch, which will bring us to mile twenty, which is where I've been told things are supposed to *really* get hard. But from mile seventeen on my splits — the time it takes me to run each mile — rise in steady increments, never to recover.

"No margin of error," Carl had said the day before in our hotel room. A white sign announces mile eighteen. Carl looks at his watch and shakes his head.

"Good try, buddy," he says. "You gave it a shot."

∞

Foster's Daily Democrat. *February 26, 1977:*

Now, sitting in his office, he describes what it is like to run so far. He often makes his point by unconsciously putting the thumb and forefinger of his right hand together and accenting his words with that hand.

His blue eyes, not unlike Paul Newman's, make him look younger than he is. He is wearing a peach-colored shirt and a blue-and-orange tie. Although he says he never thinks about his office's colors, the orange of his tie and his peach-colored shirt match the orange hues that accent much of his office.

Thumb and forefinger touching, he begins describing the 26-mile race. The first 10 miles were almost effortless, he says. He ran them in 67 minutes. The next 10 miles were not so easy.

Powell says, "It was starting to be an effort to run. I was starting to get physically tired. I couldn't figure out if it was the pace or the rain and slush."

☙

By the time we loop off the waterfront, up to a middle school water station and then back down T-shirt alley, I've entered a survivor shuffle. Mile twenty: 9:15. Mile twenty-one: 10:00. Mile twenty-two: 10:30. The sun is high now, warm and bright. Salty sweat crusts on my shoulders. Red sugar water that missed my mouth bakes on my face and my singlet and my shorts. I ingest my last goo, simply because the schedule says I should.

"See that guy in the white up ahead?" Carl asks. "Just pass him." Carl had stepped off the course for a bathroom break. A few minutes later he caught back up with me, easily, absently surging far ahead. When he realized he was dropping me, he actually turned around and ran backwards to again sync up. He throws out simple strategies now, short-term thinking. "Focus just on that, on passing the guy in the white."

I do focus. But I can't catch him, the guy in white. I can't do anything but plod forward, slowly, obsessively forward. I jiggle my mental stick shift, trying to find an extra gear. It's just not there. The guy in the white remains safe. Every runner in my sight is safe. Our plan, as we'd conceived it, was to finish strong, passing runners left and right as we surge toward the finish line. In reality, on the warming blacktop of Kings Highway, plenty of runners pass me. I watch them pull away, thinking about how much I hate running. Thinking about how I've never seen my dad fail.

∝

Foster's Daily Democrat. *February 26, 1977:*

At 18 miles, any long-distance runner comes up against "the wall." The wall is that point at which the body's excess energy has been burnt up. The body begins to metabolize the substances in its own tissue. At the 20th mile of the Silver Lake Marathon there was a three-mile hill that Powell had to negotiate.

He says, "For three miles it was all uphill, and going up that hill just physically exhausted me." Powell says the force of gravity is responsible for getting him down the other side.

When he reached the bottom of the hill, he was so exhausted that a police officer had to point out the direction he was to run. The same kind officer told him it was just another two miles to the finish line.

Of that point he says, "The exhaustion you feel is total and complete, there is nothing left physically. You literally have to tell your feet to move each step."

Finally, he reached the finish line. In the tone of a person who had just experienced a religious conversion, he says, "It's the most overwhelming feeling one could experience."

❧

Failure arrives, officially, at mile twenty-four. The course has returned to Confederate flags and Confederate flag beach towels and Confederate flag bikinis and that Hooter's restaurant with the fried pickles. We approach a large digital clock clicking out our time in neon numbers. The math is not good. To make it to Boston we must run the last 2.2 miles in less than a minute. Carl, who has been a few yards in front of me for a while now, swings his arms wide then claps his hands together. Not applause. Not for my benefit, either. Just an acknowledgment. It's not going to happen. He knew it for eight miles. Now it's official. It's definitely not going to happen.

It's true, what Carl realized at mile eighteen. It's true, what my dad feared when he saw me shuffling my feet just past the halfway mark. My sister won't be pulling her boys out of school to celebrate Patriot's Day with me in Massachusetts. Rich won't be bragging about how he took my novice ass and got me to Boston in one year. He'll have to call that guy at the *Denver Post* and tell him to spike the article about our incredible training odyssey, the article that's all set to run — newspaper profiles are for people who accomplish things. There will be no announcement over the PA at the cross-country nationals in San Diego. When I get back to the hotel room here in Myrtle Beach I'll have to call my brother in Seattle to tell him I didn't do it. That I definitely didn't beat dad's time. That well into his seventies our dad remains the family's top dog.

My brother once told me how much he'd like me to write a bestseller someday, perhaps something along the lines of the Harry Potter series. He also admitted how much he'd like to fall into a computer start-up that generates him a Google-type windfall of Internet millions. In either case, for either of us, money would change the dynamic. The structural setup in which our dad has the cash and the control that goes with it. Our father, the guy who rose from very little to become the very best at whatever it was he did for a living.

"That's probably for the best," my brother will tell me when I relay no change in the pecking order.

❧

I remember the day. I remember the snow. Serious snow, fat and wet and everywhere. It was cold, obviously. I remember the trophy ceremony after the race. In my mind it was dark. Could the sun have already set by then? What time did the race start? We were inside a banquet hall. All the runners were toweling off and defrosting. I picture my dad in fresh, dry sweatpants and a dry sweatshirt. He may have been wearing a jacket by this point, a water-repelling Windbreaker, maybe. Red? I don't really know; I might be inventing that detail altogether. There was a guy on a small stage holding a microphone. At some point he called my dad forward to collect his award. A plaque. Masters Champion. First place in his age group, a winner in his very first marathon. I recall the smile on my dad's face when he marched back from the stage to show us his award. The calling of his name, his smile, his brisk walk back with hardware. It would become familiar to us, his victory routine, repeated after every race.

"Almost there, yellow!" bleats a woman on the curb outside Myrtle Beach's minor-league baseball stadium. Less than a mile now. Just finish. Don't walk. Carl and I cut into a grove of pine trees, following the course to a parking lot we'd previously scouted in our car. Up a hundred yards to the orange barricades, then a last turn and a last stretch to the finish line. This is where my dad finished wobbling out his herky-jerk gait in the 5K last night. Seeing my own finish line, I pick up the pace almost reflexively. Where was that energy at mile fifteen? Carl falls back a step, on purpose, so I can cross the line first. Orange barricades flank us on both sides. There's a bank of porta potties. Fifty feet. Twenty. Ten. I stop as soon as I cross the line. I look at the time on the official clock. I check it against my wristwatch. About twenty minutes slower than I'd hoped for. Not even close.

Carl is slapping me on the back. Now he's pulling my shoulders the way he did after our long training runs in the snow. He's bubbly. He's saying something about achievement and guts and, I think, respect. I don't care. I tune him out. Not now.

For the past three hours and thirty-six minutes, I've had one aim, forward. Now what do I do? Where do I go? The chip on my shoe for timekeeping needs to be cut off. Okay, I can do that. Over there, to that woman with the scissors. I walk over. After she snips off my chip, I ask her if she might please untie my shoes; I can't bend down. Behind her, behind orange barricades, stands a scrum of people three or four deep. An audience looking at the runners, looking for their wives or husbands or brothers. I'm scared to look into their faces. Maybe, I think, he's not even here.

"What happened?"

"How come you didn't qualify?"

"You blew it, kid."

"You had a flat course, good weather, a training partner, a coach in Colorado, and a year to pull this off. You don't have a single excuse."

"Three thirty-six doesn't get it done, son."

Or worse, he won't say anything at all. That's the most likely outcome. That's what I'm expecting. He's a polite guy, a gentleman. Too polite to tell me I suck. Or fully certain I know the score already, that he doesn't need to vocalize my failure. That I'm anything but a mission-accomplished kind of guy. That compared with him, compared with the standard he set, I'm second rate. I'm nothing. I'm a runt. I can't handle my shit. I'm still a goddamn little boy.

"Gonna have to try harder next time, Robert."

I know the score. I know where I stand. I limp a few steps forward in my untied shoes, first thanking the woman with the scissors.

"Your mother and I flew all the way down for that?"

I'm scared to look into the crowd, afraid I might see him. I lift my head a little and turn to the left, away from the barricades. I notice a tent where they're handing out free cups of Michelob Ultra beer. No thanks. Up ahead wait cookies and bananas and servings of the same red sugar water that's splashed over my yellow tank top, making it look like a tie-dye. I see Ashley, the woman with the fish tattoo and the goal to run negative splits. She sees Carl and me and throws up a V for victory. Mission accomplished, she indicates. I see the table where they're handing medals to all of us who've finished.

"What are you going to do now son? Cry?"

I raise my head all the way up, finally, all the way. I force my eyes to my right, scanning across the orange barricade. I first see yellow flags advertising the race sponsors. Then I see a grove of pine trees. I see people. One of them is a man around my age, with short brown hair and a blue sweatshirt. I see another man wearing a leather bomber jacket, like a fighter pilot in the Great

War. I see a girl of about seven. She's wearing a puffy pink coat and pink canvas tennis shoes. Pink ribbons weave through her fine white hair.

Maybe he's not even here.

And then I see him. Right there. Watching me, as he has been this whole time. The moment I meet his eyes, I burst into tears.

24

AT A HIGH SCHOOL reunion a couple of years ago, a former classmate told me that his biggest surprise when he ran his one recreational marathon was the way he cried at the finish line. He hadn't anticipated that physical response. As he ground his way through miles twenty-four, then twenty-five, and right up to the end, he hadn't noticed tears coming on. Yet when he crossed the finish line, his eyes opened up.

I *did* anticipate my tears in Myrtle Beach. I'm a crybaby, as my mom taunted me on my drive out to Boulder from Miami. She said I'd thrown away a perfectly good life and all I think about is myself and I'm going nowhere. I cried when I left my wife, finally, for the last time. I sat on my bed in my temporary apartment, staring at my swollen face in a mirror and telling myself to remember the night forever, which I have. I cried when Mrs. Wisconsin left me rolling on my floor and again when my rebound relationship upgraded to a doctor, telling me on the way out the door that my entire life was going to be one crisis after another. I cried when I didn't get the job at the *New York Times* and I cried when my last two assignments in Miami fell through, making me feel like a total failure and fueling my flight to Boulder.

I didn't want to cry in Myrtle Beach. I tried not to cry. But as

I death-marched my way to the finish line, I felt the tears coming on. I thought about all the people with whom I'd shared my Boston Marathon goal, and how public my failure would be. How public my failure *is*. I thought about my father and what he was going to say to me. I didn't buckle down like my dad would have. I didn't address the task with his intense focus. I surfed the Internet instead. I dogged it at too many Tuesday runs. Yet after I crossed the line, the tears still shocked me with their power. I stood there sobbing. Everyone could see me. My lips and nose and cheeks twisted into a Halloween fright mask.

Carl watched the whole thing.

"I was about two steps behind you. I was waiting to have the chip cut off my shoe when I heard our names called out. I looked over and there was your mom and your dad standing together, with a look of pride and happiness. Your dad was kind of blinking his eyes. He looked a little red eyed and misty-eyed. Really, for sure. He looked like he was holding back tears. I can see the pride on his face, too. It was like, his kid just did something amazing."

My dad reached over the orange plastic barricade, calling me to him. Come here. I did what I was told. In three steps both of his arms wrapped around my chest and back. He moved one of his arms up to my neck to cradle my head, which fell onto his shoulder. His head touched mine, and I remember thinking his gray hair was going to be contaminated by my sweat. I cried, cradled in my dad's arms like a toddler. Like a baby. His lips hovered right near my ear.

"I'm proud of you," he said. He held my wet and salty skull tight on his shoulder. My chest heaved. He tapped my back with his other hand, his lips still close to my ear. He said the same thing again, perhaps to make sure I could hear it.

"I'm proud of you."

25

THERE IS THIS bicyclist, very celebrated, possibly a drug cheat (or so Frank Shorter intimates).* A guy who won seven difficult, prestigious races in France. When he retired from cycling, he ran his first marathon, in New York City, in just under three hours.

"Never again," Lance Armstrong exclaimed after he crossed the finish line in Central Park. The marathon was the hardest thing he'd ever done physically, he said, harder than climbing the Pyrenees, even harder than surviving cancer, which he's also done. Never again. Yet the next September he ran New York for the second time, finishing fifteen minutes faster. He then proceeded on to the very Boston Marathon I failed to qualify for. Once people finish their first marathon, it's almost a cliché: they say Never Again, then a few weeks pass and they return to their training.

When I get back to Boulder I contemplate running another marathon right away. I am as fit as ever. I've proved my body can withstand twenty-six miles, and I know if I stop training, or if I merely cut back on my weekly miles, the fitness I've earned

---

* Definitely a drug cheat, as finally admitted in 2013.

will dissipate. *Maybe I can still qualify, for next year.* Back in the Chicken Coop, back on the Internet, I scout marathons held in May: Green Bay, Wisconsin, flat and sea level and finishing on the Frozen Tundra of Lambeau Field. Ogden, Utah, where I served my only newspaper internship and where the marathon course winds almost entirely downhill. All the running books advise against this impulse to quickly run a second race. Wait. Don't push it. My running friends in Boulder relay the same advice. They tell me racing too soon caused them to pull muscles in their stomachs and/or buttocks and/or the insteps of their feet. So I let the marathon impulse pass. I wait. I don't push it.

"You'll run another one," Carl tells me. "I guarantee it. You're just getting started."

I don't run at all for ten days after Myrtle Beach. I spend a night finally investigating Pearl Street, staying up past midnight and drinking as many pints of Avery's brown ale as I can hold. I sleep late for the first time in a year. If I feel like doing anything physical, I drive to the gym and laze through a half hour on an elliptical machine, focusing more on the *Today* show than on the stiffness in my legs. I soak in the hot tub, carefully.

On the Wednesday after we return to Boulder, instead of immediately rejoining the group run, Carl and I walk Mapleton Hill for an hour. It's cold, with gray skies and bare trees and spring still several months off. Carl gives me a number, four hundred, which, in dollars, is my half of the hotel room and the plane tickets and car rental from our trip. That's on top of the race entry fees and restaurant meals already on my credit card. No problem, I tell him. We proceed to talk about the next phase of my athletic evolution, about running seven-minute miles, about increasing my turnover — the number of steps I take per minute. What I should really try to do, Carl says, is improve my time in a shorter race, like a 10K. That's what I should concentrate on.

I can't help but concentrate on the bill he's delivered. I'll cut him a check tonight, but it is the last check I'll write for a while. I have no money left. I am totally, officially broke. For one year, when people asked me what I was up to, all I said was the marathon. I was training. I was trying to qualify for Boston. When they'd ask what I was doing for income, I'd just shrug my shoulders. Don't worry about it, I'd say; I'm not. I was training for a marathon. I was like Frank Shorter back in his Olympic days, focused only on the running, training hard-core.

But now that original marathon dream is dead, and I'm broke. My dad e-mails me, saying to stick with it. My mom also writes to encourage me to continue running, primarily so she and my dad can take trips to watch me race. Rich sends out his regular Boulder Road Runners mass e-mail. In it he relays results from the USA Cross-Country Nationals in San Diego. He mentions an upcoming pasta dinner at his favorite new Italian restaurant off Twenty-Eighth Street. As usual, he reminds everyone about the Tuesday and Thursday training sessions. He makes no mention of me, or of Carl, or of Myrtle Beach.

I don't bump into Rich until more than a week after the race. I find him at the Flatiron Athletic Club. He is on the floor near the racquetball courts, stretching after a Tuesday workout I've skipped. Casually as I can, I sit down next to him. I watch him work a kink in one of his thigh muscles. He notices me. I wait for him to say something about my race but he keeps the focus squarely on himself. He doesn't think he is up for next Saturday's long run, he says. His body is too beat up from his race in San Diego.

"Maybe it's time you transitioned into the next phase of your career," I say, trying to make a joke. "Maybe it's time you become a full-time coach."

Rich doesn't respond immediately to my suggestion. Instead,

for a few long seconds, he only stares down at the gym's black carpeting. He never looks up. He never locks his eyes onto mine.

"I'll never coach anybody ever again," he says.

∂

"Life Is Good in Boulder." That's the headline the *Daily Camera* has slapped across its lead story. The subhead: "Life in Boulder is good and getting better, according to the results of a new city-sponsored survey." The subsequent story, which seems a bit redundant after those headlines, reports that overall quality of life in Boulder is up seven percentage points in the past seven years.

I had filled out that city-sponsored survey. There were four or five pages of questions printed on yellow paper (and green paper, if I'd wanted to reply in Spanish). I was asked to answer each question by circling a number from one to five, with number one indicating "very good" and number five indicating "very bad." I answered every question as honestly as possible, which meant I circled the number one over and over again.

"Taking all things into consideration, how do you rate your overall quality of life in Boulder?" I circled the number one. How could I not?

"How do you rate the overall quality of your neighborhood?" Number one. It's fantastic, obviously. Big, attractive, and safe houses, lots of trees and landscaping. Several parks and an elementary school within walking distance. Chautauqua just up the street, right next to the Flatirons. It's all good.

"How do you rate Boulder as a place to raise children?" Number one. Of course. Kids are everywhere around here, and they're all wearing trendy plastic shoes and organic cotton sweaters and they all look healthy and happy and I bet every single one of them is fluent in at least one foreign language, probably French.

"Safety of Neighborhood?" Number one. No one has yet slashed my knee with a sword. Over the past year, no one broke into my apartment or into my car. In Miami that would earn me a plaque from the mayor.

"Access to bike paths?" Number one. They're everywhere and easy to get to.

"Access to bus services?" Number one. I can hop on the Hop at Delilah's Pretty Good Grocery, just a block away.

"Access to library services?" Number one. The fantastic main library is a short walk down the Hill.

"Opportunity to attend Art and Cultural events?" Number one. Hello? Chautauqua? CU? The Dairy Center and the Fringe Festival? Concerts every night at the Boulder Theater and the Fox? C'mon.

"Opportunity for higher/continuing education?" Number one. Jeez. Of course. There's that big-assed flagship campus of the state university right over there. And Naropa, for people into that sort of thing.

Finally, there was an open-ended question for which I didn't have to limit my answer to a number: "What, if anything, do you think makes Boulder a great place?"

"Boulder's obviously a great place. Obviously. It's the greatest place I've ever been. It's sunny three hundred days a year. The coldest days aren't that cold, and they're soon replaced by warm days anyway. There's access to skiing and ice-skating and miles of running paths. The community centers all have pools. There's a bunch of dog parks, and all of them are fantastic, especially that one in South Boulder with the pond. The human population around here is stocked with intelligent and passionate people. Everyone is generally friendly. The Front Range, especially when viewed in the morning, can be breathtaking.

"So let me touch on what I don't like. I don't like how conservative Boulder is, culturally, especially for a city that's politically so liberal. Yes, I can smoke pot freely here, which is good even though pot's not my thing. And if I commit a crime, like, say, murdering my six-year-old beauty-pageant princess, I won't have to go to jail or anything like that—the very sensitive state's attorney will probably figure I've suffered enough. And that's good, too, I guess, if I had a six-year-old I wanted to kill. But I can't fit in here without two kids and a Subaru Outback and either a trust fund or a job at Sun Microsystems. I don't hold people's incomes against them in general, but I don't like how wealthy this town is. I don't think I can afford to live here, basically. Ever. Oh, and the people in Boulder can be smug. You know that, right? The wording of this question alone makes me feel like you've been contaminated with this smugness yourself.

"The demographics work against me, that's for sure. At the few parties I've attend, all everyone talks about is home repair. Or their kids and their investments — specifically how their decision to buy this or that stock has paid off handsomely. They also brag about the ever-increasing value of their homes and weren't they so shrewd to buy when they did? That gets old, believe me.

"But Boulder is perfect. No doubt about it. So perfect, so wonderful, it can feel oppressive. Miami, where I used to live, was real. It was dirty and dangerous and slick and shady and exciting. Boulder is real, too, but only in the sense that it's real nice. I'm not trying to be glib. It's really, really, really nice here. Boulder is where prosperous outdoorsy-types move to raise their kids. Objectively, I've never lived anywhere better. It sure beats the Chicago suburb where I grew up, where we had to drive half an hour just to get to school or a store, where there was neither bus service nor any cultural amenities. Boulder has all of those things, and if there's anything missing Denver's just twenty-five minutes away.

"So Boulder's perfect. It's spooky perfect. I'm not worried about anything in this town. Life here is very, very good. It's just that I'm not upper middle class and I don't have an investment portfolio nor a house and kids and I'm way too old to be a student at the university. So I think I've got to get a-movin' on."

In a way, I thought this marathon, and this move to Boulder, was a last chance to get with the program, a final opportunity to live a stable, normal life like my dad's. But it's already too late. I needed to catch the train for a life like his — and for a town like this — fifteen years ago. Boulder is not a place for people to liquidate their 401(k)s and chance a reinvention. That's what Miami is for, I'm afraid. I'm a perfect candidate to move back to Florida and concoct a new life. I know the ugly way those stories can end, of course. I still gotta get on with mine

❧

Niwot was chief of the Southern Arapaho, one of the first tribes known to settle along the Front Range foothills. His band wintered in caves on Mt. Sanitas, enjoying the relative warmth of Boulder compared with the icy high plains stretching to the east. If you stay in Boulder for a year, supposedly, so everyone tells me, you'll be affected by Niwot's Curse. The original curse was a warning about Boulder's eventual demise: "People seeing the beauty of this valley will want to stay, and their staying will be the undoing of the beauty." I like that original prophesy, especially because the man who said it, Niwot, was murdered by white men who arrived in Colorado after him, and who wanted Boulder for themselves.

People don't like to think of themselves as part of the problem, though, so in Boulder nowadays the Indian chief's prophesy has been spun into something more palatable. To suffer Niwot's contemporary curse is to be unable to live anywhere else. Anyone who spends a full year in Boulder is at risk. Frank Shorter contracted a standard issue of the modern curse, as I learned flipping through all those old newspaper clips at the Carnegie Library. He left Boulder soon after winning his gold medal, in 1972, but came back almost immediately, he and his wife at the time concluding there is no better place to live. My running partner Carl has been infected. He was only passing through Colorado on a postcollege joyride when he decided to stay, enroll in graduate school, then take a government job at an agency in town. Thirty years later he's still here.

My family seems to have contracted a case of Niwot's Curse by proxy. My father lobbies me to stay in Boulder. A veteran of many moves, he says it's rare to find people as helpful and friendly as Carl and Rich and everybody else here. (I certainly agree.) My sister in Saratoga Springs thinks Boulder sounds about as perfect as indicated by that city survey. My mother says I'm doing better in Boulder than I have in years. I'm happier. She wants me to stay, or at least not travel backward.

"Just, please, tell me you won't be going back to Miami," she writes in an e-mail.

Before I leave, my dad visits one last time. My mom, too, as they usually move in a unit. They are driving to Seattle to play grandparents to my brother's baby. "Driving" because my dad wants to break in yet another Cadillac. His newest luxury car features a satellite navigation system, a DVD player, a built-in hard drive for his music, and, as always, a small silver nameplate on the glove compartment announcing that the sedan was custom built especially for Thomas A. Powell.

My parents' hotel sits right next to the Flatiron gym, making it easy for my dad to join the Road Runners on a Tuesday-morning workout. I arrive at the gym only a couple of minutes before seven a.m., as is my nature. My dad is already waiting for me under the canopy outside the gym's front door, as is *his* nature. Club members emerge from the lobby and we fall in with the crowd, going slow for the first twenty minutes, as always. The trail feels soft with each step, its dirt darkened by a recent rain. The Flatirons glow in the dawn, a daily gift to Boulder early risers.

I watch my dad run. The guy's got his good form back. He leans forward like a runner is supposed to. His legs shuffle in compact steps, his feet barely lifting off the ground. He looks a bit like he's hovering, which again is exactly the right way to look. We're taking it easy on the warm-up, going slowly, but I notice my dad struggling. He's failing to keep up with everyone else, which he clearly wants to do. He wants to run with the pack.

By the time we reach the cow gate — the place where we start our real workout — my dad is already done. He badly needs water, which I'm relieved one woman has brought with her. Everyone else takes off, but my dad stays at rest. Eventually, instead of continuing up the South Boulder Creek Path, he and I turn back toward the gym. I wasn't expecting this. Anytime I've run with my dad he's been way out ahead. I've always been the one fighting to keep up. Now *he* is laboring. Jogging then walking then jogging then walking. I watch him closely. He is small and thin. He looks vulnerable, frankly. Fragile. He looks human, this guy, this mythic ghost who lives in my brain. He looks beatable, for that matter. Where is the monstrous invulnerability? Why isn't he crushing me just to prove a point? He appears to be simply a man, a cute man even, a guy I like.

We reach the gym long before everyone else. In the lobby, my dad gulps down more water while I find a space near the racquetball courts to stretch my legs, which are barely fatigued. He joins me. Much later, so do Rich and Carl and everyone else back from the regular workout.

"Once I get adjusted to the altitude, you guys are in trouble," my dad says. He's not joking. He means it, even though today he couldn't complete more than the warm-up. It's the trash talk that everyone in the club shoots at everyone else, every morning. They are all competitive. They all run races to actually win them. I can see my dad here, as a Boulder Road Runner. He'd fit in, agewise. Most members of the club are retired, as is he. All of them really love to run.

My dad invested his money wisely and worked hard every day of his adult life and stayed married and raised his kids, then put all four of them through college, including grad schools. Boulder is Valhalla for guys like him. This running club is the group he's been looking for ever since he first laced up his waffle-tread Nikes back in New Hampshire. I can see him here, easily. I bet if *he* spent a year in Boulder he'd never want to leave.

Walking together the hundred yards back to the hotel to meet up with mom, my dad is upbeat, energized by his short workout. When we approach the hotel's main door, I put my hand on his back to signal he should go through the door first. I keep my hand there for a moment longer than necessary, I notice. I like touching him. I like feeling his back muscles fire when he moves. I like connecting with him physically, however gently. When I finally slide my hand off his back, it falls in an arc that meets up with his right hand, which I grab; he might have grabbed my hand first. We hold hands for a moment — just a moment — and we both squeeze. It's an escalation of our traditionally silent communication. By squeezing my hand he signals that I'm on track and that I'm doing okay even as I struggle and that I'm a son in good

246

standing. I think. To him I signal affection and respect. For both of us, it's about as close to expressing love as we've ever come. I'm glad you're here Dad, and not just because you're paying for all my meals. I'm glad you're you. I appreciate, deeply, what you said to me in Myrtle Beach.

26.2

CARL INVITES ME over to his house for dinner. His wife, a Master Sommelier, cracks open *three* bottles of really good red wine. I'm offered a thick slab of steak, a baked potato, and a green salad topped with sliced avocados. Ice cream awaits, to be enjoyed while we watch *Survivor* and *Bones,* their favorite TV shows. Just before we sit down to eat, Carl goes to fetch something he wants me to have.

When he returns from a bedroom, he hands me the T-shirt he received when he last ran the Boston Marathon, in 2001. He also hands me his official finisher's medal from the same race. He's noticed the way I grit my teeth when Boulder runners show off the Boston shirts they've earned. So he is giving one of his to me.

"Now if people ask if you ran Boston, you can say, 'No, but I have a hell of a story!'"

❧

Summer is coming. Boulder warms. I won't be here much longer. After a Sunday group run I take Valentine hiking up in Nederland. We launch our ascent on a trail of melting snow. The higher we climb, the more stable the footing. Slush gives way to crunchy sheets of white still covering the ground and hanging from evergreen trees. Even so, the sun shines so strong I can strip down to a T-shirt. After maybe three hours of hiking, I sit on a rock for a while and rest. I eat a sandwich and pour Valentine some drinking water.

I think about what brought me to Boulder. I'd let my divorce and its aftermath sink me, basically. That's what I've concluded. I lost years cursing Mrs. Wisconsin because she didn't rescue me from the rubble. And cursing myself because I'd divorced in the first place. The fear of my dad and his high standards was a false front, I've come to believe, a way for me to feel worse about my situation. I don't have a steady job. I don't have a house on a golf course. I divorced, as he never would. Therefore I'm a failure.

But I'm not my dad. I've learned that, too, definitively. I thought I could blast through my torpor by acting more like him, by "getting back on track." Yet Boulder has made the divide between us sharper. I'm a totally different dude. I don't know if I even want a house and kids, really. Or the nine-to-five he clocked for more than forty years. I don't think it's an accident I'm not living his life.

I wonder about Myrtle Beach, too. I can't help it. If I had applied myself more, if I had trained with even more single-minded focus, I could have pulled it off. I'm certain. If I would have spent less time playing Scrabble on the Internet and reading magazines late into the night I could have shown up at my workouts alert and eager. Or maybe it was my diet. If I just would have eaten even better and dropped ten to fifteen more pounds, I could have made it to Boston. I could have obtained tangible proof that I'm a winner, which is something I still would have liked.

When I tire of the self-flagellation, my attention wanders to random topics. Cheese. Soccer. Southeast Asia. I drift to something Frank Shorter told me when I stopped by his house, a reminder not to be so hard on myself. In his living room, during the time we talked about his father, I asked Shorter why in his 1984 autobiography, which was published seven years before he alleged abuse, he was so respectful of the man.

"Well, the social time wasn't right," he said. "Society wasn't ready, and then it became sort of fashionable [to claim abuse]. Again that's not the point, the point is not that it happened but how you deal with it."

Shorter could be talking about the Montreal Olympics as easily as he could be talking about his father. He lost the gold medal in Montreal and he has good reason to suspect the man who won it, Waldemar Cierpinski, ran while pumped up on steroids. How is Shorter dealing with it? Constructively, it could be argued, in his work to clean up all of sports. And yet his loss in Canada clearly consumes him. He has not let it go. He wants his gold medal. Because he doesn't have it, he's bitter. He's isolated. He's let his convictions about the injustice of the 1976 Olympic Games isolate him even further.

"I've always been someone to go by negative example as opposed to positive example," Shorter told me early in our interview, when we were still talking about running. "In other words, you can emulate people but you can also see what other people have done and know that you don't want to do it that way."

This is what I see in Frank Shorter: A family history of alcoholism and, he says, abuse. His two divorces. His difficulties maintaining relationships with the runners in Boulder, who clearly just want to be his friend. My friend from Illinois, Dan Skarda, speculates that the silver medal in Montreal ruined Frank Shorter's life. I'm not prepared to go that far. *Ruined*, to me, is homeless on the street, drunk and toothless and dirty. Shorter lives in a nice house. He's tan and trim. Outside Boulder, in the world of running, he remains a big deal, an icon. But, *damaged?* Yeah, I can see that. He's become a negative example. He's taught me that isolation is a bad idea. I've learned that the worst thing I can do is sit in the Chicken Coop alone — or even high on a mountain with my dog — stewing over past slights and old guilt.

The Coop isn't even an option anymore. I am kicked out the day after the Bolder Boulder 10K, on June 1. A man wearing a dust mask knocks on my screen door in the morning. I need to leave immediately, he says; he is not allowed by law to tear off the rest of the Coop's supposedly harmless asbestos shingles until I am off the property. I've already moved out the little stuff I still own. In a minor encore to my purge in Miami, I've again eliminated everything I possibly can. I've given away my two collapsible bookshelves and my old boom box. I leave behind the mattress and my one table and the used denim couch with the crayon stains. I've surrendered the speakers I'd attached to my computer, and the two space heaters that warmed up the storage shed when I tried to work in there. I've also abandoned the scale with which I'd been measuring my weight and body fat, as I'm not interested in that information anymore. I left Miami with what I could fit in my car. This time I even sell my car, to an electrician down in Fremont. Just before I move out for good, I open the *New York Times Sunday Magazine* to see an ad for the AARP:

"Founded on the simple premise that no one should have to live in a chicken coop."

The marathon had been my only focus in Boulder, and while I trained for it I'd suspended all decision making. When people would ask me what I was going to do next, I never knew what to say. I joked that I was going to embark on an ambitious research project: *Sloth: Seven Years Living One of the Seven Deadly Sins.* It doesn't help that the economy has since cratered. Good magazines have folded, and more threaten to fold every week. News-papers, once the places I most wanted to work, are all but done; even the *Times* has laid people off. Things look bad. Worse than when I left Miami, and back then things were so bleak I felt para-lyzed. What, again, is my motivation to get out of bed?

Because I have to keep going. That's the takeaway from my time in Boulder. *There is nobility in not quitting.* Maybe I'll never string things together as competently as my father always has. Maybe I'll never grasp stability or prosperity or any of those talismans that tantalize me. Still, I'm finding I *want* to do things. Again. Several things. I have at least five projects I'm eager to start. In the short-term I need to make money to support myself, and I'm excited to address that challenge. I want to set up a home base. I want to start up with a new woman even, if I can. Don't quit. The point is not that it happened but how you deal with it. Keep running.

Simple, right? Easy to say, too. It's a lesson I still need to revisit, often. I remain overwhelmed. I still doubt myself. My attempt to turn my life around on my thirty-seventh birthday was derailed by a stranger with a sword. I once left Cabo San Lucas optimistic and excited only to sink down deeper than ever before. When I sink down now, when I feel like quitting — what I'm doing, what I'm planning, everything — I think back to Myrtle Beach, to the survivor shuffle I plodded through the last ten miles of that race. I think of the reward I received when I finished. I must continue moving forward. Always.

That's the new story, the "hell of a story," the narrative that has displaced my father's ghostly running history in my psyche. When I play this new story back I see myself still in Boulder. It's my last weekend in the city, and my last long Saturday run. I've already sold my car and have borrowed a Volvo station wagon from a friend I've crashed with until I can fly away. Sitting behind the wheel of the boxy car, my friend's snowboards stacked in the back and a pair of ski goggles dangling from the rearview mirror, I look, for the first time in more than a year, like I belong in Boulder. Maybe I do belong. I'm wearing a green tank top purchased at a Bolder Boulder clearance sale. Instead of the long and baggy running shorts I prefer, and which Rich Castro never liked, I wear my small black racing shorts from Myrtle Beach. I recognize my wardrobe is a symbol of some kind. My way of indicating that maybe, in some manner, I have become a runner.

The club gathers at Neva Road as usual, coalescing a bit before seven a.m. It's very hot out, July. The summer sun has long ago baked the green from the foothills, leaving them brown and so dry they sometimes burst into flame. There aren't a lot of cars in the lot, probably because of the heat. Rich and his second wife are in Scotland, attending the cross-country world championships. Carl shows up, but he's deep into training two other runners for fall marathons, the rebound relationships he entered after my career ended prematurely. One of his new disciples is a cop from Orlando, a man who moved to Boulder solely to train. I size up the guy after I step out of the Volvo. Good luck with that dream, officer.

For the warm-up, I run with Clarence, the carpenter who doubted I'd qualify for Boston, and who was justified in his doubts. He turns off early to take care of a family matter, leaving me alone for most of the morning. After taking a drink at the regular water stop, I continue on to the Altoona Grange, then west toward US 36 and a tracing of the four-mile loop. It is a significant, telling decision. No one is monitoring me and I'm not training for anything and I can stop short, no problem. But I've decided to put in the loop, setting up a total run of twelve miles. That's long. And I'm running it by choice, completely voluntarily.

Not that I'm killing myself. I'm just putting in time on my legs. A car rumbles toward me, then past, kicking up a bowl of dust that takes a while to settle down. I continue, breathing in through my nose and out through my mouth. Summer sun burns into my neck. A rabbit scampers from the shoulder into my path, then quickly back into the tall, dry grass.

Halfway into the loop, I turn south onto 36 and back toward Boulder. In the distance I can make out Chautauqua and the Flatirons and beyond that the hill to Superior I crested when I first drove into the valley. There's Frank Shorter's house on Wonderland Lake and the Victorian wainscoting of Mapleton Hill, the brick storefronts of Pearl Street and the stacks of Italian flagstone that compose the university. Bicyclists pass in packs of five and six, swerving around me on the wide shoulder, sometimes waving, sometimes not.

In my mind, in the new story that lives in my head, I'm thinking about the Quarter Pounder with Cheese that waits in my immediate future. Or how about something regional from Good Times? I'm contemplating just how boring running is, how painful. If running is a metaphor for life, I muse, then life sucks.

Enough of that! "All that negative talk is ego. It's all sabotaging." "*The great coach Bobby McGee says, 'When a bad idea floats into your head you have to say, Thank you for coming, thank you for visiting, now get out of here.'*" I think instead of a statement recorded in my journal after my very first run on the Miami Beach boardwalk, back when everything started: "Running is practice for not quitting." It really is, I can now confirm. Whatever my shortcomings out here in Boulder, I never quit.

After about a half mile on US 36, the highway slopes downward sharply, which I so welcome. I keep my head up, my shoulders down, my feet close to the ground. I try to glide like a hover-craft, like my dad. I've got my lungs and I'm flexing my gratitude muscle and I'm embracing the Mentality of Faith. Gravity boosts my speed, carrying me beyond Plateau Road with a bit of momentum.

Acknowledgments

First, a shout-out to my mother, an accomplished and pioneering woman with her own interesting story. She's an important person in my life, and I love her. Thanks to everyone in Boulder, of course, especially the many friends not named in the text. Special thanks to Steve Almond, Dan Baum, Jane Caporelli and the staff of the Miami River Inn, Joyzelle Davis, Tom Finkel, Glenn Gaslin, Ashley Gelman, Lauren Guydan, Carmen Johnson, Douglas Johnson, Tris Korten, Janet Lopez-Vilsack, Priscilla McCutcheon, Kirk Nielsen, Johanna Ojeda, Chris Parris-Lamb, Nick Riccardi, Linda Robertson, Kirk Semple and the two not-previously-acknowledged Umbdenstocks: Emma and Kenny Wayne. Out of pure affection, I wish to also recognize CU Buffaloes Chris Deaton, Andrew Krautheim, and Will Menzies from Gnarnia on Hamilton Court, my temporary home in Boulder after the Chicken Coop's demolition.

A very small portion of the text, pertaining to my divorce, originally appeared in *Miami New Times*. My reporting on Frank Shorter and his antidoping crusade was conducted on behalf of the *New York Times*. I began working on this book in earnest at the Corporation of Boyacá writing colony, which is really just a farmhouse in rural Colombia that I beta-tested for my friends Steve Dudley and Juliana Martínez, whom I can't thank enough.

And finally, a correction: Immediately prior to the marathon in Myrtle Beach, a Boulder Road Runner named Lois Calhoun gave me a small silver circle embossed with the word *courage*. I'd gotten confused about who gave me the pendant—it came to me through a third party—and I ended up never thanking Lois, ever. I thank her now, quite belatedly. I sincerely appreciate the thoughtful present.